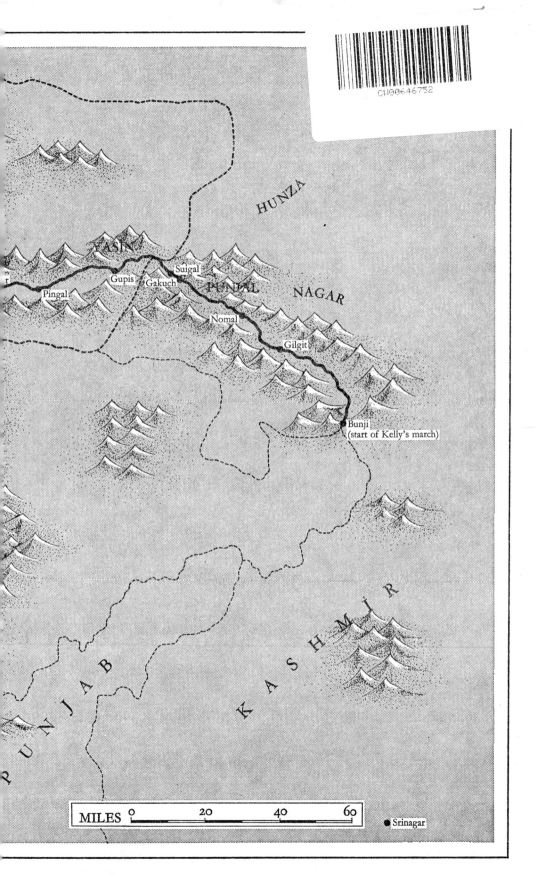

HUNZA

YASIN

Suigal

Gupis

Gakuch

PUNIAL

NAGAR

Pingal

Nomal

Gilgit

Bunji
(start of Kelly's march)

PUNJAB

KASHMIR

MILES 0   20   40   60   ● Srinagar

Much Sounding of Bugles

Also by John Harris

Novels

The Lonely Voyage
Hallelujah Corner
The Sea Shall Not Have Them
The Claws of Mercy
Getaway
The Sleeping Mountain
The Road to the Coast
Sunset at Sheba
Covenant with Death
The Spring of Malice
The Unforgiving Wind
Vardy
The Cross of Lazzaro
The Old Trade of Killing
Light Cavalry Action
Right of Reply
The Mercenaries
The Courtney Entry
The Mustering of the Hawks
A Kind of Courage
Smiling Willie and the Tiger
Ride Out the Storm

History

The Somme: Death of a Generation
The Big Slump
Farewell to the Don (as editor)
The Gallant Six Hundred
The Indian Mutiny

For Younger Readers

The Wonderful Ice Cream
The Sword of General Frapp
Sir Sam and the Dragon
Sam and the Kite
A Matter of Luck
The Fledglings
The Professionals
The Victors
A Tale of a Tail

JOHN HARRIS

Much Sounding of Bugles

The Siege of Chitral, 1895

Hutchinson of London

Hutchinson & Co (Publishers) Ltd
3 Fitzroy Square, London W1

London Melbourne Sydney Auckland
Wellington Johannesburg and agencies
throughout the world

First published 1975
© John Harris 1975
© Maps Hutchinson & Co (Publishers) Ltd 1975

Set in Monotype Fournier
Printed in Great Britain by The Anchor Press Ltd
and bound by Wm Brendon & Son Ltd
both of Tiptree, Essex

ISBN 0 09 124590 7

Contents

Each night there were alarms, when the garrison, still wanting in experience, responded with unnecessary commotion and much sounding of bugles.

SURGEON-MAJOR GEORGE S. ROBERTSON

Illustrations

Between pages 192 and 193

MAPS IN TEXT   *Page*

Author's Preface

There was 'no campaign so rapid, brilliant and successful' since Lord Roberts' march from Kabul to Kandahar. So wrote Captain George John Younghusband about the struggle to relieve the sorely-pressed garrison at Chitral on the north-west frontier of India in 1895, a campaign in which he took part with his more famous explorer brother, Francis. 'No element,' he claimed, 'was wanting to call forth the keenest instinct of the soldiers or to arouse the anxious interest of those who watched with breathless suspense.'

A later, more cynical historian put it another way. 'If only there had been a blonde . . . in the fort,' he wrote, 'the story would have been dramatized and fictionalized ad infinitum.'

It has another important point in its favour to make it worth re-telling. The siege and the campaign which followed provided an episode of high adventure that offered a magnificent opportunity to prove their worth to a few able and daring young soldiers who happened at the time to be straining at the leash of promotion. Just how able they were and just how courageously they grasped their chance was proved by the number who later rose to high rank. They included a future field-marshal and at least nine future generals, while a surprising number of them received knighthoods for military or civil achievements, and one of the defenders, Captain C. V. F. Townshend, as Major-General Townshend, was to put to such good use the knowledge he had gained that he held off the Turks in another siege at Kut in 1915–16 for 143 days – one of the longest in history.

The Chitral campaign took place at the peak of Victoria's 'Happy and Glorious' so that England's good name and military pride – that strange emotion the British had evoked from a whole string of disastrous defeats – were involved. There was therefore little wonder that it produced the sort of response it did, because to the staid Victorians in England it provided the vicarious excitement they loved as they went about their business and good works, and brought a whiff of adventure into their sometimes dull lives.

It was fought in a savage area still noted as 'queer' by General Lord Rawlinson, commander-in-chief, India, in the 1920s – for whom a local war there was once politely stopped to allow him to ride through unimpeded – and it took place in an age when courage was judged by other standards than today's. Patriotism is no longer a word to conjure with, and it is no longer regarded as good sense to die for such ideals, so that young soldiers posture no more with bandaged heads and blazing eyes in front of tattered flags – not even in pictures. *That* was a brief phenomenon that lasted only from the day when newspapers learned to reproduce heroic pictures for the titillation of their readers until artillery barrages, improved photographic techniques and the Great War finished it forever.

Although outdated nowadays, however, such behaviour wasn't at all odd in the last years of Victoria's reign, when it was firmly believed that such incandescent courage had built the British Empire. To the Victorians the Chitral affair symbolized all the nineteenth century derring-do of besieged forts, savage foes and noble officers defying terrible odds. It was the very essence of small Victorian wars and again and again typified the gallantry, stupidity and heroism of such things as the defence of Lucknow, the broken square at Abu Klea, and Gordon at Khartoum. Yet, in the fin-de-siècle attitudes of the young men involved, it also had a spicy dash of twentieth-century down-to-earthness.

Among others, my thanks are due to Colonel A. J. Barker; the Ministry of Defence Library; Colonel P. S. Newton, of the Army Museums Ogilby Trust; the Royal United Services Institute; Major C. R. D'I. Kenworthy, of The Gordon Highlanders; the India Office Library and Prints and Records Department; Mr. R. R. Mellor, of the Library and Records Dept. of the Foreign and Commonwealth Office; the National Army Museum; my neighbour, General H. Essame, for advice and pithy comments on the frontier and for reading the manuscript; the Central Library, Bradford; and, once again, the staff of the West Sussex County Library in Chichester, who never seem to grow tired of my nagging demand for books or information. I'm also grateful to my publisher, Gerald Austin, and to John Foster White, for all their editorial assistance.

Chronology

1892

30 AUGUST   Aman-ul-Mulk, Mehtar of Chitral, dies. Succeeded by Afzul-ul-Mulk.

6 NOVEMBER   Afzul-ul-Mulk murdered. Sher Afzul becomes mehtar. Nizam-ul-Mulk claims mehtarship. Sher Afzul flees.

1893   Mortimer Durand and Amir of Afghanistan decide position of Afghan border.

1894–5   Richard Udny setting up Durand Line.

1895

1 JANUARY   Nizam-ul-Mulk murdered. Amir-ul-Mulk, his brother, becomes mehtar. Demands help from Umra Khan of Jandol.

6 JANUARY   News of murder reaches Surgeon-Major G. S. Robertson, British agent, at Gilgit.

15 JANUARY   Robertson leaves for Chitral.

23 JANUARY   Robertson crosses Shandur Pass. At Mastuj learns from Lt. Gurdon that Umra Khan is already in Chitral.

31 JANUARY   Robertson arrives in Chitral with Shuja-ul-Mulk, younger brother of Amir-ul-Mulk.

19 FEBRUARY   News received that Sher Afzul is also in Chitral.

27 FEBRUARY   Sher Afzul demands that Robertson leaves Chitral.

1 MARCH   Occupation of Chitral fort. British garrison comprises Robertson, Capts. Baird, Campbell and Townshend; Surgeon-Capt. Whitchurch; Lts. Gurdon and Harley.

2 MARCH   Robertson deposes Amir-ul-Mulk in favour of Shuja.

3 MARCH   Sher Afzul reported advancing. Sortie from fort. Last message leaves.

4 MARCH   Siege begins.

5 MARCH	Information received that Pathans have joined besiegers. Lts. Edwardes and Fowler head for Chitral with engineering supplies and ammunition.
6 MARCH	Edwardes and Fowler reach Reshun.
7 MARCH	Attempt to fire water tower at Chitral. Edwardes and Fowler besieged at Reshun. First news of uprising reaches Peshawar.
8 MARCH	Capt. Ross leaves Mastuj to help Edwardes and Fowler. Attacked in Koragh defile with heavy loss. Besieged in caves.
11 MARCH	Ross attempts to break out.
14 MARCH	Gen. Low's Division mobilized.
15 MARCH	Edwardes and Fowler taken prisoner.
17 MARCH	Beginning of truce at Chitral.
22 MARCH	Col. Kelly ordered to lead relief force from Gilgit.
23 MARCH	Kelly's first troops leave. Moberly besieged at Mastuj. Truce ends at Chitral.
27 MARCH	Kelly's main column leaves.
1 APRIL	Low's division moves north. Kelly's first attempt to cross Shandur Pass defeated by weather.
3 APRIL	Low forces way through Malakand Pass.
4 APRIL	Capt. Borradaile crosses Shandur.
5 APRIL	Low reaches River Swat.
6 APRIL	Borradaile's advance once more stopped by weather conditions, but Kelly's main column crosses Shandur.
7 APRIL	Gun tower fired at Chitral. Low bridges Swat. Enemy retires north.
9 APRIL	Kelly's fight at Chakalwat. Mastuj relieved.
12 APRIL	Edwardes and Fowler at Mundiah. Low's clash with Umra Khan's forces at Panjkora River.
13 APRIL	Edwardes reaches Low. Kelly's fight at Nisa Gul.
16 APRIL	Mining heard at Chitral.
17 APRIL	Harley's sortie at Chitral.
18 APRIL	Mundiah captured. News of imminent defeat of Robertson reaches Low. Gen. Gatacre pushes ahead.
19 APRIL	Gurdon sorties from Chitral.
20 APRIL	Kelly's advance guard reaches Chitral.

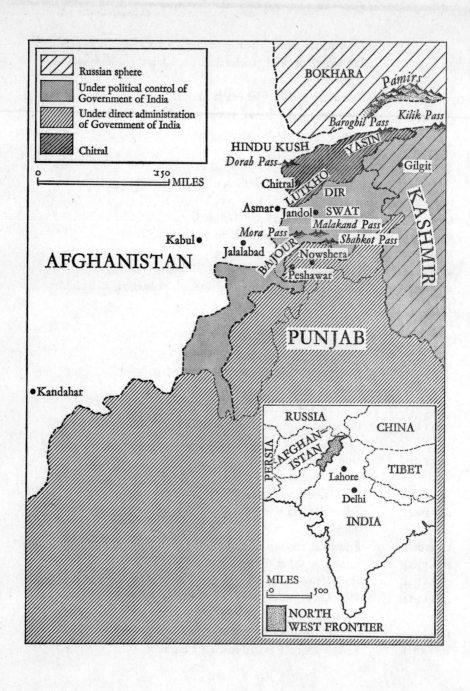

The land of mirth and murder

It is fashionable in the late twentieth century to sneer at the now defunct British Empire. On the whole, however, its record was as good as – or even better than – most, and it should be judged in the context of its own time. At the end of the last century, every country with money, industry and an army was at the same game of expansion – in China, Africa, India and anywhere else that hadn't already been worked over – and the young Englishmen who administered the northern borders of India were no different from their contemporaries doing the same job for other nations elsewhere.

Most of them came from the army. It had always been the practice in India for the most vigorous and intelligent officers to be snatched away for the civil or political posts that were constantly being created by the 'Forward Policy' of the government.[1] To a few of these men the border tribes gave their devotion, and the young men returned this devotion by administering their territory with common sense and intuition rather than with arid laws and regulations. 'This is the way I treat these things,' John Nicholson once said, kicking a bundle of papers across the floor. Colonel Algernon Durand, political agent in Kashmir in the nineties, put it another way – 'You want men on the frontier, not machines to grind out files of paper.'

The service was always undermanned and the quality of the administration slipped. General Sir Ian Hamilton, who served on the frontier as a subaltern in the seventies, noticed that the junior ranks of the British army did more for goodwill than any government official, spending their long leaves – sixty days or even six months – in the Himalayas, 'talking, walking, risking their necks', in close touch with the tribes, spending their savings in the country where they earned them, instead of – as the government seemed suddenly to prefer – taking a long sea trip back to England and spending them in Leicester Square and Piccadilly.

Very often the families of these young men had served India for generations, and as one of later vintage[2] said, those of their menfolk who did not 'were dotty or became parsons'. For the most part they loved the frontier and almost everyone who wrote about it spoke of its beauty with real feeling. But the frontier was always exciting too, of course, and sharing dangers and hardships with their men, they dealt with murderers and high diplomacy, and made and broke princes with a wave of the hand. They were as gallant as they were skilful at the double-talk of the tribal khans, and, like their opponents, they were so completely *au fait* with the niceties of siege courtesies that, at times, the exchanges seemed either medieval or farcical. They were dealing, however, with men to whom treachery meant little and human life even less, and whose happier pursuits included castration, flaying and roasting alive, and, well aware of the dangers they faced, they were fond of Kipling not because he was an imperialist but because he knew their job. '*The flying bullet down the Pass, That whistles clear: "All flesh is grass"* ' was a quotation they used almost to a man but they also knew the blunter one about '*And the men of the First Shikaris Picked up their Subaltern dead, With a big blue mark in his forehead And the back blown out of his head.*'

In a strange way they admired the tribesmen they were opposing – for their courage and fierce independence – in the same manner that the tribesmen admired the British – for their wealth, daring and 'bunderbust', or administrative ability. Mistakes were made, of course, and things sometimes went wrong because the British were often arrogant in their attitude to foreigners. They were occasionally even thick-headed and chanced their luck too much because they were not always as skilful in war as they thought. Nevertheless, they always led from the front and the one thing they never lacked was courage.

Contrary to common belief, the end of the nineteenth century was not a golden age of peace, prosperity, and tranquillity. It was an iron age of 'strident nationalism and imperialism, militarism and monarchism, devious diplomacy, espionage, unrest and crisis', and for all-conquering Britain, astride the northern border of India, there was a great deal of envious dislike. The British Empire was 'larger than that of the Romans, larger than the former dominions of the Spanish kings: over thirteen million square miles of territory stretching into five continents'; a population of over 400,000,000, with Queen Victoria ruling over nearly a quarter of the world's people. 'The statistics were overpowering and the vast areas of red on the map, which the British accepted with anything from pride to near in-difference, were to many Europeans . . . an affront and a challenge and a permanent nagging source of jealousy.'[3]

In an era of expansion and colonization, this jealousy caused the European powers to look round for areas where they might emulate the British with their influence. With their navies, Britain, France and Germany had been able to expand overseas but, without an ice-free port, Russia had been able to expand only by land. Already she had occupied Finland and Poland and driven to the far borders of Mongolia and Manchuria. Because she could go nowhere else now but to the south, it was always firmly believed by the British that she posed a threat to India. It was a belief that had troubled relations between the two countries for generations and had brought them to war in the Crimea when the British had thought that the Russians were threatening India through Turkey. In 1878 new Russian moves against Constantinople had been countered when Disraeli had moved the Mediterranean Fleet to Besika Bay and the two countries had again been on the brink of a conflict. The acceptance of a Russian diplomatic mission by the Amir of Afghanistan had provoked the second Afghan struggle which had resulted in a virtual British protectorate over that country; and when in 1885 the Russians had clashed with Afghan troops at Penjdeh, the British cabinet had actually drafted a declaration of war.

This wasn't the end. When it became known that Russians had been crossing into the border states north of India, the prize jewel in the British Crown, it at last seemed time to let it be seen that Britain was fully alert to the dangers. As General Sir George MacMunn, a frontier soldier himself, said, 'Enterprising Cossack officers had . . .

poked their noses into Hunza and Chitral and . . . it was desirable that Kashmir should . . . see to it that its control of its feudatories – the lesser fleas of our feudatory – should be sufficient to ensure that neither the amir nor the Russians from the Pamirs should come a-meddling.' With the British government concerned with these mountainous areas, and determined to close the Killick, Baroghil and Dorah Passes in their face, arrangements were made between Great Britain and Kashmir – a Sikh state enjoying British support – that a joint Indo-Kashmir Mission should work from Gilgit in Kashmir.

There were two border lines on the north-west frontier of India, the 'Administrative' border up to which the British occupied and policed the country and levied taxes, and beyond it the 'Political' border to Afghanistan, up to which the British exercised 'influence'. The long strip of territory in between these two lines contained tribes who provided what were, in fact, buffer states between British India and the Russians to the north. Though they were under British influence these tribes could be expected to break out in rebellion at any time and were kept quiet only by the devotion of young British officers who spent months in the wilderness with no other company but their Indian troops, gifts of rifles and what General Sir Bindon Blood, another famous frontier fighter, said were 'euphemistically called "subsidies" but what no doubt might be called blackmail by irresponsible critics'.

Chitral itself – the name sounds like a shot from a rifle echoing down the craggy slopes of a frontier gorge – was on the main and shortest line of communication between the Punjab, Afghanistan and the Russian districts of the Oxus, and lay close to the passes over the Hindu Kush, a circumstance that gave it an outstanding strategical importance. Tucked away in the very north, it was only a little larger than Wales with a population of only 70,000 to 80,000. Both the state and its capital bore the same name, and the fort at the latter, which was also the home of the ruling family, was only forty-seven miles from the main watershed of the Hindu Kush. Traders, pilgrims and tribesmen constantly traversed the country on errands of peace – *and war* – and the Indian government therefore considered it a place to hold, 'to secure an effective guardianship over its northern passes'.

Its dominant note was size and desolation; vast silent mountains cloaked in eternal snow, wild glacier-born torrents, cruel precipices and pastureless hillsides where the ibex and the markhor found a precarious subsistence. According to Sir George Scott Robertson – in 1895 a surgeon-major acting as British political agent – it took time for the mind 'to recover from the depression which the stillness and melancholy of the landscape' at first compelled. General Sir W. G. L. Beynon, in the nineties a mere lieutenant with the 3rd Gurkhas, thought 'the startling sensation of the immensity . . . in comparison with man's minuteness strikes home with almost the stunning effect of a sudden blow.' All colour was purged away by the glare of the sun and no birds sang, while cruelty, the predominant emotion in Chitral, was symbolized by circling eagles and vultures and the straight purposeful flight of the hawk.

Enclosed in such a mighty frame, the space for human life, as both Beynon and Robertson noticed, 'seemed almost microscopic'. Only about one per cent of the country was cultivated and this consisted of tiny fan-shaped oases of soil deposited by mountain torrents which provided life and nourishment to parched fields. These fertile patches, dwarfed by the limitless expanse of rock, glacier and mountain, were the only relief in the monotonous grey of vast slopes of shale and shingle; and the willows and plane trees and the soldier-like poplars of the valleys were the only points of coolness after the fierce light and dust of the hillside.

It was an area of sudden seasonal changes. One week the earth was frozen hard and the next the almond trees were covered with blossom and the lines of willows were like strings of green beads. Ian Hamilton described 'a hot little valley just stuffed with wild olives, pomegranates, walnut trees and mulberries. . . . Towards Chitral you look . . . up a narrow valley like a funnel with the black water racing at the bottom of it. And far in the distance the funnel is closed by a heavy belt of dark blue mountains. When there are clouds on these mountains you see nothing more. But . . . if those clouds should lift... the astonished traveller beholds towering in the background the most stupendous bulk of . . . pure snow . . . At first he fears no earthly mountain can be so vast and wonderful. Then he realises he is gazing at Tirich Mir, the fourth largest . . . in the world.'

The country was probably at its best in autumn with the leaves of the plane trees standing out 'as if stamped from copper'. Winter was harsh, dry and windless, though there was always the possibility that the hanging masses of snow would topple into the valley in thunder and smoke. Even this period had its beauty, however, with the frozen cataracts, fantastic snow wreaths and whitened branches, and the red dried rhubarb leaves stacked for fodder in colourful bunches in the trees.

Fashioned from the ridges and spurs – what writer after writer called 'a tossing sea of mountains' – that ran down from the Hindu Kush, Chitral lay between Kafiristan and the Amir of Afghanistan's other territories and the Gilgit frontier districts of Hunza and Punial. It was mountain-locked, bounded on the south by the high range that formed the northern watershed of the Indus, and level ground was at a premium. Where it existed it was often swampy or crusted with saltpetre, while a great mass of mountains ran from the Hindu Kush to the southern boundary range and divided the little state into two very separate halves.

Because of the terrain, the difficulties of travel were enormous and all baggage and stores had to be carried on the backs of ponies or men. Food, Robertson said, was so scarce 'a fat man had never been seen and even the upper classes looked underfed, and the most effective of bribes was a good meal'. The hill tracks, the main lines of communication, were often difficult and sometimes even dangerous, with precipitous overhangs that made good nerves essential. The bridges, which were usually untrustworthy, were sometimes constructed of ropes, three of them bound together to make the footway, with others for hand-rails chest-high on either side in the form of a V. Since the bridge sagged in the middle the side ropes hung outward so that a tall man had to stoop forward to cling on to them, with a resultant horrifying view of the drop below, while to add to the fun the ropes had a habit of perishing. Sometimes the bridges were of wood but they were still regularly swept away after the winter thaws – if they hadn't already been destroyed by some evil-intentioned tribesman with a 'pan full of charcoal and a bundle of dry straw'. The fords were always rocky and difficult, even when they were placid, and they usually required a guide because the unwary traveller was always likely to be carried into deep water or find himself in a quicksand.

The Chitralis matched their country. They smiled a lot and enjoyed singing and music, and at the end of a day's march there was always a band, dancing boys to attitudinize or prance, or at least a sitar player to sing of love in the high-pitched sustained notes full of quavers so admired in the area. Sometimes a play would be enacted by the fire, the plots invariably concerning princes beset by the darker-skinned aboriginal men of Kafiristan who were usually depicted as evil elves. Broad comedy, however, was always an element enjoyed by the watchers. They loved stories of fairies and the supernatural, and the singing boys would listen with wide-eyed enjoyment, 'pressing together like shy maidens to hear the excitement of the tale'.

Yet, despite their pleasant manners and their engaging light-heartedness, despite a passion for simple-minded ostentation and an instinctive yearning for the softness and luxury that their unforgiving country denied them, there were, in the words of Robertson, few people more treacherous than the Chitralis.

According to Sir Olaf Caroe, who spent half a lifetime on the frontier, the old enemies of the British, the Pathans, were admired for their courage, gallant bearing, and courtesy, and their preference for fighting honourably to the bitter end. The Chitralis, their next-door neighbours, who were not Pathans, had inherited all their inherent cruelty without their honesty, and the early history of their country was 'a crimson-stained record, a monstrous tale of murder and perfidy – the slaying of brother by brother, of son by father'. No gleam of generosity or magnanimity, Robertson claimed, illuminated the lurid pages, and the naked treachery, wholesale betrayals, and remorselessness were only varied by the intrigues that cemented them into a connected story. The case was much the same, of course, in many eastern countries, and putting aside their avarice, cruelty and treachery, Algernon Durand found the nobles pleasant enough to meet, fond of sport, swimming and their own wild country, while the ordinary people were bright, cheery, and impervious to fatigue, splendid mountaineers who liked to sing as they walked along and gather wild flowers to stick into their turbans.

Sir Francis Edward Younghusband, the explorer, who was assistant both to Robertson and Durand and political agent at Chitral in 1893, said the Chitralis 'were like children – impulsive, gay, careless, easily roused and easily soothed.... They were fond of shooting and hawking and played polo with great dash and spirit, old fellows of sixty galloping and shouting as hard as any....' Their bad points were the same as children's – 'they were always wanting presents and the more they were given the more they wanted'.

Their legal customs demanded the satisfaction of the aggrieved rather than the punishment of the guilty. Murder had to be avenged by another murder and when a man who killed his wife because he found her with another man was brought before his prince he was told, 'Go away and don't come back until you've killed the man, too.' 'It is considered,' Younghusband said, '. . . to save subsequent feuds if both parties . . . are killed and the matter once and for all settled.'

Despite a strong affection for relations – 'when cupidity or jealousy did not intervene' – the Chitralis, Robertson claimed, had such a wonderful capacity for cold-blooded cruelty that when enraged or envious they were far from averse to cutting the throats of their own children, parents or brothers. Even their stories, pleasantly told by people who were outwardly gentle, were, he noticed, invariably of cruelty or hatred. They told of shameless perfidy and of sudden disasters to travellers overwhelmed by avalanches, and even their fairy tales had a crimson tinge because, despite their simple appearance, their apparent happiness and the loveliness of their children, the Chitralis were 'guilty of sensuality of the grossest kind while murders, abominable cruelty, treachery or violent death were never long absent from their thoughts'.

They were the products of their environment. 'The life of a frontiersman is hard,' wrote Lord Zetland, twentieth-century Governor of Bengal and Secretary of State for India, 'and he treads it daily on the brink of eternity,' and in a cruel land, in Robertson's opinion, there were no men crueller than the Chitralis. One of the few 'convenient' traits they possessed was that there seemed to be a complete absence of religious fanaticism.

Perhaps he was seeing the Chitralis only through the sophisticated eyes of the West but events proved that he was not far from the truth and it was these 'implacable, treacherous' people operating in their own harsh country – what Algernon Durand called 'the land of mirth and murder' – who in the early months of 1895 were to create such a hubbub in India that their name flashed across the world while thoughts of defeat at their hands caused British prestige to be invoked with talk of a serious military reverse.

That pattern meant war

There had been rumours of trouble as early as the spring of 1891 when Algernon Durand, British agent at Gilgit, had felt that 'mischief was brewing'. 'The threads held in my hands,' he said, 'persistently wove themselves into one pattern, and that pattern meant war.'

The Amir of Afghanistan, Abdur-Rahman Khan, had watched the British moves to counter the Russian threat with increasing concern in the last few years. In 1895, he was a stout man of about fifty-five, with an active brain and courteous manners, but he was also shrewd and utterly ruthless and was quite prepared to kill with his own sword any man who reviled him. When a regiment of his soldiers mutinied he had the eyes of every man put out.[1] It was his habit to cut off the hands of thieves and highwaymen, and when an elderly spinster complained that he had given her in marriage to a man with no teeth, his grim humour led him to have every one of hers drawn too, to make them equal. British officials at his court were usually glad to leave at the end of their tour with their heads still on their shoulders.

The Afghans resented the intrusion of foreigners and, despite a projected visit of Abdur-Rahman's son to Queen Victoria and the friendly cartoons and jingles in *Punch* that followed the announcement, there was little love lost between the two sides. Hearing that the British wanted a more exact delineation of the frontier, in 1893 Abdur-Rahman approached the Indian government for a formal conference at Kabul. The Indian government suggested Sir Mortimer Durand, Algernon Durand's brother, as administrator, and when the conference was over, according to the amir's diary, 'the misunderstandings and disputes . . . were put to an end'.[2] He had renounced long-standing claims to Chitral, Bajour, Swat, Buner, Dir, Chalas, Kurram and all other places south-west of a line drawn by Durand, and from the spring of the treaty a joint commission worked for two years – in 1895 under Richard Udny – setting up pillars along the thousand miles of the frontier to mark the border.

The Durand Line has often been criticized for having few advantages and many defects. It should have facilitated frontier administration but, in fact, it increased the responsibilities of the government of India and the chance of a collision with the tribes and war with Afghanistan. It was not based on sound topographical data and certain places marked on Durand's map did not even exist. 'Many ethnic absurdities were perpetrated', several bad blunders were made, and it was never a tripartite agreement for there was no evidence whatsoever that the tribes themselves were consulted. 'In the light of subsequent events,' one historian said, 'it is difficult to understand the reasons which prompted the amir to sign. . . .'[3] In many cases it was possible to travel long distances without knowing whether one was in British tribal territory or in Afghanistan and the tribesmen knew little about the line, anyway. To add to an already difficult situation, in Chitral, just to the south of the line, the death of its ruler had left seventeen ambitious sons all eager to get their hands on the reins, and the country was virtually in a state of anarchy.

The ruler, or mehtar,[4] of Chitral from 1857 to 1892 was Aman-ul-Mulk, known to Chitralis as the Great Mehtar. Labelled by one British administrator as 'a truculent old savage',[5] he had climbed to the throne by steps slippery with blood, but, strong, brave and cunning, he was far-sighted and ambitious and knew exactly what he wanted. He had murdered two brothers to get the throne and when he died in August, 1892, from being merely a younger son of the Mehtar of Lower Chitral, he had gained possession of the whole of the hill country bordering the south of the Hindu Kush from Gilgit to Kafiristan, and held authority – even if unofficially – in Darel, Tangir and Eastern Kafiristan. Without a standing army or even the means to support one, he had persuaded others to fight his battles, disciplining his turbulent nobles and relatives by assassination or by working on their greed, lust and vanity.

Three years before he reached the throne, Chitral had been in dispute with its next-door neighbour, Kashmir. In those days all the mountain land between Kafiristan and Gilgit was divided between two chiefs. The western half, Katur, or Chitral proper, was reigned over by Aman-ul-Mulk's father, Afzul II, whose death was remarkable in Chitrali annals because it occurred naturally. The eastern portion, the Kushwaktia, was ruled by a mehtar of whose vicious temper Kashmir authorities were so afraid they formed an alliance with Afzul. In 1855 Katur seized Mastuj, the headquarters of the Kushwaktia chief, sixty-five miles from Chitral fort and on the Chitrali side of the 12,400 foot-high Shandur Pass which divided the country in two. They were driven out the following year but in 1857 the place was captured again. Three years after Afzul's death and the appearance of Aman-ul-Mulk, the eastern mehtar died also and part of his territory, the Gilgit valley, was acquired by Kashmir, while the dead man's sons fought over what was left till the border reeked with blood.

By treachery and cunning, Aman's power and influence increased. In 1885 and 1886, and again in 1888 and 1889, by which time he was at the zenith of his power, he entered into negotiations with the government of India which were highly profitable to him in guns and money. Only with Afghanistan did he suffer a relationship that was other than friendly, but an agreement with the government of India had led to the amir being informed by the British that no claim by him to the overlordship of Chitral could ever be recognized.

At the time of his death, Aman was a big man, with a strong clever face spoiled by the loss of his front teeth. Handsome in his youth, he had a charming expression when he smiled and a habit of embracing people who pleased him – 'A dreadful ordeal,' Durand thought '. . . for the Chitrali . . . does not wash too much, and his clothes swarm with vermin.' Despite his charm, however, Aman was steeped to the lips in treachery and his refugee brothers would never return because they knew they would receive short shrift.

He made money by forced labour; interfered in trade; levied prohibitive taxes; bullied passing merchants to sell him their goods at his own price; and sent presents of slaves to neighbouring chiefs. Nevertheless he was a devout Mohammedan, a kind and indulgent father to his younger children, and 'in a country where unnatural vices were rampant he was unstained'. He was reputed to have had eighty children, every village containing at least one of his sons or daughters.

Bright clothes delighted him. His court was a confusion of different garbs and only his dancing boys – 'the corps de ballet', Algernon Durand called them – dressed alike, in blue sleeveless coats and white shirts with huge red spots. This troop of dancers and singers was a great favourite with Aman, and for public occasions he even had an official whose sole job was to belabour over the head any spectator who did not applaud loudly enough.

The only member of his immediate family to die in peace and the fullness of years, his end came, as Robertson dryly pointed out, in an odour of sanctity because in his declining years he had begun 'to turn his diplomacy heavenwards' and had sent pilgrims to Mecca on his behalf. As he had chosen as allies the infidel British instead of his co-religionists along the frontier, however, he was detested by his people. His authority had rested chiefly on British subsidies of breech-loading rifles and money, and even as he breathed his last, the seeds of strife were germinating and his kingdom was 'to reel through a period of battle, murder and sudden death'; his sons, their hands red with each others' blood, were to go down in rapid succession to the grave, and six of them were to sleep in crimson shrouds.

In the words of Winston Churchill, Aman's sons were 'all equally ferocious, ambitious and unscrupulous' and, since the pernicious habit of parcelling out a kingdom into governorships for sons invariably led to civil war, they were all well aware that after their father's death it would be a case of kill or be killed. Indeed it was constantly a major problem for the British that you could never count with certainty on the succession. They were all half-wild[6] and only three were regarded as legitimate, and it was accepted that whoever won the throne, the inexhaustible hatred of all classes in Chitral for Aman would visit the sins of the father on the sons.

The most intelligent and best educated was Shah-ul-Mulk, at that time about twenty-eight years old. Aman's other two most likely heirs – more likely even than Shah-ul-Mulk because of the seniority of their mother – had both been to India to meet the viceroy and were in receipt of small subsidies. Nizam-ul-Mulk, the elder, was an amiable, good-tempered homosexual, a keen sportsman and polo player but also an utter coward. Afzul-ul-Mulk, the younger, was fearless, implacable, and as secretive as his father, a good-looking young man with handsome eyes but his father's heavy lower lip. While Aman was said to have favoured Nizam, in fact he feared both his offspring as much as they feared each other and him, and he had always been in the habit of sitting with a drawn sword across his knees whenever they had visited.

As it happened, the question of the succession was quickly resolved. When Aman died unexpectedly of heart failure, Nizam was shooting in the Chitrali province of Yasin, 160 miles away on the Gilgit side of the Shandur Pass, where he was governor. Afzul-ul-Mulk, who was governor of Mastuj, on the Chitral side, and in Chitral fort at the time – a fact that gave rise to stories that Aman had been poisoned – immediately seized the fort with its arsenal and treasure, and butchered Shah-ul-Mulk and two other brothers, Wazir and Bairam. This appeared to settle the matter and Afzul promptly wound round his head the enormous turban of the mehtar, with whose folds every personage of consequence had to help as an indication of his acquiescence in the investiture, and sent off messages to Gilgit, claiming friendship and affection for the British, and demanding recognition. Nizam became angry, frightened and warlike in turn but when he discovered that Algernon Durand, the British agent at Gilgit, proposed to remain neutral, his courage evaporated. Nevertheless, his reaction had frightened his brother who made overtures all round for assistance and, withdrawing the Chitrali garrison from the fort at Nursut – which was promptly occupied by his brother-in-law, Umra Khan, the restless and ambitious ruler of the Pathan state of Jandol and Dir, just to the south – had set off to Yasin after Nizam who fled to Gilgit.

Always on the look-out for the main chance, the Chitrali nobles were now in a dilemma. They had a strong mehtar they loathed who could only be replaced by a weak one they despised. Nizam was a miser, however, and was believed to have treasure with which to bribe, while Afzul had given everything away and had no reserves. Now, hurrying back to Chitral fort, he let loose the savage instincts he had inherited from his father and began to torture women suspected of knowing where treasure was hidden.

The British remained neutral. Afzul was still expected to become a good ruler while, because of his weak character, Nizam had hardly one Chitrali noble behind him to support his claim. In his anxiety to ingratiate himself with the Raj, however, Afzul now began to offend his nobles by forcing them to make roads for the hated British. Sure of himself, he dressed his bodyguard in a blaze of colour, and appeared to be completely in control but, according to Durand, while the death of his brothers would have passed with little comment, the announcement he now made that what he had done was nothing compared with what he was about to do set the whole country against him. Knowing the weak character of his brother, Nizam, the Chitralis turned their eyes to another half-forgotten candidate for the mehtarship, Sher Afzul, Aman-ul-Mulk's half-brother who, having fought unsuccessfully for the throne against Aman, had become a fugitive soldier of fortune at the court of the Amir of Afghanistan. At this time he was a short grizzled man of about fifty with a hawk nose and what was called 'a very Jewish face'. His manners were good and he had the courtesy of the hills, but he was as predatory in behaviour as all the rest of the frontier princes and at that moment, 'by the strangest of coincidences', he was just crossing the Dorah Pass from Badakhshan and passing into the Lutkho valley with a hundred men.

Afzul-ul-Mulk had no idea of the moves being made against him and went to bed on 6 November, 1892, never dreaming of danger. When at midnight the alarm was raised and men wearing tall Kabul-made caps appeared over the walls, Afzul's women tried to persuade him to escape in their clothes but he refused and, by the light of a fire he had lit to discover the extent of the danger, he was shot down as he tried to rally his men. As he was hacked to pieces, the shouts that were raised over his body hailed Sher Afzul as mehtar.

They weren't there for a change of air 3

It became part of Surgeon-Major Robertson's job to sort out the results of this imbroglio.

At the time of the coup Durand happened to be at Buni, about forty miles from Chitral fort, and to this dreary tumbledown place whose troops, Durand said, were 'forty per cent useless and the fort wholly so', came the governor of Mastuj, a man normally seen only in silks and cloth of gold. He arrived breathless and travel-stained and with his favourite son on the saddle, and he had ridden 140 miles at full speed to save his life. Refugees were also beginning to pour in now, and to a man they said that the country around Chitral fort was in the wildest confusion with no one's life safe.

The British still preferred not to become involved. The Chitralis were sorting out their problems in their normal bloodthirsty way. Sher Afzul had taken possession of Afzul-ul-Mulk's treasure, rifles and ammunition, and assumed the reins of government. But while refusing to be involved, the British were also not yet recognizing Sher Afzul. Without doubt, Afghan intrigues were playing no small part in the struggles in Chitral[1] because princes rarely left Kabul without Abdur-Rahman's knowledge and it seemed even that he might well be backing the usurper.

Since there was no communication between Gilgit and India, Durand had to decide what to do. With his brother dead, Nizam, who had been living at Gilgit on an allowance from the British, claimed his right to try for his father's throne. Through the skill and cunning of a minor chieftain, he defeated Sher Afzul's son in a skirmish at Drasan when most of Sher Afzul's 1200-strong army changed sides and, in panic and concerned only with their own skins, the nobles of Chitral at once demanded that Sher Afzul should return to Kabul. It was significant that when he did he fled to the camp of the Afghan commander-in-chief at Asmar. With difficulty, Nizam was induced by his supporters to move on to Chitral fort but, in terror, he sent messenger after messenger to Gilgit, offering his country to the British with both hands if they would only give him protection.

During his short and bloody reign, Afzul-ul-Mulk had also asked for a British official to visit him to give recognition to him as mehtar and Robertson had been sent. He had been stopped by Afzul's death but now, when Nizam wildly began to demand someone to hold him on his throne, Robertson was again ordered off.

Beyond Mastuj the people were bitterly hostile to Nizam and cordially detested the British, and the country was in a turmoil. Robertson's escort consisted of fifty men of the 15th Sikhs, and as his assistant he had Francis Younghusband, the explorer. Since, as a minor complication, the province of Yasin had risen against Nizam, with him also was the seventeen-year-old prince who had been proclaimed ruler.

As they crossed the Shandur Pass, it was so cold one of the Sikhs of Robertson's escort was brought in frozen stiff and Robertson's horse, which was well used to the bitter weather, died despite the thick clothing that was piled on top of it, the fires that were lit around it, and the frequent doses of hot rum and water that were administered.

Following the icy roads on the Chitral side of the pass, they reached Mastuj and as they turned into the Chitral valley, Nizam, unpopular and far too weak to follow in the ruthless Aman's footsteps, met them with his retinue. Since the rocks were covered with silent watching Chitralis, however, his military adviser had to forbid the normal salute for distinguished visitors from second-hand Snider carbines, matchlocks and ancient jezails in case the Chitralis used the occasion to mow Robertson and his party down.

Nevertheless, a great show of welcome was put on and games were played, though the polo was somewhat different from that enjoyed by British subalterns to the south. On the frontier very few flat areas existed and the polo grounds were merely terraces and often very small. Any number of men took part, the limit usually ten-a-side and a band of horns and drums played at full blast throughout. The game

B

was rough and produced a wild mêlée in which the players hit the ball and each other 'with fine impartiality', so that Durand had never been able to understand why it didn't end in sudden death and a general free fight.

Following the polo, high poles were set up, on top of which were gourds full of dust. Horseman after horseman then dashed past at full gallop to fire at these marks, the haggard Nizam, watching with horror, always careful to keep Robertson between himself and the marksmen.

Despite the outward gaiety of the celebrations, in Robertson's view everyone in Chitral was clearly uneasy. The successive revolutions had shaken the country to its foundations and nobody trusted anyone else. Nizam had not character enough to make himself respected and, because he had promised Durand not to indulge in the usual carnival of slaughter, it was assumed by his subjects that he was afraid.

Dozens of men were swaggering about with their chins in the air, scowling defiance and armed to the teeth, most of them with weapons collared during Sher Afzul's short reign, so, as they bedded down for the night, Robertson and his military advisers took care to see they were well provided with water and food and worked out schemes for loopholing the building they were in, in case they were attacked. Well aware of the Chitralis' hatred for the British and the family of Aman-ul-Mulk alike, Robertson realized the 'electric atmosphere' had reached the point of detonating spontaneously. 'Everything was wrong,' he noted, 'and an onslaught of fanatics seemed inevitable.'

It was very worrying because at this moment in time, apart from Robertson's group, the only other British officer on the Chitral side of the Shandur Pass, the only route from Gilgit, was Lieutenant Henry Kellett Harley, a cheerful and good-looking young Irishman, with his detachment of the 14th Sikhs. So concerned indeed was Robertson with the possibility of trouble, he requested that the agency at Gilgit should be strengthened so that it could control Chitral, keep Umra Khan and his Pathans – with the occupation of Nursut now an important factor in Chitral political affairs – from causing trouble, and persuade the Amir of Afghanistan to keep Sher Afzul from returning. Because of all these problems, however, he was committed also to the wretched Nizam who now seemed to have no other rival in the field, and, like the rest of the British, he was obsessed by the problem of the Russian threat from the north.

According to a Second World War general[2] who served his apprenticeship on the frontier, 'there was never a threat – it was pure imagination'. He was more than likely right because the Russian administration was always hopeless and they were never in a position to move against a country as powerful as Britain was at the end of the nineteenth century.

In fact, the threat was always regarded with more concern in London than in Calcutta, because they could not forget there that, while once 2000 miles had lain between the Russian and British frontiers, now, with minor principalities swallowed up by both sides, they were divided only by Afghanistan. However, the threat was always a convenient excuse for maintaining a field army which could be used outside India if necessary and the authorities there did little to discount it and the idea remained firmly entrenched in British minds.

Durand had no doubt about it and could not overlook the fact that in 1885, when war hung in the balance, Russian troops were moved towards the Pamirs. 'They weren't there for a change of air or to shoot big game,' he insisted. Had war broken out, he felt, there was nothing to prevent a Russian officer with a thousand Cossacks reaching Kashmir, a threat to India that would have been enormous. A born leader like Skobeleff,[3] he thought, could have made a great deal of such a chance, especially with no British troops within 200 miles. Francis Younghusband was also in no doubt. In 1889 in the Pamirs he had met a Russian officer escorted by Cossacks who had told him that, although the English did not believe the Russians intended to invade India, the Russian army – officers and men – thought of nothing else. The government of India claimed that it was this very thing that explained all the frontier wars they had to fight, whose object, they said, was to prevent at any cost the establishment within this outlying country of the political preponderance of any other power.

Right or wrong, the attitude called for a strong man in Chitral but, unfortunately, in Nizam the British had the worst of all possible worlds.

Some subterranean conspiracy had exploded

Known to Durand as 'Prince Hal' and far more royal in appearance than any of his brothers, Nizam-ul-Mulk had always been feckless by nature and from the day he had succeeded to the throne of Chitral he had been busily throwing away his chances of success by spending a great deal of his time drunk. With liquor forbidden to the followers of Mohammed, this habit so infuriated his subjects that probably not a dozen men in the whole of Chitral were behind him and Robertson had no great expectation of success in his mission. As it happened, however, largely through the skill of a native attaché, the cupidity of the nobles and the absence of fanaticism, he was able to win the Chitralis round. Though it was impossible to detach Umra Khan from Nursut, Yasin was restored by diplomacy, and Robertson was able to leave Francis Younghusband with a hundred men to back Nizam and return to Gilgit through a countryside as quiet as an Indian district.

By 1894, Robertson, now agent in place of Durand, was a tall, strong-featured man going bald but with the inevitable heavy moustache of the period. Possessed of a wry humour, intelligent and honest, he had been born forty-three years before in London, though with an ancestry deep-rooted in the Orkneys. He had married twice – his second wife a daughter of Samuel Lawrence the painter – and after training as a doctor, had entered the Indian Medical Service in 1878. After serving through the Afghan campaign of 1879–80, he had transferred his allegiance to the Indian Political Office and, following two dangerous journeys into Kafiristan, had become political officer for the Hunza-Nagar expedition of 1891–2 when he had taken over from his superior officer, Algernon Durand, wounded at the siege of Nilt.

A born soldier, he was said by Durand to be a man with 'a sublime disregard for odds', and his experience of the northern tribes was wide. While he could deprecate their villainy, cruelty and treachery, however, he could also still admire their good looks, their boisterous high spirits and their grim magnificent country. He was also honest enough to be aware of the arrogance of the British in ignoring the tribes' wishes, and of the fact that the Indian government's frontier policy, developed from day to day by the fortuitous dictation of events, was rarely logical or consistent, especially to the tribes who had to suffer it.

His base, like Durand's, was at Gilgit in Kashmir and, returning there after a year's leave in England, he was surprised by the apparent prospect of peace along the frontier. When he had left, Nizam had been so universally unbeloved that, suspecting upheavals, Chitralis of importance had fallen into the habit of sleeping in the daytime and passing the night with a loaded rifle across their knees, while a trusted servant guarded the roof over the central smoke-hole.

This phase seemed to have ended by the middle of 1894, and in proof of the fact many of the neighbouring chiefs and notables were now arriving in Gilgit with their followers to play polo, watch pony races and join in the general festivities of the British garrison to mark Christmas and the New Year.

Gilgit had a strange and enduring charm. Shut in by mountains, traversed by a fine river and 'adorned by a chain of lovely lakes', it contained plane trees, every imaginable species of fruit tree and the magnificent chenars so beloved of the Moghul emperors who planted them wherever they chose to dwell. Eternal snows reflected the sunlight and every season had its own peculiar beauty while, despite its height of 5000 feet above sea level, the temperature was mild and severe cold was practically unknown.

Headquarters consisted of a fort – described by Robertson as 'picturesque but useless' – which contained an arsenal and barracks for the troops of the Maharajah. It lay on the river bank and was surrounded by fields and orchards dotted with drab villages of crude hovels. Robertson's home was a snug, gabled house not far from a range of double rooms serving as offices or lodgings for bachelor officials. The European inhabitants of Gilgit were *all* officials, except for a solitary white woman, the wife of a transport officer.

From September to June they were cut off from the world because the passes to India were blocked by snow, and mail bags sometimes did not arrive for thirty or forty days at a stretch. Northwards there was no outlet, and southwards only to picturesque Srinagar up the Indus valley was there a track – through an area inhabited by cut-throat tribes with a fanatical hatred of Europeans. A telegraph line was supposed to connect them to civilisation but it was invariably destroyed by winter avalanches, and the men of the telegraph service suffered endless hardships and risk to their lives in a hopeless endeavour to keep it open for more than three or four days at a time.

The British-Indian troops at Robertson's disposal were few and the Kashmiris had always been considered indifferent soldiers.[1] Not only were they poor specimens in terms of morale, but when Durand first became agent they were also half-starved, and suffering from cholera epidemics and commanders who took no military precautions whatsoever. Their food was vile, the officers rarely visited their men, and so many of them were corrupt the honest ones had little chance. Among them, however, were mercenary Gurkhas from Nepal and Dogra Rajputs from Jammu, and with the Kashmiri army now being remodelled and trained by British instructors, service at Gilgit, 'long deemed the last word in horror and exile', was beginning to wear a very different aspect.[2]

With the army in the safe hands of the British and the frontier apparently quiet, the end of the year celebrations were enjoyed. Into Gilgit came horsemen perched high on doubled-up blankets to protect them from the hardness of their wooden saddles, their stirrups so short their knees reached almost to the withers of their mounts. Followers on foot used these stirrups or the pony's tail to help themselves up severe inclines or to steady the pony on a descent. The horses were richly caparisoned in tooled leather decorated with silver, and their riders carried hawks on their wrists. The men on foot were often in tatters – strong-faced men mingling with youths with smooth cheeks and fine eyes whose heads were bound in the untidy turban of the hills.

The political scene still seemed good – though there were one or two clouds on the horizon to give Robertson cause for anxiety. The Liberal government had issued instructions back in 1893 for the withdrawal from Chitral of Francis Younghusband, the political officer. Yet on a visit only a month before the games Lieutenant B. E. M. Gurdon, his successor on Robertson's staff, had not been slow to find a strong anti-British party. By this time, too, Nizam had begun to follow the crimson footsteps of his predecessors. Secret murders had multiplied, while whole families had been sold into slavery.

Gurdon's information had been disquieting, particularly as bazaar reports in Peshawar had begun to insist on the certainty of a frontier war as a result of Udny's boundary commission, at work in the nearby Kunar valley trying to put flesh on the bones of Sir Mortimer Durand's proposals. Insurrection seemed somehow to be in the very air again. Convinced that the danger would fall on Udny, Robertson decided that Gurdon should remain in Chitral and keep in touch with the Kunar valley, but he had also taken care to advise him to summon his agent's escort from Mastuj where Lieutenant Harley waited with 100 men, and to make certain that if anything happened he could quickly send the news to Gilgit. At the same time the senior British officer at Gupis, in Yasin, Captain C. V. F. Townshend of the Central India Horse, was ordered to repair roads and be ready to rush reinforcements to Mastuj at any moment.

Robertson's worries were still undefined, however, and as the Christmas and New Year festivities ended, he had no idea how near the frontier was to the spontaneous combustion he feared. While the notables who had arrived to watch and take part in the games were still heading homewards with their strings of followers, on 6 January 1895, an exhausted messenger on a jaded pony galloped in from Yasin. He brought an unconfirmed rumour that Nizam had been accidentally shot dead while out hawking at Broz, twelve miles from Chitral fort. He also brought a letter from Townshend saying that the rumour was well and truly believed by all the men of substance in Yasin and that refugees, fearing that attempts to seize power would result in the usual blood bath, were already flocking in.

Robertson recognized at once that 'some subterranean conspiracy had exploded', and he did not doubt for a moment that Nizam had been shot. Knowing Chitral, however, he was also under no delusions that the affair had been an accident.

This was a bolt from the blue!

It was always the tendency of earnest-minded Liberal governments in England at the end of the last century to consider first and foremost the delicate susceptibilities of their pacifist and anti-imperialist followers. By modern conventions these attitudes were correct but in the context of their own times they had the effect of constantly putting in jeopardy the lives of the soldiers who tried to administer the territories which, rightly or wrongly, the British had annexed. Policies were changed overnight, expeditions were sanctioned and then cancelled – with unfortunate results for the men on the spot – and bloody frontier outbreaks exploded for the simple reason that the troops on whom peace depended had been withdrawn.

For the rest of his life Francis Younghusband was of the opinion that if he had been left at Chitral in 1893, instead of being withdrawn, the events that followed would never have taken place. Fortunately, in Lieutenant Bertrand Evelyn Mellish Gurdon, Robertson was extraordinarily lucky. A blond, good-looking and utterly unflappable young giant, Gurdon had first joined the Manchester Regiment but had later transferred to the Indian Staff Corps and then to the political branch. He was well-known for his temperate and thoughtful judgments and it was because of this that the reports he had sent to Gilgit had been so disquieting.

Captain Townshend at Gupis was also worried. Gazetted to the Indian Staff Corps, he had first gone to Gilgit in 1891 on Durand's invitation to 'knock a couple of Kashmiri regiments into shape'. When the Thum of Hunza had headed, with Russian encouragement, into Kashmir and been forced to back down, he had been made military governor of Hunza, but on the murder of Afzul-ul-Mulk, he had moved to Gupis, 'a rat-trap' at the entrance of the Yasin valley where one of his jobs was to collect and collate information on Russian, Afghan and Chinese moves beyond the frontier.

He wasn't very happy at Gupis, which he thought an 'awful place', but he was intelligent enough to scent trouble almost at once. 'Nothing of excitement has occurred here yet,' he wrote home, 'only there is every appearance of a row. In fact I don't see how we shall get through the winter without a pantomime . . . of sorts.'[1] Like Robertson, he had also been badgering the authorities for more troops, better roads, a telegraph and a political agent at Chitral, and by November – again like Robertson – he had become convinced that trouble was coming; since he would be in command, he was ambitious enough to hope that it would.

No reports came in on 7 January, and everyone began to be aware of a growing sense of calamity, but the next day a letter finally arrived via Lieutenant Harley at Mastuj, displaying all the incredible sang-froid Gurdon always showed in a crisis. Nizam-ul-Mulk, it seemed, had been murdered on 1 January by his half-brother and the heir to the throne, Amir-ul-Mulk, a sullen nineteen-year-old who was clearly sharper than he looked because the British annual subsidy had just been increased to 30,000 rupees and the Chitrali treasury was full.

Fond of hawking, Nizam had ridden to the top of a mound to watch his falcons working and while descending his turban had become unfastened. Occupied with re-arranging it, he was shot in the back by one of his attendants who had a loaded Snider hidden under his robe. As he fell screaming from his horse, attendants ran to cut down the assassin, but Amir rode forward and claimed responsibility and, in the fashion of the Chitralis, loyalties changed sides at once and guns were let off in salute. Amir was acknowledged mehtar even as life slipped from the wretched Nizam who, had he not been murdered on the hill, was to have been despatched while he sat at his midday meal.

In Chitral, the murder was being everywhere applauded and the new mehtar, astounded at his own success, had now begun to wonder how he could dispose of Gurdon who had been out shooting when he learned the news. Returning to read the instructions Robertson had left with Francis Younghusband, to be followed in the more than likely event of Nizam being assassinated, he had carefully never allowed the Chitralis to know what was in his mind. At interviews with Amir – now terrified by his own temerity – he had remained unruffled, placing the seven or eight Sikhs he had with him in such a position that they could not be despatched without great loss, and smiling cheerfully on the armed men with rifles at full cock who crammed into his apartment eager to slit his throat. To Amir's demand for recognition, he would only respond by stating he would have to refer the matter to Robertson and by demanding to be allowed to summon his normal escort of fifty Sikhs from Mastuj.

Gurdon's unemotional persistence overcame the passionate Chitralis but now a new complication entered the affair.

It seems unbelievable that into this already tangled skein of murder and frontier politics there could be yet another element to confuse it further. But on the frontier anything could happen and very often did, and now Umra Khan of Jandol appeared once more.

When Sher Afzul had fled to Kabul after his unsuccessful coup against Afzul-ul-Mulk in 1893, Amir-ul-Mulk, Nizam's murderer – who had also joined in the plot – had fled to his brother-in-law, Umra Khan. After much negotiation with Nizam, Amir had returned to Chitral, professing to have escaped. He was well received but Nizam drew the line at the provincial governorship he demanded, because he looked on Amir as an idiot. Slow of thought but not lacking in cunning, Amir was, however, all the time a member of a new conspiracy to remove Nizam, his job being to make his brother feel secure by acting as a half-wit, a role he played so well Nizam was actively ashamed of him. The conspiracy had had as its sole object the return of Sher Afzul, for whom Amir was only keeping the throne warm, but, because he was uncertain of the reaction of the government of India to Nizam's murder, Amir had written in a panic to his brother-in-law, Umra Khan, for help.

Umra Khan was more than willing to join the fun. But he was far too ambitious to play second fiddle to Amir, and instead of considering how he could advance Amir's cause, he began instead to wonder what he could get for himself.

Known to Sir William Barton as 'the most striking military adventurer on the border' and to Algernon Durand as 'the Napoleon of Bajour', Umra Khan had been born about 1860, a younger son of Aman Khan of Jandol. Turbulent and restless, he had married a daughter of Aman-ul-Mulk, of Chitral, but after failing to unseat his brother on the death of their father in 1879, he had 'prudently retired on a pilgrimage to Mecca'. Returning secretly in 1881, he stole a rifle from the British lines in Peshawar and headed for Jandol where, dressed in women's clothes, he hid in the women's quarters at his brother's fort at Barwar and shot him dead as he passed through the gate.

Then, putting on the turban of rule, he obtained as many rifles as possible and, raising a band of well-drilled deserters from British-Indian regiments and a small troop of horse, began a series of wars on his neighbours. Scarcely a month passed without a fight and he had soon defeated the Khan of Dir who lost a large slice of his territory.

In the habit of extracting a tithe from all merchants and farmers and changing the money into gold – much of it Russian, which filtered across the border – at a rate fixed by himself, Umra had grown wealthy. He was tall with a powerful chest and arms, round shoulders, and a face that was long and thin with a big nose and firm mouth. Dressing without ostentation, he was religious but by no means a fanatic and, frugal of habit, was very popular with his followers.

All in all, he was a formidable enemy. The 'most expert and enterprising soldier on the North-West Frontier', he was spoken of in a Gilgit Agency report of 28 April 1890, as 'the most important man between Chitral and Peshawar'. Unfortunately he had been lost to the British by Mortimer Durand's arrogant re-shaping of the frontier and the decision that the little khanate of Asmar – formerly Umra's territory but now occupied by Afghanistan – should remain with Kabul. His Pathan sense of honour wounded by Durand's decision, he was determined to get back, if not Asmar, then some other territory to take its place.

Chitral, clearly a ripe plum ready to drop into his lap, seemed to be that territory. But, though he probably conspired in the murder of Nizam, it is unlikely that he chose the time and place, because at that moment he was preparing to fall on someone else and would hardly have chosen the season when the 10,000-foot-high Lowarai Pass between his own territory and Chitral was blocked by heavy snow.

Towards Umra Khan the attitudes of the Chitralis varied. Those who had supported Amir were prepared to welcome him because many of them, including Amir himself, considered the British the real enemy, anyway. Others remembered that the Pathans were their hereditary foes and were prepared to resist. Either way, they had no leaders, and no stomach for a fight and Umra himself was far less concerned with helping Amir than with securing the western half of Chitral, the fort and the rifles it contained.[2]

In this already complicated web of frontier treacheries, even Umra was being fooled by the Afghans who were eager to take advantage of the confusion to press the claims they had made against Aman-ul-Mulk in 1874; but though all these people were traitors to each other, they had been agreed on the necessity of removing Nizam, and here they had had the sympathy of all Chitralis. Now, however, with Umra Khan beginning to cast covetous eyes over the country, the dull-witted Amir began to speculate on the chances of keeping the mehtar-ship for himself. His senior chiefs had considered it prudent to await events, so that his sole advisers were two or three reckless young nobles not much older than himself who encouraged him to follow the usual procedure on ascending the throne and put to death all the people he disliked.

Tasting power, they began even to behave as if they were the actual rulers. Deciding that Sher Afzul might never return at all, and that if Umra Khan *did* appear it might well be difficult to get rid of him, they composed a letter to Umra telling him he was not wanted and decided to ingratiate themselves with the British. It was as a result of this attitude that Lieutenant Gurdon had been permitted to send word to Robertson and to increase his escort of a few Sikhs with fifty more from Mastuj as he had requested. Coolly he also used the opportunity to put an end to the bloodshed by saying it would alienate the government of India.

As Gurdon had probably suspected, the government of India was far from eager to compound the already confused political scene by recognizing as mehtar a youth whose capacity to rule was by no means evident, who was liable to be kicked off the throne at any moment by Sher Afzul, and who was in any case guilty of the murder of their own nominee. Nevertheless, Gurdon – feeling it better for a British officer to be at Mastuj to keep the chiefs quiet and hold open the route to Chitral – had no wish for the eager Harley to come pounding down to his aid. Captain Townshend was instructed to hold Ghizr, on the Gilgit side of the Shandur. This was a fortified place known as a darband or 'closed gate', a good defensive position tested in actual combat through generations of struggle.

The troops were soon on their way. In bitter weather with sometimes thirty degrees of frost, Lieutenant H. A. K. Gough, of the 2nd Gurkhas, left Gupis on 12 January with 150 Kashmiris of the 4th Ragunath Rifles, Townshend following on 14 January with another hundred men of the same regiment. Even as they began to head west, so Robertson's own orders arrived. He was to go to Chitral but was to remain non-committal because the Chitralis seemed prepared to accept Amir – except in the province of Yasin where the Yasinis again rose and where the Chitral-appointed governor was forced to flee into the fort at Gupis by the country people who swore they were now British subjects. Robertson left for Chitral on 15 January with Captain Colin Powys Campbell, of the Central India Horse, as his military adviser. Their impending departure had thrown Gilgit into an uproar of excitement and Robertson had been besieged by officers eager to see him 'on pressing business' which soon resolved into 'earnest, even pathetic prayers' to be allowed to go with him. In all the territories of the Empire, young men were distinguishing themselves in small wars and the young men in Gilgit, no different in ambition and desperate to see action, had used every kind of argument imaginable, Captain John MacDonald Baird, of the 24th Punjab Infantry, Robertson's military secretary, a man of great courage, finally almost bursting into tears when told he had to remain behind as staff officer to Colonel James Graves Kelly, who was employed making roads in the Indus valley, in case *he* was also needed to march to Chitral. In the end, it had been agreed that Lieutenant William

George Lawrence Beynon, of the Gurkhas, should be instructed in Baird's work so that Baird might then go to Gupis from where, in the event of trouble, he could be summoned to Chitral.

Robertson's party, surrounded by their servants and accompanied inevitably by their pet dogs, reached Gupis in forty-eight hours. There Robertson interviewed the deposed governor of Yasin who had somehow got hold of the idea that the mehtarship was to be put up for auction. Robertson quickly put him right and extracted a promise from the district headman that he should not be molested, a promise reluctantly given because the governor had been in the habit of carrying off their young girls for his pleasure.

The party left Gupis on 19 January, among them – as aides to Robertson – four young rajahs. One of them, Sifat Bahadur, was an unusually handsome Puniali, fair-skinned and powerfully built and the hereditary leader of his tribe. He had already once saved Robertson's life during the Hunza–Nagar campaign by a magnificent charge at the critical moment of a skirmish, and Robertson placed great confidence in his ability in the rough fighting of the frontier.

At first the journey was not difficult. The tribesmen en route were not trusted and the troops moved in two groups, one by the road, the other over the hills in case the roads were blocked. Following ice-covered tracks which sent ponies and men sliding from the pathway on several occasions, they met Captain Townshend at the windswept village of Ghizr on 21 January, and started at once up the slopes to the Shandur Pass. Lieutenant Gough, with whom was Surgeon-Captain Henry Frederick Whitchurch of the Indian Medical Service, had already crossed at the cost of a few mild cases of frostbite.

The cold was tremendous but in the fine dry air it caused little trouble, though the ponies were often in difficulties. At Langar at the entrance to the pass, the officers crowded into one small tent, warmed by a stove stoked red-hot by a sepoy. Though the only shelter for the men was a long wedge-shaped erection of willow branches, such were the precautions the officers insisted on there wasn't a single case of frostbite.

The next day the Shandur was crossed. Fortunately the wind was at their backs and they reached Laspur on the other side to find great bonfires blazing in the winter gloom for their arrival. Mastuj was reached on 25 January, the fort bleak among the saltpetre swamps. It had 'known better days'. Though in the era of bows and arrows and matchlocks it had been a formidable place, it had recently, like Gupis, been damaged by one of the earthquakes which were not uncommon in the area and its walls had fallen into decay. Gough and Whitchurch had arrived two days earlier, and the gregarious Lieutenant Harley was delighted to find himself with so much company after months alone with his Sikhs.

The news that awaited Robertson was alarming. Umra Khan had crossed the Lowarai Pass into Chitral with between 3000 and 4000 men and had sent letters ahead to say he had entered into a holy war against the Kafirs of the Bashgul valley. He claimed he had no hostile designs on Chitral itself, though if Amir-ul-Mulk did not support him he must take the consequences.

This was a bolt from the blue. Robertson knew little about Umra Khan except that he was a disturbing spirit on the frontier who must not be allowed to commit further aggression, and once more he began to expect trouble in the debatable land of the Kunar valley where the Udny commision was still working with the Afghans.

The Chitralis were clearly afraid. Only a few of them knew that Umra Khan had actually been invited into Chitral by Amir-ul-Mulk and, his renown as a warrior beginning to create a panic, a stampede from lower Chitral was already starting. Amir-ul-Mulk was soon suspected of double dealing, and Lieutenant Gurdon could not retreat to Mastuj because the only route lay through incredibly bad country where he could not rely on transport or supplies. There was only one thing to do: Robertson had to push on by forced marches to Chitral and seize the fort. In a when-one-moves-we-all-move operation, warnings were sent to Colonel Kelly that he might have to move up to Gilgit to take command, while Captain Baird was ordered up to Ghizr with 200 men and Lieutenant Frederick James Moberly, of the 37th Bengal Infantry, was ordered to Mastuj with another hundred. Transport was rounded up and the dilapidated fort patched up, while Harley was sent on towards Chitral fort to find out the state of the roads, fords and bridges.

During the day, news came in that Umra Khan had arrived with a vengeance. He had burned the Chitrali village of Utzun and was now threatening the town of Kila Drosh a mere twenty-five miles from the capital of Chitral itself. There was no time to be lost. Snider ammunition was ordered up from Gupis, to be replaced there from Gilgit, and Captain Townshend was sent off to Buni on 27 January with a hundred men, Surgeon-Captain Whitchurch acting as his subaltern. That day for the first time Robertson learned that it was Amir-ul-Mulk who had invited Umra Khan into Chitral.

It had been hard to provide transport animals for Townshend and it was harder still to move the second detachment under Harley, who took command of thirty-three Sikhs and a hundred men of the Kashmir Rifles. It was an appalling journey over icy paths and through freezing fords, and though Robertson and Campbell got into Townshend's camp at Buni in the evening, Harley, abandoned in the bitter weather by his half-frozen guide, did not arrive until the following morning with several of his men frostbitten.

The baggage was delayed by the awful roads but they dared not wait because news now arrived that Umra Khan had defeated the Chitralis at Kila Drosh, killing and wounding thirty of them. Since the defeat meant grave peril for Gurdon, a messenger was sent ahead to tell him to move out to meet Robertson's party.

The road, at this point so narrow and dangerous it could be destroyed in a dozen places, consisted chiefly of shingle slopes and *paris*. On the shingle slopes every heavy rain or thaw brought down avalanches of rock so that the traveller always had to keep a wary eye open. A *pari* was a cliff path often barely more than a foot wide, sometimes even consisting only of a single shaky plank or bundle of tamarisk or logs set in steps, with a sheer drop below. They were impossible for animals and made excellent defensive positions.

Harley and his men were detached for much needed rest while Townshend was sent on ahead to Baranis. It required a very difficult march to rejoin him. The path followed a cliff face that curved out above the river and at one point it had broken away so that they had to crouch in darkness until it was repaired by the light of flaring torches[3]. Robertson's party were not unhappy to put such an area behind them and throw themselves down on the dirty straw of the native huts at Baranis.

Despite the freezing nights, the days were insufferably hot with a blazing sun, though the frozen snow underfoot constantly brought men and horses down, and on one occasion Captain Campbell, riding a diminutive black pony 'hardly bigger than a rat', suddenly found the animal shooting forward from between his knees so that he was 'left standing on his feet and gazing in surprised enquiry at his boots'.

As they pushed on they met men carrying the bodies of relatives from the fight at Kila Drosh. The road at Baitari five miles from Chitral fort ran for a considerable distance on galleries constructed by driving branches into holes in the cliff face and packing them with earth. A break could stop a pony for hours and there was always the prospect of being caught there and having the gallery cut before and behind so that they could be sent toppling into the valley by rocks hurled down from above.

They arrived in Chitral on 31 January to find that Umra Khan was now besieging the fort at Kila Drosh but that the garrison seemed to be defending themselves sturdily. Lieutenant Gurdon, imperturbable as ever, rode out to meet them, and aboriginal Kafirs, old friends from Robertson's journeys into their country, skirmished round his horse, kissing his fingers or pressing his hand to their foreheads in salute. The day was close and cloudy as they occupied Robertson's old house on the high ground on the south bank of the river.

The first shot . . .
always to be dreaded

Chitral was not a town as most people would understand the term.
The valley in which it was situated was one of the few large stretches
of land in the country that could be cultivated, and in the middle of it
the fort, the home of the mehtars, squatted by the river. This was the
centre of Chitrali society and round it were a number of scattered
hamlets and houses. In normal times the population was a mere few
thousand but at the moment it was swollen by the tribesmen who had
come in from the outlying districts, as well as by less patriotic tigerish-
looking types looking for loot. The atmosphere was electric.

Sixteen miles south of the fort was the village of Gairat, which was
said to be the place where the fairies who were supposed to inhabit
Tirich Mir gathered every Friday night to say their prayers.[1] More
important, however, it contained a rocky position pierced by the
river which was another darband like Ghizr, and here Amir-ul-Mulk
had stationed himself with several hundred men. The position was
easily defensible in the prevailing wintry weather and even if Umra
Khan captured the fort at Kila Drosh, ten miles further down the
river, he could be stopped at Gairat so long as the men holding it
remained dependable.

Amir-ul-Mulk excused himself from receiving Robertson's party in
person. He claimed military responsibilities but Robertson hadn't the
slightest doubt that the real reason was because he was wondering if it
would not be better to do a deal with Umra Khan. However, his only
full brother, a grave little boy called Shuja-ul-Mulk,[2] had met them at
Mastuj and, travelling almost all the way with the party, had made
himself very popular.

The day after the British arrived it rained heavily, turning the dirt roads into quagmires, but Lieutenant Gurdon set himself the task of collecting supplies, while with Rab Nawaz Khan, an elderly Multani cavalry jemadar formerly of the 15th Bengal Lancers and now employed in Chitral as 'news writer' or junior political representative, Campbell and Townshend went to inspect Amir's shabby fortress and make rough plans in case of trouble. Like most frontier forts, it was a drab place with decaying luxury alongside sheer filth. The Chitralis had no idea of cleanliness or hygiene. Refuse was merely flung into the alleys and left to the scavenging birds, while the dust that drifted everywhere blurred the expert filigrees of craftsmen and dulled the colours of both foliage and clothing. Even the royal quarters were mere drab rooms where chipped furniture and neglected wood carvings rubbed shoulders with threadbare drapes and unrevered ornaments, the mud walls all too often visible through gaping holes in the panelling which sometimes ended in scuffed boards inches above worn dirt floors. The whole place had suffered from years of neglect and, with every wall overlooked from the surrounding slopes, huge trees had even been allowed to grow just outside to shade and dominate the courts in summer.

Nevertheless, they were able to feel satisfied with what they saw, though according to Rab Nawaz Khan, who had spent many years in Chitral and knew the Chitralis intimately, every one of the nobles with Amir was a follower of Sher Afzul at heart and only awaiting his return. Stranger still was the report that Umra Khan had as many as eighty Chitralis of this faction in his camp. There was clearly a conspiracy afoot that puzzled Robertson, though the possibility of Sher Afzul appearing once more was discounted because Udny, working with the Afghans in the Kunar valley, had felt he would learn of any move that was made.

One hundred men under the command of a Kashmir major were sent to the fort with the excuse of guarding stores but in reality to hold the main gate, while Amir's women – what Captain Townshend, who had always had an eye for a good figure or a pretty leg, called 'sheeted bundles' – were moved to Robertson's old house. Meanwhile Captain Campbell reconnoitred the neighbouring hills and Lieutenant Harley marked out ranges. These moves were explained away to the Chitrali notables in the fort and a message sent to Amir at Gairat who that evening rode in to see Robertson in person. He proved to be a stupid-looking youth with sulky ill-manners whose young nobles conducted the conversation on his behalf. Their object was to persuade Robertson to send part of his escort to Gairat – to give confidence to the defenders, they said – and the argument went on throughout the evening and all the following morning. In the end Robertson agreed to send fifty more men and, clearly assuming that Robertson might put Shuja in his place on the throne, when he left Amir took his young brother with him. Almost immediately news arrived that Chitrali resistance at Kila Drosh had suddenly collapsed.

It seemed high time to occupy the fort at Chitral completely. No help was given with the baggage, however, and tremendous arguments were put forward to prevent the move. Amir's nobles and his men established themselves inside. To make sure of a water supply, Campbell constructed a covered way from the fort to the river, and also put in a state of defence a corner of the garden to the south where there was a summer-house. Gurdon had meanwhile been more than successful in gathering supplies, though – since all the villagers were at Gairat or Kila Drosh – there was no one to carry them in.

The information coming from Kila Drosh suggested the fort there had been surrendered through the treachery of the Chitrali governor, Kokan Beg, Amir's uncle, and many breech-loader rifles and match-locks had been given up.[3] Treachery was clearly in the air and, since the eastern Chitralis from the Kushwaktia area had always hated the domination of the western Chitralis, many of those on duty at Gairat now broke into open rebellion and, hurrying back to Chitral, claimed that henceforward they would accept no other rule than that of the government of India. In this, Robertson thought shrewdly, they were probably actuated more by their dislike of Amir than by any senti-mental attachment to the British. Amir also reappeared, wearing a dove-coloured suit embroidered with gold that had belonged to the murdered Nizam, and to match him Robertson put on his agent's uniform of frocked coat, spiked helmet, high boots, spurs, sword and sabretache. Amir was indignant at the occupation of the fort and, when his objections were overruled, suggested that at least the southern half should be reserved for him and his women. Since this half commanded the northern half, Robertson again had to refuse.

With Amir sullen at his proposals being turned down, they turned to the rebellion of the Kuskwaktis. To Robertson it was clear that the western nobles were willing to settle the matter there and then with their weapons, but he managed to prevent a fight and they all eventually started back for Gairat. He was feeling more secure now because he had a feeling that at least a proportion of the Gairat garrison would oppose Umra Khan if he advanced, and to put backbone into the Kushwaktis he sent Townshend down with a detachment of the Kashmir Rifles and the means of signalling the enemy's approach.

Robertson joined him on 17 February, accompanied by Baj Singh, a Dogra soldier who was a Kashmiri general. Their escort, in true Chitrali fashion, knocked up their horses badly en route. Though constantly in the saddle, the Chitralis were always poor horsemen, preferring to use every one of the few available level stretches of their tortuous countryside for furious gallops that gave their horses sore backs and themselves bruises and abrasions.

By this time, with all the precautions they had taken, things were looking better. The British officers at Gairat reported the defenders full of confidence and the only storm cloud seemed to be at Kila Drosh. That night, however, 'that first shot . . . always to be dreaded' was fired against Lieutenant Gurdon and his small escort while reconnoitring along the river bank south of Gairat. Captain Campbell hurried off to take command of the darband. Almost at once, he sent back word that the enemy had appeared; but that it was not just Umra Khan but Sher Afzul also!

This was a startling item of news, but the story was corroborated soon enough by a horrified Amir-ul-Mulk. Unconvinced, Robertson thought it was just a Jandoli trick. Had not the Amir of Afghanistan 'solemnly declared' after Sher Afzul's last and abortive venture that the Chitrali prince's stay in his country would now be permanent? Two days later, Robertson's scepticism seemed to be confirmed when Campbell reported that Umra Khan's men were deserting and that Umra himself was becoming worried. Despite persistent rumours that the men hurrying away from Kila Drosh were not deserters at all but Chitralis eager to greet Sher Afzul, now supposed to be at Dir,

Campbell went so far on 22 February as to say that Umra was about to throw up the sponge. Townshend also reported large-scale desertions, but, on 23 February, Campbell reported again – this time that Sher Afzul had actually ridden into Kila Drosh! Robertson couldn't believe it.

Captain Baird, who had been moved up from Mastuj convoying ammunition, had marched in on 20 February and been sent off with a hundred men to Aiun, a mile or so from Gairat, to support Campbell, and now Robertson actually managed to get in touch with Umra Khan. Unfortunately, the letters he received in reply were unintelligible, a fact that was blamed by the envoy who brought them on Umra Khan's secretary. He was a Persian, he said, and 'badly educated'. On 24 February despatches arrived from India instructing Robertson to deliver an ultimatum to Umra Khan. Clearly assuming that the primitive Chitralis would regard him as being against them if he were not actively for them, the government also instructed him to help them turn Umra Khan out. The orders were pointless. Robertson had already done as much as he possibly could.

Puniali and Hunza levies were, however, sent for from Gilgit. These were valuable troops who had been raised for rough local work when it was found that the Indian army was growing too formal and was losing its readiness for swift action. It was felt that, in the doubtful event of Umra Khan still not having retreated, they would encourage him to do so.

By this time, Robertson was convinced that Sher Afzul was the only possible mehtar. Amir had still not been recognized, even as a temporary mehtar, and Sher Afzul's reappearance had reduced his followers to the smallest possible number, while to Amir's fear of Umra Khan was now added a terror of Sher Afzul, whom he had cheated.

Robertson, however, still couldn't understand the connection between Sher Afzul and Umra Khan and, wrongly assuming that Umra Khan would gladly retreat if he could save face in what, with the arrival of Sher Afzul, now seemed a dead enterprise, he decided it might be as well to get Sher Afzul to Chitral to put forward his not insubstantial claims, and persuade Amir to resign with the promise of a governorship.

Sher Afzul made the first move, however, by asking the men at Gairat to meet him at Kila Drosh. Hearing of it, Robertson sent him an invitation to Chitral, promising safety and the almost certain agreement of the government of India to his claims, but just before the letter arrived, all his plans were thrown awry by a few headmen at Gairat who persuaded the defenders to leave their posts to escort Sher Afzul to Chitral, so that the position was left to the care only of Campbell's men and a few Kushwaktis.

With Robertson still aghast at the news of this treachery, that evening two letters arrived, one from Umra Khan, of which only the opening greeting, 'To the brave and great colonel of Chitral', was decipherable, and one from Sher Afzul, 'To his kind friend, the Colonel Sahib Bahadur', professing 'with complimentary hyperbole' undying friendship and a willingness to co-operate with the government of India, but failing entirely to reply to Robertson's invitation to visit Chitral. Robertson wrote again and when this also failed to produce a reply he began to grow anxious.

Their eyes on the hills that surrounded them, the British watched for signs of trouble. An army could hide itself in the folds of land above them and they looked for the small things that might show they were there – a layer of floating dust over one of the ridges, a flock of birds disturbed from their roosting. But nothing moved and they began to wonder if they were being unnecessarily edgy.

A worried reconnaissance down the right bank of the river next day showed everything to be quiet. A string of horsemen moving along the opposite bank was discovered to be a mission from Sher Afzul and, finding the people at Aiun overjoyed at what seemed a peaceful end to the crisis, Robertson rode to Gairat on 27 February to meet the deputation. It comprised a single gorgeously-dressed Afghan with one dirty attendant. The Afghan haughtily presented his credentials and said Sher Afzul had escaped from Kabul without the knowledge of the amir. The only place fit for him as mehtar, he claimed, was the fort which Robertson should therefore evacuate at once. Coldly, Robertson answered that neither Umra Khan nor Sher Afzul could impose a mehtar on Chitral but, though the Afghan moderated his tone, he refused to shift his position and merely reiterated the demands. He returned without any promises.

That night, with the weakened force at Gairat expecting to be attacked at any moment, it was decided that the only thing to do was get them back to Chitral as fast as possible. The baggage was a problem and darkness magnified the distance, the difficulties and the shortage of troops. On this western side – Robertson's side – of the Shandur Pass there were at this time only eighty men of the 14th Sikhs and sixty-seven of the 4th Kashmir Rifles at Gairat; eighty of the 4th Kashmirs at Aiun, 150 at Chitral, and 102 at Mastuj, while en route to Mastuj from Kashmir were ninety-five men of the 14th Sikhs and twenty men of the Bengal Sappers and Miners. At Ghizr, on the other side of the pass there were 106 men of the 4th Kashmirs and 100 of the 6th Kashmir Light Infantry. Their enemies numbered thousands and more were arriving all the time.

Early on 28 February, Amir-ul-Mulk appeared, half-distracted, at Aiun and an interview was held on the roof of one of the houses flanking the polo ground. Pressing on all sides, agitated Chitralis watched Robertson carefully and all ears strained to catch his words. Amir gave no trouble and was even persuaded to bawl out a few orders which sent porters to Gairat. At 2 pm Captain Campbell signalled that they had arrived and that he hoped to start back in half an hour, and about 4 pm Captain Baird galloped off to help and every pony that could be found was sent after him, whether it belonged to a prince, a British officer or a common Chitrali.

Another night of stringent precaution followed. It was as well, because Sher Afzul's men were waiting nearby and as the British left Gairat, one body of them marched in so fast they walked bang into the middle of the rear-guard of Kashmiris who promptly took them prisoner.

Daylight on 1 March was doubly welcome. Amir-ul-Mulk was still being watched carefully. Though he knew the road to Mastuj had been destroyed by Sher Afzul, he continued to suggest that Robertson's force should retreat there to await reinforcements, his hope obviously being that the British force would be trapped on the galleries of the Baitari cliffs.

All day rain fell without ceasing, lashing into the puddles and saturating baggage and clothing. There was another terrible delay over porters, but Baird had wisely sent a message to Gurdon at Aiun to hold the bridge over the river and to send a detachment to command an awkward length of road just before the Chitral plain. By keeping control of these dangerous points the party crossed safely, though some precious food stores had to be abandoned.

In a continuing downpour, feet squelching in thick mud, wet through and miserable, and with Robertson wretched with dysentery contracted at Gairat, the party finally stumbled into the fort. The sky was heavy, the ground was saturated; the old fort, cheerless in the gloom, looked grey and forbidding. Robertson, however, was not too alarmed by the prospect of a siege. He had been trapped for a week once before, at Sherpur near Kabul in 1879, at the time of Sir Frederick Roberts' advance to Kandahar, and he felt that things would work out all right. Work was therefore immediately set on foot to bring in the food that had been gathered and to prepare defences, while Gurdon wrote to Lieutenant Moberly at Mastuj informing him of events and warning him that if letters arrived irregularly for a few days he was not to be surprised.

This time, however, the siege was to last rather longer than a few days and the message Moberly received, concealed in the lining of the messenger's breeches because it was already known that mail bags were being stopped, was the last news to get through to the outside world.

When you meet an Asiatic, go for him

Despite their dangerous situation, Robertson's men were in good heart and worked hard at carrying in the supplies. There were over five hundred of them to feed, including camp followers, clerks, messengers, commissariat workers, transport personnel, those Chitralis who – willingly or unwillingly – were to remain with Robertson, and the Indian servants whose capacity for loyalty had always survived the worst of British ignorance.

Thanks to the efforts of Gurdon and Futteh Ali Shah, the Askogol of Shoghot, a ragged-bearded man of middle age who constantly clutched a sword to his chest because the triumph of Sher Afzul would have meant certain death to him, it was considered they had sufficient supplies for three months. Food still remained important, however, and when one of the princes, whose house was full of grain, went over to Sher Afzul, the petulant Amir-ul-Mulk was told to detail men to seize it. But Amir was still toying with the idea of making his peace with Sher Afzul and destroying the British, and he held back so long that in the end the supplies were lost.

Still sick with dysentery, but pleased to have got everyone into the fort, Robertson was worried about Amir and even more worried about Umra Khan whose alliance with Sher Afzul he still failed to understand. Some reports indicated that he was only waiting for a chance to seize Sher Afzul and regain the favour of the government of India; others said that Sher Afzul was just as eager to desert to Robertson but was held back by Umra Khan. In fact, the basis of their alliance was simple – united hostility to the British – but whoever was to be mehtar, the real ruler of Chitral would always be Umra Khan.[1]

Robertson was still trying to work it out when another letter arrived from Sher Afzul demanding a subsidy from India and that no Europeans should remain in Chitral. With winter covering the passes with snow, he pointed out, the British could not hope to be reinforced and the only thing left to them was to head for Mastuj up the right bank of the river. 'It was the old plan warmed up,' Robertson thought, guessing that it was intended to catch them on those terrible galleries five miles outside Chitral. It was too late by this time to escape, anyway, and he arranged to present his answer at a durbar. The Chitrali chiefs were received in a large inner room in the fort, with Amir-ul-Mulk in an armchair on Robertson's right. All the British officers were present but every precaution against treachery had been taken and the headmen had to squat on a carpet below them. Then Robertson dropped his bombshell and announced that, since Amir had not once shown the slightest sign of sound government, he was going to make his younger brother, Shuja, head of state subject to the approval of the government of India.

The decision was ruthless and the silence which greeted it profound. Amir's youthful followers stared in astonishment with dropped jaws while Amir himself sat speechless. There was nothing they could do, however, and after a time they recovered sufficiently to offer homage to Shuja and kiss his hand, but when Amir rose Shuja refused to permit him to come near.

Robertson then pointed out that the princes and headmen would be held responsible for the good advice and instruction of the new young mehtar, while Amir would remain in the fort since his life outside could no longer be considered safe. This, of course, was manifestly true. Now that he no longer possessed the divinity that hedged a mehtar around, the implacable hatred of Nizam's household would follow him wherever he went, and from that moment he became virtually a prisoner.

Amir was quite unprepared for his sudden downfall. He had been so certain of his power, he had even brought into the durbar the man who had shot Nizam. But he had been noticed, and as he left Captain Campbell arrested him. His carbine was found to be at full cock. As he was dragged away, Shuja made his first experiment in power and demanded to be allowed to deal with him in his own way; the

wretched man was eventually marched to the river bank and despatched
with a sword.

As soon as the durbar ended, Shuja ordered men to the house
where the royal women were living to collect treasure, horses and
rifles. Captain Townshend sent twenty sepoys to help, at the same
time – on the excuse of needing them for defence – collecting thirty
valuable rifles and ammunition from the Chitralis. Not only did this
add to the number of weapons the British could use if necessary but
it also had the effect of disarming the untrustworthy Chitralis.

In the afternoon, Shuja held a durbar of his own in the public part
of the fort. Drumming and piping and rejoicing 'of a not very
enthusiastic kind', took place and the Chitralis came in to make their
obeisance. The last word remained with Sher Afzul, however, and at
4.30 pm news arrived that, escorted by a strong force, he was only
ten miles away at Aiun.

They were all aware of the growing suspense. Would Sher Afzul
jump or would he back down? As they went about their duties,
aware of the silent hills around the fort and the hostility of the village
of Chitral a quarter of a mile away, the prospect was cheerless.

The distant huddle of houses was quiet and there still was nothing
about the chiselled hills to indicate that they were full of eyes, though
they all knew they were there, staring down on the shabby fort,
watching silently what went on – the passage of mules and ponies,
the arrival of tradesmen, the movement of soldiers, even the mounting
of guards, their positions and probably even whether they stayed alert
or dozed at their posts. It had been going on ever since they had
taken possession, and the garrison had never seen any movement that
wasn't intended to be seen, so that the silence was intense and nerve-
racking. The present friendliness of the Chitralis, they knew, would
last only as long as Sher Afzul kept his distance.

The following day a letter from Sher Afzul, in reply to one sent by
Robertson telling him of Shuja's accession to the throne and warning
him to make his obeisance, was brought to the fort by a prince called
Yadgar Beg, who also brought a document alleged to have been sent
to Sher Afzul by Chitrali headmen. Both demanded that Sher Afzul

be made mehtar and that the conditions he had set down should be agreed to. Because his dysentery had grown worse, Robertson received Yadgar Beg in bed. Though intelligent and influential, Yadgar Beg was a plausible scoundrel and Robertson had to work hard to force him to be frank. Bribed by gifts he admitted that the letters he brought had no real meaning because negotiations were still going on between Sher Afzul and Umra Khan.

Yadgar Beg's admission increased Robertson's worries. Staring at the dark screes and slopes that surrounded the fort, with the white bulk of Tirich Mir beyond, he tried hard to decide how his enemies were thinking. Though cattle and flop-eared goats grazed nearby, the hills were terrible in their silence. There was no sound from them, and barely a tree or a blade of grass on them, and in their magnificence they looked as unreal as a stage setting. He knew there were men there even though he couldn't see them – men with an indifference to death, men who would show no weakness because they themselves had no fear of wounds or mutilation. The border tribes were a resentful people who owed their allegiance to Allah and, though they were often courteous and laughter came easily to them, they would never hesitate in their hostility towards the infidel Europeans.

As the hours of 3 March trudged by he was still uncertain what opposed him. He had heard the day before that Sher Afzul's advance guard was not more than three miles away but a few loyal Chitralis had ridden out under Wafadar Khan, one of Shuja's supporters and advisers who had always opposed Sher Afzul as a usurper, and had returned with the news that the countryside was devoid of enemies. Wafadar was a young man of considerable intelligence and courage, handsome, slender, wiry, always tidily dressed with a neat turban, tunic, trousers and curved sandals. Since his life, like Futteh Ali Shah's, was in grave danger if Sher Afzul triumphed, there was no reason not to believe the report, but information now arrived that a dozen of Sher Afzul's horsemen were actually in the bazaar, a serai-like enclosure of low ramshackle shops and violent smells and colour only 750 yards from the fort.

This was worrying. The fort was surrounded by wooden buildings, together with a musjid – or Mohammedan temple – stables and guest and store rooms where the supplies of grain had been placed. It was not safe to leave these buildings standing, but to demolish them, a task taking three days or so, before the last hope of peace was gone, was also dangerous because in Chitrali eyes these royal adjuncts to the fort were considered almost sacred. Robertson was desperately in need of time. The buildings stood in the way of the garrison's field of fire and commanded the parapets where Campbell's men waited, and in the end he decided to ask Campbell to make a strong reconnaissance across the Chitral plain.

At 4.15 pm on that day, therefore, 200 Kashmiris of the 4th Ragunath Rifles, almost half the garrison's fighting strength, marched out to find out what was really in the wind. They were fully equipped, and dressed despite the heat in long black overcoats that stretched from neck to ankle. With them were a few horsemen, Sifat Bahadur and the other Puniali rajahs, Rab Nawaz Khan, medical attendants, and the usual assortment of servants, clerks, orderlies, grooms, bearers and pet dogs.[2]

With Captain Campbell in overall command, and with Gurdon as his political agent, the sortie almost emptied the fort. When the anxious Robertson threw a horseman's cloak over his pyjamas and rode after them himself, not a single fighting officer was left behind because Harley was already outside with his Sikhs. With treachery about, it was a highly dangerous thing to do, but Surgeon-Captain Whitchurch – despite a shy, quiet manner – was highly dependable and could easily take over the duties of an army subaltern at any time; and when Harley returned to post his men with what was left of the Kashmiris on the ramparts the danger passed.

There was still a tension in the air, however, that seemed to call for strong measures. Campbell detached fifty men to seize the bazaar-serai, and despatched Captain Baird with a section under a subadar to investigate a number of armed men in a ravine which carried a stream from the hills about a mile south of the fort. The main body under Captain Townshend held the road to Aiun and Robertson's old mission house, with a party thrown forward to keep in contact with Baird. Wayfarers were interrogated and it became quite obvious from their replies that Sher Afzul himself, with a party of armed men, probably 400 strong, was in a hamlet hidden from view on the far bank of the stream overlooked by Baird.

The few native horsemen under Robertson's command were sent forward to investigate. In the prevailing tension they were distinctly nervous and did little more than ride backwards and forwards, 'looking very gallant with their long spears, but doing little good'. The men facing Baird across the stream in the ravine were variously described as 'timorous' and 'spoiling for a fight', but, despite the fact that they carried banners, the balance of opinion was that they were merely country folk terrified by the appearance of armed soldiers. In his experience, Rab Nawaz Khan preferred to think otherwise but felt that the waving of banners was merely bravado, and it was decided to push Townshend further forward with a hundred men. They marched in an extended double line towards a house indicated by Campbell, but unfortunately the movement carried them to lower ground where they were at a disadvantage. Campbell sent a messenger forward to change their direction, but for some reason the message never arrived.

Meanwhile, Lieutenant Gurdon, reverting from political to military duty, was sent off to Baird with a message that a single shot was to be fired over the heads of the armed men across the stream who, if they proved to be enemies were to be steadily volleyed at until they were driven back. The eager Baird seemed to misunderstand the instructions and, when the single shot was answered at once by a volley, he decided he was intended to descend from the secure position he held, cross the stream and attack up the opposite slope of the ravine with the bayonet.

The land in front of him – a tangle of gullies, ravines, boulders and stunted bushes – called for a great deal of circumspection but Baird was itching to prove himself and in no mood to be cautious. He was a gentle man, but there was no more dashing officer in the army and like most Britons of the period he regarded Asian enemies with contempt. 'When you meet an Asiatic, go for him,' he always insisted, but Gurdon, whose head grew cooler as danger increased, suggested he had not read his instructions correctly and that he, Gurdon, should be allowed to bring up supports before the forward movement was made.

Baird answered briskly that the orders were quite clear, but as they descended their side of the ravine and crossed the stream to the other side, they found they were followed up the slope by only thirteen of their Kashmiris, the rest having divined that it was safer to take cover. Their guess was a good one. As Baird and Gurdon had moved forward, the Chitralis on the opposite side of the ravine had retreated higher up the slope but now, unexpectedly, they scrambled hurriedly down again to cross the stream and climb up the other side to seize the very ground Baird had just left. Immediately, the whole Chitral plain exploded in a ragged outburst of musketry.

Taken in flank by the men they had been attacking, Baird's party was caught by a shower of rocks and a blast of fire from riflemen who had been invisible up to that moment. Baird went down at once and only Gurdon, Subadar Badrinar Singh, a Gurkha, and three sepoys were left standing. Even Baird's fox terrier was killed. Crouching out of the blast, Gurdon at once sent off one of the three unwounded sepoys to fetch Surgeon-Captain Whitchurch. Then, leaving the other two with Baird, who was badly wounded, he calmly climbed farther up the hill with Badrinar Singh to a point where he could see the troublesome riflemen above and keep down the fire coming from the ground Baird had so unwisely abandoned.

Eventually Whitchurch arrived but, though Baird was carried off in a litter, Gurdon decided to hang on a little longer. As he waited, his groom was killed and his pony caught by the enemy, but he coolly continued to hold his ground until he felt Whitchurch's party was out of danger. Then, seeing them safely on their way, he hurried back, collecting as many of the sheltering Kashmiris as he could as he went.

With Badrinar Singh's help, he had just got them in some sort of order on the bank of the stream when a mass of men from Sher Afzul's main party in the hidden hamlet climbed the bank of the stream and burst through the middle of the line. By sheer weight they forced Badrinar Singh and half the Kashmiris back down the road Whitchurch had taken while Gurdon and the rest were pressed uphill.

With the enemy also above, they were completely surrounded.

C

Like wild dogs round a failing deer

8

While Baird had been making his reckless and ill-advised advance, Townshend was pressing forward with his men – led by Colonel Jagat Singh and Major Bhikam Singh and accompanied by the Kashmiri general, Baj Singh – towards the house pointed out by Campbell. Campbell had remained behind with Robertson on higher ground to the right but, as the firing that had started began to grow heavier and one of the men alongside Townshend fell with a bullet through the head, he moved forward to direct Townshend's attack. Robertson's party remained on the edge of the high ground and as they moved slowly along it they became witnesses to the disaster to Captain Baird's party.

Low down on the spur where Baird had disappeared a group of men were seen moving. Since none of the Kashmiris were believed to be there, they were at first assumed to be Chitralis, and Robertson was just about to order a volley to be fired into them when he recognized Lieutenant Gurdon's long legs.

'Stop,' he shouted, just as rifles were being settled to shoulders. Then Baird was seen stretched on the ground with the dead fox terrier at his feet. Robertson was too far away to do anything but send a messenger to bring up Surgeon-Captain Whitchurch who, in fact, was already on his way. By this time Robertson's party had reached a small walled orchard and, because of the increasingly heavy firing, the horses were led to the rear and Robertson crouched down to wait. The men with him were the Gilgiti rajahs who had been so pleased to escort him from Gupis, the little cavalryman, Rab Nawaz Khan, a few Mohammedan clerks and orderlies, and two or three loyal Chitralis who formed a rough escort.

The house Captain Townshend had been approaching had been found in the meantime to be empty but in front and to the right lay a hamlet enclosed by a wall where Townshend saw men dodging among the trees. Just then, the sound of firing from Baird's party to the right was heard and, deciding that the men he could see must be the enemy, Townshend ordered his detachment to fire a volley and push on. Their fire was immediately furiously returned from the hamlet.

Townshend had only a hundred men and of them he kept back a couple of sections under Jagat Singh and Bhikam Singh as a support. About 250 yards from the enemy, his men found cover behind a low stone-revetted bank and spread out, firing industriously; but the Chitralis were shooting well and there were several casualties. Townshend kept up a steady fire, firmly expecting Baird to come down from the high ground to the right to attack the hamlet from above – in which case he could catch the enemy as they ran – but as time passed and there was no sign of Baird, small groups of the enemy began to move round his left and enfilade him from the direction of the river. It was also possible to see them creeping round to his right and, since it was now 6.30 pm and almost dark, he sent off a note to Captain Campbell to say he was in danger of being outflanked.

Campbell hurried up. 'Rush the village,' he said, and Townshend ordered up his supports. As the firing had started, however, most of the craven Kashmiris had flung themselves down behind walls 150 yards to the rear and refused to move, so that Campbell himself had to go back to bring them up. He was only able to drag forward a mere half-dozen and, as he reached Townshend again, he had to climb a fallen wall where, pausing on top to use his binoculars, he was bowled over with a bullet in the knee. The hamlet facing Townshend had meanwhile turned out to be a large village with a high wall a hundred yards long, behind which the enemy sharpshooters waited. Jagat Singh had also gone back to bring forward the supporting Kashmiris, but no more than sixteen had arrived and Townshend decided he must storm the village with the men he already had. It was a disaster. Baj Singh was shot dead on one side of him and Bhikam Singh was mortally wounded on the other. Several others, including Townshend's orderly, also fell. The rest flung themselves down again behind what shelter they could find.

Neither cajolery nor threats could push them any further. It was hopeless to persist, and Townshend had to crouch behind a tree with the bullets plugging the ground about him. Finally, realizing that the battle had become a disastrous muddle, he led his men back, telling Campbell it was time they started the tricky business of extricating themselves. Even as they talked, the orderly dressing Campbell's wound fell dead, shot through the chest, and it grew very clear that time was running out.

Despite the pain he was suffering, Campbell calmly wrote a message to Lieutenant Harley to bring his Sikhs from the fort to cover the retreat and told Townshend to give everyone time to get moving and then fall back himself. Townshend tried to bring the line of sullen Kashmiris to the point of moving but they were clearly scared stiff, though with the help of Jagat Singh he eventually got them in some sort of order. As he started to withdraw them, leap-frogging one section over the other, the excited Chitralis saw the move and rushed forward from one cover to another, yelling and firing rapidly. In the growing dusk it was impossible to spot anything more than rare glimpses of white clothing, a head-dress, a banner, or the puff of smoke that indicated a rifleman.

The march became a run. Fighting to prevent a panic, Campbell pushed away the four scared Kashmiris assigned to help him who were hurrying him along faster than his men, and, throwing away his scabbard, hobbled along on his own, using his sword as a stick. Bullets ripped into the struggling group and, as the men fell, the tribesmen were on them at once, hacking and yelling, to snatch up their rifles and ammunition. An Indian hospital assistant carrying the fort's medical supplies fell badly hit. Groaning, he offered large rewards to the Kashmiris to carry him in, but he was a heavy man and already dying, and the frightened soldiers refused to listen. Eyes wild, firing haphazardly and throwing away their equipment as they pushed past him, no one noticed that the medical supplies had been left behind.

One of the Ragunath Gurkhas insisted on grabbing Campbell's hand to help him, and had to be furiously shaken off as they reached a wall where Campbell needed both his hands to help himself. Rolling down the other side, he was picked up by the Gurkha while the white-robed Chitrali swordsmen and riflemen, 'running in like wild dogs round a failing deer', drew closer.

It was a horrifying situation. Men cut off from their comrades could expect short shrift and, as he kept the enemy at bay with his revolver, Campbell knew very well what would be done to them if captured alive. It had always been enough to give them nightmares and the shaken Kashmiris were now not far from a rout.

The firing had become heavy by this time, the noise echoing among the hills, the valley catching the waves of sound and passing them on to the next cleft in the slopes until the whole region rocked with the tumult. It was extraordinarily accurate, too, and in the orchard Robertson and his men were having to keep their heads down as the bullets swished and whined overhead. Robertson had his fur cap slit, and the Kashmiris with him required no urging to lay low. As it happened, the half-combatant little company had been assumed in the growing darkness to be the real attacking force, yet their lightweight enfilading fire was holding the Chitralis back long enough to enable the other parties to withdraw.

Robertson was desperately weak with his illness, and doubled up with pain, and for most of the time had had to follow the progress of the struggle by the shouts of Rab Nawaz Khan. 'Now they fly,' the cavalryman yelled. 'No, they don't! Yes, yes, they do! Hurrah!' Each cry increased in optimism until suddenly the cavalryman's eyes stared and his mouth dropped open. Pointing to the right, he began to shout again. 'They are on us!' he yelled, and Robertson saw a small party of Gurkhas who had been with Baird racing back on his left.

Ordering Rab Nawaz Khan to hold back the men moving in from the right, he went to halt the Gurkhas. The cavalryman actually stopped the advancing Chitralis for a while before his rifle jammed and he was cut down and his weapon snatched up by howling tribes-men. Meanwhile, running to intercept the retreat, Robertson's weakness caused him to stumble and fall. 'You are hit,' he heard someone say, and Sifat Bahadur ran up to offer him an arm.

'No, Sifat,' Robertson panted. 'Not hit! For God's sake, try to get my pony!'

As he spoke, a Gilgiti groom, normally the most timid of men, was seen bringing up his big Galloway, an animal with a tremendous stride, at that moment snorting with terror. They could hear the bullets thudding into the ground like a hailstorm and, half-maddened with fright, the horse was difficult to approach. Even after Robertson had been pushed into the saddle by Sifat and the groom, he expected at any moment to be flung out of it again, and when he caught up with the retreating Gurkhas he couldn't stop the horse and could only haul it round with both hands on one rein. In the end he had to throw himself off but as he did so the Gilgiti groom, still remarkably cool, ran up again and seized the bridle.

Nearby was a small enclosure. It was only a few yards square, but Robertson hurried every man he could stop into it. The Kashmiris behaved steadily enough, and Robertson peered about, wondering what had become of Campbell, Townshend and Gurdon. Only the wounded Baird was believed to have been got safely away.

The enemy seemed to be all round them and now a few of the sepoys who had slipped past Robertson began to run back to him, indicating that he was surrounded. Then one of the sepoys on the south side of the enclosure shouted and fired into a mass of men emerging from the gloom. Fortunately the shot went high and the next moment Townshend fell into the enclosure, followed with the last of the men by Campbell in a picturesque state of fury. He had lost his cap and his knee was roughly bandaged, while the sword he carried seemed to vibrate with his rage. [1]

He dismissed his wound as of little importance and continued to rally his men. Three of the horses had been brought up by this time and Robertson bawled at him to mount one, but, thinking he was being ordered to leave his men, Campbell refused and had to be almost forced into the saddle.

Ordering Townshend to bring the detachment towards the fort, Robertson — not knowing that Campbell had already sent an order to that effect — decided to hurry back ahead of him to bring out Harley and his Sikhs. Once again, quite calm and unruffled, the Gilgiti groom brought up the Galloway and, aided by Sifat, pushed Robertson into the saddle. The frightened animal started off with huge bounds, while Sifat ran behind yelling that the walls about them were dotted with enemy swordsmen. But the horse was out of Robertson's control by this time and, eyes wild and flecked with foam, it cleared both walls of a narrow lane to leap down a series of small drops from one terraced field to another to the polo ground. A group of Chitralis on foot surged forward, waving swords, but the horse was going too fast and burst past, the firework-like sparks from the ancient matchlocks only serving to drive it faster.

At the opposite end of the polo ground, Robertson managed to drag the animal round for a final rush through the hamlet that still lay between him and the fort. Two loyal Chitralis, mounted on ponies and armed with long spears, were waiting for him there. The three of them splashed through a stream, and, heads low and crouching in the saddle, ran the gauntlet of the narrow lanes between the houses.

Near the fort they ran into Lieutenant Harley advancing with his Sikhs in line. A few long shots from across the river had wounded one of the men he had posted on the ramparts but there had been no attack and soon afterwards Campbell's orderly, Duffadar Mohamed, a Punjabi of the Central India Horse, who offered to act as guide, had brought Campbell's message to lead his men out. A hundred yards from the walls they ran into the returning Robertson who was concerned that the stragglers following him would mistake Harley for the enemy in the darkness and fire on him. Two men were sent off to warn them and, thinking of riding back himself to make sure the job was done properly, Robertson shouted to Harley to ask how many men were still in the fort.

'About forty,' Harley shouted back.

As it happened, he had underestimated but the words, in Harley's rich Irish brogue, took Robertson's breath away. Forty! To guard the whole fort? It seemed incredible and he could only assume that some of the men he had left behind had either been ordered out by Harley or had deserted. Fortunately the bridge across the river was still held by Gurkhas but an enterprising enemy could easily have approached through the trees on the west and rushed the fort.

Hurrying inside, Robertson found a scene of utter confusion. Harley had handed the place over to a Dogra officer who, 'paralysed by his own responsibility', could only reply to Robertson's orders with a graceful bow, oddly combined with a military salute. A few sepoys were trying to close the gates, but a Gurkha officer came to the rescue and men were pushed outside to cover the entrance while others were sent to take the Sikhs' place on the parapets. As the dispositions were being made, Lieutenant Gurdon arrived.

By the grace of God it had been almost dark when the remains of Baird's party had been rushed and the imperturbable Gurdon, never losing his nerve for a moment, had actually led his own little group *back into the middle* of the throng of shrieking tribesmen who were panting to cut his heart out. Silently, their steps slow, their hearts thumping, they had slipped through the screaming men in the gloom and, heading between the temple and Robertson's old mission house – by that time crowded with Sher Afzul's warriors – they had reached the bank of the river and had run down the incline to the water's edge. Hurrying along it for several hundred yards, they had waded through a stream and made a final dash for the fort.

As soon as he had recovered his breath, Gurdon collected a fresh detachment and hurried off to give cover for the main gate to help the retreating coumn which was just beginning to appear from the darkness. Fired on all the way from the mission house on a spur above, Campbell and Townshend had brought the terrified Kashmiris along the east side of the polo ground, exposing them as little as possible to the enemy's skirmishers and rallying them to cross the bridge over the stream and enter the serai. They were quite out of hand by this time, however, so that when Harley, advancing to their aid, saw the confused mass stumbling out of the bazaar enclosure in the dark he could only assume from their ragged formation that they were the enemy.

His Sikhs were in line, their bayonets fixed, and shots were falling all around while matchlocks were sparking in every direction. The Sikhs were several hundred yards from the fort with no supports and were being shot at from three sides, so it would have been understandable if they had become excited. Fortunately they didn't.

'Present!' Harley shouted.

By great good fortune Campbell heard the order from among the approaching mass of men and shouted a warning at exactly the same moment that Harley recognized the grey horse Campbell rode. It was a close shave but the Sikhs were so well under control not a single rifle was fired, and Campbell and his party passed to safety between the line of fixed bayonets. Harley gave him 200 yards' start. Then, after two or three volleys which effectually stopped the more adventurous of the pursuing enemy, he retired slowly, giving the stragglers who were now coming up time to reach the fort.

As the gates slammed shut, by the light of flaring torches that flung huge shadows on the walls everyone was shouting at once. They were all over-excited and breathless, their hearts stampeding as they noisily discussed narrow escapes or the death of friends, and listened to the screams outside where wounded Kashmiris crouching behind rocks and in hollows were dragged out and butchered. Huddled in a corner was the Gilgiti groom who had brought up Robertson's horse. Pushing Robertson into the saddle a second time had used up the last of his unexpected courage and he had collapsed in a motionless daze, his limited stock of bravery too severely tested. For days afterwards he hardly moved.

In the hubbub as they went to their posts, a hasty and informal roll call showed to their horror that Whitchurch and Baird and their little group, who were supposed to have headed back long before the rest of the reconnaissance party, were still missing. So were a large party of Kashmiri Gurkhas under Badrinar Singh who had been separated from Gurdon in the rush of tribesmen at the beginning of the fight. With darkness and the situation that faced the garrison, there was nothing that could be done for them. It was an agonizing decision but, listening to the cries outside, the gates were kept firmly closed and the grim-faced Robertson occupied himself with getting Campbell to the hospital they had hurriedly set up in the durbar room.

It was obvious that the defeated Kashmiris, who had been badly shaken by their losses, would need a few hours to recover themselves but the parapets and towers were manned, the trustworthy Sikhs keeping a sharp eye on the main gate and the river front where the greatest danger lay. Going to see what amount of skill was possessed by the native dispenser who – with Whitchurch missing – was in command in the hospital, Robertson found that Campbell's injuries were much greater than they had believed. His knee-cap was shattered and even worse damage to his leg was suspected. Desperate emergencies seemed to demand desperate cures and, trusting to half-forgotten surgical remedies he had for years put aside for his political duties, Robertson seized a bottle of carbolic acid diluted with water and poured it over the wound. The pain was hardly less than Campbell's indignation.

The writhing victim was still alternately cursing and catching his breath when it was learned that Whitchurch was outside the fort at a small gate that led to the garden, and there was a frantic scramble to unbar it. Whitchurch was there all right, tired, breathless and white, his hands clasped under Baird's arms, his heaving chest supporting the sagging head of the injured captain who had received a further bullet wound – this time in the face – only a moment before. With them were Badrinar Singh and the missing Gurkhas, who had helped carry Baird in.

Whitchurch had just got Baird into a litter when Badrinar Singh and the other Gurkhas, separated from Gurdon by the rush of tribesmen, had arrived, but as the litter was being carried back across the polo ground, three of the four bearers were shot dead and the other mortally wounded. As the litter fell to the ground the Gurkhas were forced away again, leaving Whitchurch entirely alone with Baird. Baird was thickset and heavy and Whitchurch couldn't lift him, but, pulling the wounded man's arm over his shoulder and circling his waist with his other arm, he had dragged him towards the fort alone in the darkness until Badrinar Singh and his men fought their way back to them. Cut off by the tribesmen, Whitchurch had decided to head for the river, but the ground was very difficult and before they could reach safety the party had had to charge with the bayonet and carry several stone walls behind which groups of Chitralis were posted.

By now the courtyard was a chaos of hurrying men and anxious helpers bent over moaning figures. Baird was carried to the hospital while Townshend began to prepare a message to Udny, and Gurdon and Robertson wrote notes to be sent to Mastuj. They were still busy when the sentries reported that a dying man had been left in a litter at the main gate. It was found to be Rab Nawaz Khan. Stripped and left for dead with nineteen sword cuts, one of which had missed his carotid artery by a hair's breadth, he had been found by two of Aman's illegitimate sons, Asfandiar and Shahi, who realized he was still alive. With the help of servants they had brought him to the gate and, though they refused to enter, they asked that if the British won, their action should be remembered.

Even now the garrison was not complete. There were men still outside guarding the bridge over the river. It was these men, resolutely holding their positions, who had made the precipitate retreat possible because the enemy swarming on the opposite bank could not cross to join the mob surrounding the struggling Kashmiris. Campbell and Townshend wanted to bring them in at once but Robertson felt they had a better chance in daylight. As it happened, the orders were misunderstood and the men came in anyway – fortunately without loss. The enemy immediately occupied the position they had held, screaming and beating their drums in triumph while the shocked men in the fort at last began to count noses and tot up their losses.

Impossible ever to improve them

9

The reconnaissance had been a disaster. They had allowed themselves to be ambushed by between 1000 and 1200 men – 500 of them Umra Khan's Pathans, most of whom were armed with excellent Martinis and Sniders – and instead of the advantage they had hoped to obtain they had lost thirty per cent of the men engaged. With the dead left on the field, spirits in the fort were at rock bottom, and the hasty retreat was, in Robertson's opinion, 'a confession that we were completely defeated'. It was clear the Chitralis thought so, too, and several princes who had been quartered outside the summer-house in the garden promptly went over to Sher Afzul, as sure as he was that the fort was now untenable.

Robertson's responsibilities lay heavily on his shoulders. Though Captain Campbell had been in military command, the chief accountability remained his. As political adviser in direct contact with the government of India, his demands always had to be met and the reconnaissance he had requested had brought death to twenty-three men and wounds to thirty-three more. Instead of discouraging Sher Afzul it would merely persuade him to attack the fort itself.

Ten years after Chitral an army handbook[1] was published which waxed strong on the disadvantages of this kind of reconnaissance in force. 'Not a man nor a horse more than is required should be employed,' it said, and critics of the sortie always felt that a patrol or two could have gained all the information required, without loss of life or morale.

Without doubt they had brought the defeat on themselves by launching the sortie too late in the afternoon so that a daylight advance had ended as a headlong retreat in darkness. They had also probed much too far forward, and, despite the fact that there had been British agents at Chitral for several years, constantly hunting and riding in the surrounding district, and that Campbell had reconnoitred the surrounding hills only a few days before, there seems to have been no discussion about danger spots and remarkably little information about the terrain. There had also been a confusion of orders in the fighting, and, in attacking across the stream, Captain Baird had compounded the errors already made.

Robertson did not attempt to excuse or delude himself. They had lost fifty-six men they badly needed for the defence of the fort. What was probably worse, these included good leaders like Rab Nawaz Khan, who had shown himself as steady as a rock in a crisis, Baj Singh, Campbell and, of course, Baird. Setting down the causes of their defeat in his diary, he pointed out how Sher Afzul's men had used all their skill to keep under cover, hiding behind rocks and trees and walls, and dashing from one place to another with so much agility in the deepening gloom that they were practically invisible.

On the credit side, some of the Kashmiris had behaved splendidly. They had been hampered by their greatcoats and had had to fight a numerous, better-armed, more active enemy while armed with Sniders whose rifling was so worn they were known as 'gas-pipe rifles'. But if some had behaved well, an almost equal number had behaved indifferently. 'It was clear,' Robertson wrote, 'that the Kashmir sepoys had not the faintest idea of musketry. Their shooting was terribly wild – atrociously bad. They fumbled with their rifles, let them off at all manner of unexpected times, dropped their ammunition about, and behaved as if they had never before fired a shot.' There was even reason to believe that some of the men had been shot by their own comrades in their panic.

He quoted one brave man who had smiled at him as he displayed a shattered arm, saying, 'All right, Sahib, but I am wounded, see.' Yet there were others who had pretended that they had no more cartridges and, twisting their fingers in the eastern gesture which meant 'I have nothing', had rushed on 'with wide-open eyes and dilated pupils like a hunted animal's'. It was really not surprising, he thought, that the Chitralis in the fort considered the Kashmiris were 'not only no better than they had always been but that it was impossible ever to improve them'.

The following day the siege began.

A dropping fire was kept up all day from sangars – stone fortifications thrown up on the hillsides – from the slopes all round them, from the village of Danin across the river, and from Robertson's old house and the house of Rab Nawaz Khan which were within easy rifle range and on higher ground. It was so bad, in fact, Campbell had to be moved from the spacious durbar room to a dark but safer room on the south side where he found it poor fun to lie in bed with the bullets whacking into the walls alongside him. No man who could move at all was too weak to be of help, however, and it was decided to use his new room as a store. Although unable to leave his couch, Campbell could at least keep watch on their most precious supplies.

Left now with Robertson were only three active British officers. Captain Charles Vere Ferrars Townshend, on whom the defence of the fort had fallen, was an odd ugly young man. He was thirty-four years old and a great grandson of the first Marquess Townshend who took command of the British at Quebec when James Wolfe fell in 1759. Born into an impoverished branch of the family, his parents had tried to push him into the navy but he had finally managed to get himself into Sandhurst and had been gazetted to the Royal Marines in 1881. Like Robertson, his experience of war and sieges was not small. He had been attached to Wolseley's column which had marched up the Nile valley in an attempt to relieve Gordon in Khartoum in 1885, standing in the square which had been broken by the Sudanese at Abu Klea, and had been involved in the retreat and battles when Khartoum fell. Restless, 'obsessively ambitious'[2] and convinced that only action would bring him the promotion he wanted, he had transferred to the Indian army and the Central India Horse in 1886. He was a curious character with actors and actresses among his friends, and had made himself known to the army's upper crust by his ability at parties to sing a whole array of gay and bawdy ditties while accompanying himself on the banjo. With his good connections,[3] he had been able to pick and choose his jobs. He had already been growing bored with India, and had not wished to return there after his leave in 1889 when he had tried to wangle a posting back to Egypt.

While at Gupis, Townshend had acted as host to the Hon. George Nathaniel Curzon, that autocratic and equally ambitious man who later became Viceroy of India, who was making a tour of the north. To Curzon's surprise, he had been treated to a strong dose of Hamley and Clausewitz and the strategy of Hannibal, Marlborough and Napoleon, had noticed 'daring' illustrations from *La Vie Parisienne* on the mud walls, and had finally been regaled through what seems to have been a long evening with selections from his host's musical repertoire. It was little wonder that he thought Townshend 'somewhat unusual'.

There were also Lieutenant Gurdon, Robertson's assistant, imperturbable as he had already shown, and a tower of strength in any undertaking, military or political, and Lieutenant Harley, a cheerful youngster who had originally joined the Dublin Fusiliers before transferring to the Indian Staff Corps and then to the 14th Sikhs. After living alone on the frontier for months, he was unlikely to be put out by the thought of more months with companions. Finally there were Surgeon-Captain Whitchurch, who could be of value as a soldier, though there were so many wounded after the sortie his duties would inevitably keep him in the hospital; and Captain Campbell who, though confined to his bed, could be used as intelligence officer and store-keeper.

There were few enough of them and they had a great deal to do, their first objective being to make what was in effect an old and useless fort into a position strong enough to withstand attacks. For the tribesmen, hearing what had happened to the hated British, were already pouring in their hundreds from the hills into every hamlet and village around.

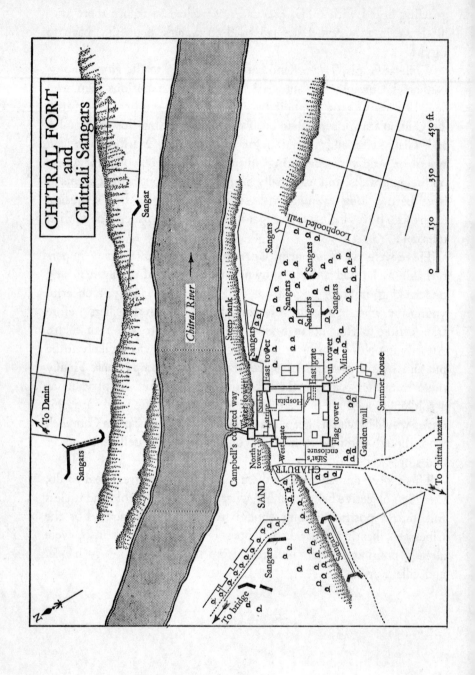

CHITRAL FORT
and
Chitrali Sangars

His bright smile haunts me still

Chitral fort, built on the same lines as many others thrown up by tribal chiefs along the frontier, followed the usual square pattern with court-yards and a tower at each corner of the outside walls. Shabby and rickety, it lay on the south bank of the River Chitral – or the River Kunar, as it was sometimes called – which at that particular spot was so scarped as to make the fort almost inaccessible from that side, except by one narrow gulley where the sunken rocky path had been earlier partly converted by Captain Campbell into a safe passage to the waterside. The route lay by an extra isolated tower known as the water tower which, for part of the way, roofed it in. This tower was linked to the rest of the fort by an enclosure containing the stables. It was not quite as high as the north-east parapet of the fort proper but was higher than the wall that surrounded the stable enclosure. According to the season, the distance between the lower end of the path and the water's edge increased or decreased and at this time it was at its greatest, and through lack of time, no attempt to roof the sunken path beyond the tower had yet been made. From the fort side of the water tower there was a short steep climb to a narrow level space separating the stables from the parapeted wall.

The tunnel formed one side of a bay of white sand that was covered with water during the period of winter thaws. The other side was a low bank of marshy land covered with the big trees which had been allowed to grow to shade the courts and whose branches in some cases actually reached over the walls. Although held by the enemy, this area was lower than the level of the fort, which was constructed of coarsely-squared timber laid horizontally to encase layers of stones embedded in mud mortar so that it was virtually two crude wooden cages, the smaller one inside the larger and the space between filled with rubble. The walls varied in thickness, strongest near the main entrance on the west and weakest on the side overlooking the south. The wooden framework was held in position by cross pieces which projected some few inches from the wall – 'like stumpy almonds from the surface of a plum pudding' – and at the corners of the towers, where the long lateral timbers overlapped and were fixed by clumsy tenons and mortises which also projected, so that wooden knobs stuck out all over the outside of the fort, in particularly large numbers on the towers. 'A monkey,' Robertson decided, 'would find them convenient steps . . . while a lithe Chitrali could follow him in most places.' These timbers had been cut from highly inflammable pine wood and in very dry weather it would be almost possible to set the fort alight with a torch 'to make it burn like a blast furnace'.

A transverse block of buildings divided the place into two unequal oblongs, the one on the river side the larger. This part was normally available to the public and was provided on three sides with a maze of living rooms. One room, of great size, with a good verandah and normally used for durbars had been converted into the hospital. On the south side of the partition was the private half of the fort and the women's quarters, and none but a very select few ever visited the mehtars of Chitral in that area. It had one large and three smaller courtyards, the rest being covered in.

The fort was not only unprepossessing but, with its history of murder, it was also no place to encourage the faint-hearted. It was in the fort that Afzul-ul-Mulk had had his brothers, Shah-ul-Mulk, Wazir and Bairam, butchered and their bodies flung into the yard. Ancient ghosts seemed to haunt it and the whole shabby structure was stained from end to end with the blood of the ruling family and their enemies.

The dropping fire that fell on the fort throughout the hours of 4 March made it imperative that some sort of roof should be made for the tunnel to the river so that water could be obtained without difficulty. To do this, however, timber had to be obtained.

It had already been decided that the old stables and buildings on the garden side should be knocked down at once to prevent the enemy approaching too close, but the Kashmiris who were given the work were clumsy and slow and their unhandiness immediately attracted the enemy's notice so that one man was badly shot through the thigh.

Captain Baird had died during the morning. Robertson had found him propped up in a sitting position, his right arm round the neck of a Kashmiri servant who had knelt for hours holding his hand from which the thumb had been severed. He was bandaged at the waist and his bloodless face was disfigured by the wound he had received at the gate. He knew he hadn't long to live but he didn't seem to mind. It was a soldier's death, he said, and he tried to tell Robertson how Surgeon-Captain Whitchurch had stuck to him throughout the whole retreat, never once leaving him except to place him on the ground while he and Badrinar Singh and his few Gurkhas drove off the Chitralis, making charge after desperate charge to clear their route. 'Don't forget Whitchurch,' he begged.

He was just making a few bequests on behalf of his widowed mother when a message came that Robertson was wanted at the gate and as he moved away Baird murmured, 'Good-bye . . . I hope all your plans will come right.' When Robertson returned he was already unconscious.

Wrapped in his greatcoat, Baird was buried that night. Lieutenant Harley, who undertook to dig the grave, tried first in the garden but his men found the soil there a network of tree roots and had to place it instead in a building immediately in front of the main gate. As they returned, the Kashmiris guarding the east tower, who did not know what was going on, fired a couple of volleys at them but fortunately their aim was as bad as ever and the bullets simply cut the tops of the surrounding trees.

The first essentials now were to learn what the garrison had in the way of supplies. It was little enough. There was sufficient ammunition but none to spare — 300 rounds a man for the Sikhs' heavy calibre Martini-Henry rifles which fired a large soft-nosed lead bullet, and 280 for the Sniders[1] of the Kashmiri troops. Both weapons were obsolescent. The Martini-Henry had a recoil that was so fierce British troops disliked using it. The Snider was even older, a muzzle-loader adapted for breech-loading. There was plenty of gunpowder, however, and Harley, who was the one man who knew anything about its use – by virtue of the fact that he possessed the only book on the subject in the fort – began to prepare it in case it was needed.

Food was scantier than expected but the little mehtar, Shuja-ul-Mulk, turned over all his private stores and it was ordered that each man was to receive a pound of ordinary flour a day as the basis of his diet. There were also a few tins of beef, four precious bottles of brandy, a few tins of tobacco, a few scanty condiments, and a good quantity of pea flour. This last was the mainstay of the Indian soldiers' diet, and, cooked into a paste called dhal, was served with chupattis, which were made of ordinary flour and soaked with ghi, or clarified butter.[2] Together with salt, they formed a substitute protein for meat and gave remarkably good value. In addition to all this, there was a little rice for the officers and a goose or two, but the few sheep they possessed had to be reserved for the sick and wounded. Finally there was tea and a little rum that enabled Townshend to settle on a dram every four days for every man whose religion did not forbid it.

It was a drab enough diet that would grow punishingly dull if the siege dragged on. It was also quite clear that the stocks they possessed could support no extra mouths, so that all unnecessary prisoners and civilians were sent out of the fort to take their chance with the enemy. With servants, camp followers, Puniali levies, clerks, messengers, loyal and not so loyal Chitralis, there were still 543 people inside the fort, however, and of these only 340 were riflemen and able to take part in a defence. And of *this* number only 83 were dependable Sikhs.

Simple-minded men – except in money matters, when they were crafty and miserly – these Sikhs were cheerful thick-headed Punjabis who considered themselves splendid, handsome fellows and could not understand why they had not aroused the admiration instead of the enmity of the hard-bitten Chitralis.[3] It was their habit to spend their spare time cleaning, nursing, even fondling their rifles – their 'fathers and mothers', they called them because, they said, 'Do they not protect our lives?' – and their chief subject of conversation was how to save or gain additional rupees. With their philosophic '*Kabbi sukh aur kabbi dukh, Angrez ka nauker*' ('Sometimes pleasure, sometimes pain, in the service of the English') they were excellent soldiers, because the profession of arms was an honourable one to them. Becoming a soldier was a family tradition and there was a close bond between them and their British officers, and they were as steady as rocks under Harley's strict discipline.

The tall burly Kashmiri soldiers who made up the bulk of the garrison were worthless and lacking in discipline and training, but among them was the usual leavening of Gurkhas, sturdy Nepalese mercenaries who were normally cheerful, independent men of Mongolian appearance as thick-headed as the Sikhs.[4] Though rarely low in spirits and normally wearing enormous grins, at that moment, however, they were subdued by the death of Baird. There were also fifty-two Chitralis who had always to be watched when there was an alarm but were necessary to the garrison for their knowledge of Chitrali methods of fighting. These included the little mehtar and six or seven loyal princes and chiefs like Wafadar. Finally there were a few women who included members of Amir's harem and the wife of Rab Nawaz Khan, still weeping over her unconscious husband. It wasn't a very big garrison because outside there were God alone knew how many fanatical tribesmen eager to butcher the Sikhs and at the very least capture the British, and these unfortunately were not the lot.

Two days after the beginning of the siege, a messenger with a white flag appeared. He brought two letters, one from Sher Afzul and one from two Jandoli kinsmen of Umra Khan who had just arrived in Chitral. They demanded that Sher Afzul be recognized as mehtar and that Robertson should immediately return to Gilgit under the protection of the two Jandoli khans. The messenger was loquacious and not unfriendly, and he let it be known that during the fight on 3 March the Chitrali losses had been even less than the British had imagined. There had been only the contemptible figure of fifteen killed and wounded compared with the British fifty-six, and the only man of mark who had died was the ill-mannered Afghan who had acted as Sher Afzul's envoy. There was one other item of news: with them the two Jandoli khans had brought an extra thousand Pathans armed with good rifles.

Without doubt this changed the picture considerably. Though the Chitralis had shown themselves skilful fighters, they could hardly be compared to the Pathans.[5]

There are several pithy sentences on the Pathans in the *Indian Field Service Pocket Book* issued to British officers of the Indian army even up to the partition of India after World War II. 'They are active, hardy and skilled marksmen,' it states, 'adept in all the arts of individual warfare, always seeking and seldom missing an opportunity. As a rule they neither give nor expect quarter and a wounded Pathan should always be regarded with suspicion.'

Many people have tried to define just what it was that made up the Pathans – the speakers of Pakhtu – and Sir Olaf Caroe put it down quite simply to their environment. 'One secret . . . is to be sought in the tremendous scenic canvas against which the Pathan plays out his life,' he said. '. . . the weft and warp of this tapestry is woven into the souls and bodies of the men who move before it.' Death meant nothing to them; they were dogged fighters, and the authority of the different empires which at various times claimed to rule the frontier really only extended to the plains and one or two passages through the mountains. Because of this, the tribal form of society persisted – and until recently still did – in a country which had known countless invaders, including Alexander, Genghis Khan and Tamerlane.

According to John Masters, who knew him well, the Pathan was 'rangy, hawk-nosed' and seemed to be made of 'whipcord and steel'. He 'walked with the grace of man-eating tiger, in long and unhurried strides', carried his head 'insolently up and his shoulders back' and he often had pale eyes, 'untamed and a little terrifying', the young men rimming theirs with kohl to match the flowers they wore in their hair.

They were incredibly cruel and tortured prisoners in a variety of hideous ways,[6] though 'this kind of cruelty was not confined to war but was . . . a part of the Pathans' normal lives'. A man suspecting his wife of a minor infidelity would happily cut off her nose, while blood feuds were waged against innocent children. Cunning and incredibly patient, they could hide in ambush among the rocks 'only two yards away and unsuspected', and if an undisciplined youngster had moved a pebble the infinite murderous patience of his elders would have called the ambush off. They were terrifying when they appeared in this fashion.

They armed themselves with razor-like curved swords, ancient bell-mouthed pistols, old jezails, gas-pipe guns they had made themselves on the Snider pattern, and stolen or captured British army weapons, many of them hacked and marked by sword cuts which showed that their original owners had perished fighting to the last. For a Martini-Henry the Pathans would pay 400 rupees, or about £25, when the actual value was no more than fifty rupees. One tribe, the Utman Khels of the Khyber Pass, made traffic in arms their special business, obtaining the weapons by theft or the dishonesty of people connected with the arsenals. Of a hundred rifles the Pathans surrendered in a later campaign, nearly a third proved to be government Martinis, which had been condemned and should have been destroyed under European supervision.

They were born warriors with a natural devilry and love of war, and all British soldiers who had to face them managed to feel for them an undoubted admiration because when beaten they 'took their licking' and bore no malice. According to Churchill they were 'soldiers from the first day they were old enough to hurl a stone till the last day they had the strength to pull a trigger, after which they were probably murdered as an encumbrance on the community', and British officers opposing them, knowing their watchfulness and remembering the number of times a rush and two seconds of stabbing and hacking had left men dead with their rifles and ammunition gone, got into the habit of never doing things the same way twice.

Despite all their strength and ferocity, however, the Pathans had a tendency to homosexuality, as their favourite song, the lilting, lawless Afghan *Zachmi Dil*[7], showed. Yet such was their character, the young political officers to whom they gave their erratic friendship grew attached to them and became proud of them, even at their murdering worst.[8] They had a marked – if cruel – sense of humour and it was said you could do anything with them if you could make them laugh, so that the extraordinary thing about their wars with the British was the spirit in which they were fought. Across the harsh and bitter landscape where death, hunger, exhaustion and thirst were always matters of great moment, there would suddenly flash 'a jagged lightning-streak of humour'. To the Pathans war with the British was a game – The Great Game – a contest with rules in which men could kill without compunction and die in order to win, but in which there was no resentment when the whistle blew and the game was over.

Behind this murderous chivalry, however, there was always a smouldering core of religious fanaticism and a determination to keep the foreigners out of the hills, and the Pathans had no fear of Indian troops whom they were said to despise because they ate rice – 'such miserable stuff it all passes away when they make water'. The Sikhs returned the loathing with interest. On one occasion when they had come into contact in a border scuffle, watching Britons decided there was no truth in the stories, because they could see a Sikh lancer carefully propping up a wounded Pathan. As they continued to watch, however, the Sikh remounted, rode away and turned with his lance lowered, to thunder down on the helpless man 'as at a tent peg, hitting him fair in the breast'.[9] The Sikhs never failed to treat the Pathans with respect, however, and the British echoed their sentiments. 'That Ghazi[10] with his gory knife, his bright smile haunts me still,' was a line from a song in a garrison pantomime at Sherpur in 1879.

Umra Khan's warriors were no exception. Proud, accustomed to fighting each other and everyone else within reach, they came from the Tarkanri group of Pathans and were great believers in revenge. They wore white or blue skull caps, white or blue puggarees, white shirts, loose embroidered waistcoats, pyjama trousers and green shoes with turned-up toes, in addition to the inevitable guns and bandoliers of ammunition, and they spent their lives 'attacking and defending the forts scattered over their country as thick as public houses in England'.

Egged on by their fanatical mullahs,[11] who always dreaded that the encroachment of a foreign power would lessen their influence, they had a reputation for reducing strongholds with ease, and the thought of a thousand of these anarchic warriors, fresh and eager to join the fun provided a daunting prospect.

Still the friend of the British

Shocked by the news of the arrival of the Pathans, Robertson managed to hide his feelings and, giving money to the messenger who brought the information, sent back with him only an acknowledgement of the letters he had received. A policy of lying low and saying nothing seemed to be the soundest course to follow for the time being. Relief, he felt, would be bound to arrive soon.

Indeed, moves *were* already being made to go to his help.

On 26 February, before the crisis had even come to a head, Captain Baird had written from Aiun to Lieutenant Moberly, now in command at Mastuj, to send on to Chitral Lieutenant John Sharman Fowler of the Royal Engineers, at that time moving up from Gilgit. The letter had also instructed that when Captain Claye Ross Ross, marching from Gilgit with his company of the 14th Sikhs, reached Mastuj and took over command there, he, Moberly, was to remain at the fort as political officer. Lastly, Baird had requested, sixty boxes of Snider ammunition, escorted by a trustworthy Kashmiri officer and forty men, were to be sent on for the Gilgiti levies who had been ordered to Chitral on 24 February and were expected to arrive in the early days of March.

Lieutenant Stanley Malcolm Edwardes, of the 2nd Bombay Grenadiers, had also been summoned from Gilgit to Chitral to help with the levies when they arrived, but on 28 February Baird had written again, ordering him to remain at Mastuj until further orders. By the morning of 3 March, however, with the clouds already gathering round Chitral, Baird had sent off an urgent despatch to Moberly giving instructions what to do in the event of communications being cut: The levies were to be sent instead, under the command of a

British officer, to seize the fort at Drasan, a position of great importance; the next day Fowler was to follow with 200 Kashmiris, accompanied by Moberly for the political work and to command the soldiers. Ross and his Sikhs were to hold Mastuj.

The road to Chitral was 200 miles long, and ran along deep river gorges and galleries of logs sticking out of the cliff side – 'a road of which the mere memory would keep men awake in their beds' – but the moves advised by Baird ensured the good behaviour of the surrounding tribes and made certain that the road from Mastuj could be kept open.

Unfortunately, as Lieutenant Gurdon had warned, Baird's letters had been intercepted and Moberly had to rely on rumour and his own common sense. The instructions about the ammunition reached him on the last day of February together with fragments of gossip about what was happening in Chitral, the oddest being that the Viceroy of India, Lord Elgin, had sent a letter to Robertson via Sher Afzul recommending Sher Afzul as mehtar, news which started an immediate stampede of Sher Afzul's opponents to Mastuj from the village of Reshun on the road to Chitral. The ammunition convoy, with forty Gurkhas of the Kashmir Rifles under the command of an excellent Gurkha subadar, Dhurm Singh, was sent off the following day to Sanogher but the rumour – already current but in Moberly's view unreliable – that Robertson had been defeated at Gairat, was repeated, and the convoy was stopped. After further consideration, it was permitted to continue.

On this day Captain Ross was reported to have crossed the Shandur Pass with his Sikhs and to have reached Laspur. Moberly begged him to hurry. Gurdon's letter about the possibility of messages being intercepted arrived the next day, followed by a note from Dhurm Singh with the ammunition, saying that, though the villagers en route were helpful, it was impossible to continue until a deliberately broken road ahead was mended.

It was on this same day, 3 March, that Ross, with Lieutenant Herbert John Jones, his subaltern, and Captain George Howard Bretherton of the Supply and Transport Corps, marched into Mastuj with 100 Sikhs and Moberly handed over command. After hearing all available reports, Ross decided that Dhurm Singh's ammunition convoy should wait at Buni and that as soon as Edwardes and Fowler, who were known to be close, arrived, they were to join it, bringing the guard for the ammunition up to sixty men. They were then to advance cautiously, repairing broken roads as they went, and if they were attacked or obstructed, Ross would set out to join them after summoning every available man from Ghizr.

It was in the certainty that such efforts as these were being made on their behalf that Robertson and Captain Townshend had applied themselves to the defence of the fort at Chitral. The news of what had happened must surely, they felt, have reached someone in authority by this time and there were plenty of men within reach who would be more than willing to take a chance to bring help.

It was obvious by now that the Kashmiris who had been detailed to demolish the old stables and other buildings were going to be useless and, in their place, Robertson organized a corps from the horse-keepers, officers' servants and low-class Chitralis in the fort. He placed them under the command of the burly, strong-willed Puniali rajah, Sifat Bahadur, who had a natural aptitude for leadership, and they became one of the sights of the siege. Almost always under fire from the sangars, walls were pulled down or defences run up, heavy timbers adjusted, or wooden pillars dragged with tremendous speed and surprising quietness from condemned roofs. The work was usually carried out at night but they also tackled the jobs without hesitation if they had to be done in daylight. Thanks to Sifat's cunning, not one of them was seriously wounded.

Under the energetic Puniali, timid men became brave. One abject Balti, who would normally have flung down his load and darted about, crazy with fear at the mere suspicion that he was being shot at, was actually seen skipping across the open ground, laughing at the dust kicked up by the bullets, as though he were playing a game. The labour corps proved invaluable and saved the troops for military duties.

The timber that was collected was needed for many things. The enemy had run up a sangar on the opposite bank of the river and their marksmen, firing at short range, were already proving troublesome.

A marble rock projecting into the river – at a point where the water-carriers filled their skins – and the foot of the water tower were the danger spots, and in the first week five men were wounded so that it became increasingly imperative that Campbell's route to the river should be covered.

The narrow confines of the fort were already growing horribly comfortless but it was found that the flat roofs of the quarters inhabited by Shuja-ul-Mulk and his followers provided a good place to walk in the dark when firing was slack. In daylight they were crossed at the double, with a nervous grin in the direction from which a shot might come. A few wags among the native servants took their time, however, making facetious remarks and pretending to jump over imaginary bullets.

Because of the shortage of hands, every single man in the fort had his allotted role in its defence, whether combatant or non-combatant. Various experiments had already been made in dividing the night guards between Townshend, Harley and Gurdon, but after a while regular ship watches of four hours on and eight hours off were organized. What sleep they got was taken during the day when they lay down in their clothes and belts with their weapons by their sides. Everyone stood to arms at dawn when most of the alarms came.

No move against them was made in bright moonlight and it was the darkness that troubled them most – for a variety of reasons; one night while making his rounds, alert for an attack and with his eyes on the defences, Gurdon disappeared through an unnoticed smoke-hole in one of the roofs.

One of Lieutenant Harley's Sikhs was a capable handyman and an attempt was made to build a corn-mill. The only stones he could find, however, were soft, so that the flour was always mixed with grit which caused dysentery and other ailments. But the Bengali-commissariat agent was a good organizer who never allowed his undisguised terror to interfere with his duty; when a man was shot dead alongside him at the scales there was no shakiness in the figures in his book. And if, as he crossed exposed places, he was always green with fear, he went none the less.

With Captain Townshend in military command, Robertson made it his job to devise new ideas for the defence and to use every available scrap of material for cover. His policy was already becoming clear. The tribesmen, always utterly reckless of life, could assemble in a few hours; when the call had gone out thousands of them had massed in the surrounding countryside. Haggard-faced men, gaunt, fierce-eyed and draped with ammunition belts or scimitar-like swords, they filled the valleys and every available cranny which might give them the pleasure of a shot at the fort. It was obvious they were too strong for the defenders to drive them away and, with the greater part of his troops still demoralized by their defeat of 3 March, Robertson decided to avoid fighting as far as possible, and concentrate instead on merely countering the stratagems of the besiegers in the hope that they would eventually be driven away by a relieving column or grow disheartened and go away of their own accord.

The bad siting of the fort, however, made it important that Sher Afzul should in the meantime be dissuaded from launching a really determined attack. Robertson accordingly initiated a campaign of false rumour to the effect that food was already becoming so scarce the garrison would soon be starved into surrender. The Indian clerks were briefed to play their part in the scheme, and the rumour itself was spread among the Chitralis in the fort. Supporters of Sher Afzul almost to a man, they were only too eager to take any opportunity of ingratiating themselves with him, and in this they were now 'encouraged' by allowing them to whisper to the messengers continually arriving under flags of truce. As a result of their constant affrays with the British along the frontier, the tribesmen had come to understand and respect the crucial significance of a white flag, and Robertson decided to use this to his own advantage. Armistices were to be encouraged, negotiations were to be prolonged, and messengers bribed to smuggle food in the hope that they would pass back information that the defenders were growing hungry. And this they did!

To cheer everybody up, on 6 March fourteen men, including Badrinar Singh, who had distinguished themselves in helping Surgeon-Captain Whitchurch bring in Baird, were put in orders for the Order of Merit, an Indian decoration which carried a life pension. There had been nothing like fourteen men in Whitchurch's party – Whitchurch himself could only identify Badrinar Singh and three others – but when Badrinar Singh was asked, with the cheerful optimism of a Gurkha he included every man in his section. Robertson was wisely generous and the recommendations stirred ambitions even among the Kashmiris.

That day, under a flag of truce, Umra Khan's diwan or financial adviser appeared. An astute-looking Hindu dressed as a Pathan, he had a large hooked nose which made his intelligent and impassive face look as fierce as a tribesman's.[1] He enlarged on the 'polite fiction' that Umra Khan's Persian secretary could neither write good Persian nor translate it into Pakhtu, and that therefore there might have been some misunderstanding in the letters that had already been exchanged. 'Umra Khan is still the friend of the British,' he said, 'and has positively warned Sher Afzul not to fight with the "Colonel Sahib".' Moreover, he went on, his two kinsmen, the Jandoli khans, and their thousand men who had been reported as arriving in Chitral, had been sent not to support Sher Afzul, 'as the vulgar might suppose', but as an act of friendship to prevent a collision.

It was unpardonable to accuse a frontier man of lying, so Robertson politely refrained from asking if the steady fire being poured into the fort by the Pathans was also an act of friendship, and the diwan continued that – as was already suspected – the Amir of Afghanistan was openly helping Sher Afzul and that all Mohammedans were united to drive out the British. He urged Robertson to leave as soon as possible for Gilgit and said that Umra Khan would be responsible for his safety.

Robertson went through the usual rigmarole of grave thanks but pointed out that as a soldier Umra would appreciate that he was not really in a position to evacuate the fort. He also expressed regret that since they were besieged he was unable to do justice to the diwan with the ceremonies his rank demanded. The inscrutable old scoundrel remained until 6 pm – something nobody minded because while he was inside the fort it could not be fired on.

Throughout 6 and 7 March, loopholes and head-covers of logs were made on the parapets. A lot of the work had to be altered later as experience showed it to be badly devised, and the loopholes had to be reduced in size as they proved useless against frontier marksmen who made a point of firing slowly, carefully and with deadly accuracy.

There was a desultory fire during the days and alarms at night when the men inside the fort hid their inexperience with 'unnecessary commotion and much sounding of bugles'. It still remained Robertson's wish to get news to Mastuj and for four days attempts had been made to encourage or bribe someone to carry letters through the tightening ring of enemies. No one would volunteer, and the British officers were growing anxious now that the convoy of ammunition which Lieutenant Moberly had been told to send might fall into the hands of the enemy.

On 7 March Robertson sent out a spy to find out if his messages had been delivered. The spy was to return at night by way of the water tunnel. Instead, he went straight to Sher Afzul and was replaced by a man under sentence of death who was offered his freedom if he would set fire to the water tower. Umra Khan's Jandolis invariably began their assault against a fort by attacking the precious water supply, and in the early hours of 8 March the arsonist was allowed to enter in the belief that he was the man Robertson had sent out. Letting in other men, they started their fire and then got clean away.

Fortunately little damage was done. A battle at night always sounds twice as noisy as during the day and the one that accompanied the fire was no more than a feint against the north-west corner of the fort by matchlockmen. As the firing broke out the flames were discovered under the water tower and, though it blazed up gaily '. . . there was never much danger'. Three water-carriers 'constituted the entire force necessary to cope with it . . .' and Townshend rewarded them with ten rupees each. The garrison was not dissatisfied with itself and it was felt that relief could not now be far away.

What they did not know was that even as they put out the last of the flames events were shaping up round Mastuj which would make relief very unlikely, and as they rose and began to clear up on 8 March all hopes of immediate relief were wiped out by a disaster that was even more calamitous than the one they themselves had suffered on 3 March.

Gallant to the verge of eccentricity

The first news of the events at Chitral reached the British authorities at Peshawar on 7 March. It was a message Robertson had despatched from Mastuj on 28 January before leaving for Chitral.

The message did not seem to indicate much more than a normal frontier foray by the Pathans. Nevertheless, to be on the safe side, preliminary arrangements were made for a relief expedition, but the commanding generals had such confidence in Robertson that another seven days were allowed to pass before any positive action was taken.

By this time the command at Mastuj had passed from the astute, vigorous Lieutenant Moberly to the less experienced but more dashing Captain Ross who had arrived with his men of the 14th Sikhs. Ross was proud of his regiment because it had been raised during the Indian Mutiny by his father, General Sir Campbell Claye Ross who had commanded it for fourteen years, and he was eager to prove himself a worthy son. According to Robertson, he was 'gallant almost to the verge of eccentricity'.

While both Captain Bretherton, the commissariat officer, and Moberly were cautious men wise in the ways of the frontier, Ross was headstrong and he had already made up his mind. Well aware that his chances of proving himself as a soldier had immeasurably improved with the crisis, he had written with eager enthusiasm to his mother on 23 February, 'We are off to the wars at last!' On 4 March he wrote again from 'the crazy old fort' at Mastuj. He was waiting for further orders, he said, but he expected to be issuing them himself within a day or two. 'I shall be senior officer for 160 miles,' he pointed out, 'and will have to organize a column. . . . A pretty job it will be!' He clearly recognized the gravities of the situation and understood what had to be done but, in Robertson's words, 'slight instinctive apathies, little personal peculiarities of temper' produced incalculable results.

He expected his column to consist of 350 men, transport and what food they could carry with them; but, even as he wrote, news came into Mastuj from Dhurm Singh, the Gurkha subadar with the ammunition column at Buni, that a Chitrali nobleman was stirring up trouble in the district and that he was expecting to be attacked. Ross resolved to start towards him with Lieutenant Jones at dusk that day in the hope of capturing the troublemaker.

Lieutenant Edwardes of the Bombay Grenadiers and Lieutenant Fowler of the Royal Engineers also set off on 5 March as arranged, with a supply of engineering equipment to join Dhurm Singh, while Bretherton recrossed the Shandur Pass for Ghizr. Jones returned late the same night with a few men and the troublesome noble who had caused all the anxiety at Buni. Ross had picked him up near the village and had then continued his march.

A great deal of false news had arrived in Mastuj during that twenty-four hours, doubtless deliberately provided by the Pathans and Chitralis with the intention of confusing the situation. It had included the information that Robertson and Sher Afzul were on friendly terms and that letters were on the way to Mastuj to announce that the disagreement between them was at an end.

Ross returned himself at 2 am on 6 March, pleased with his work and with the information that Edwardes was due to start from Buni for Chitral with the ammunition and the augmented guard that very day. Towards evening, however, a note from Edwardes, written near the village of Koragh, said that a force was reported to be gathering at Reshun, nearby, to stop him. This somewhat alarming message concluded that he would still try to push on and send back further information. Edwardes did not entirely believe the report about opposition but he suggested that if Moberly had better information Ross should move out to give him support.

The experienced Moberly considered it much more sensible to recall Edwardes and the ammunition convoy. The headstrong Ross disagreed and, announcing his intention of taking out his full company to help, sent a message to Bretherton, now at the other side of the Shandur, to hurry back with every available man. The chiefs and

D

headmen at Mastuj felt too much risk was being taken and, warning
Moberly of danger down-river towards Chitral, urged that no more
men should be sent in that direction. Moberly was entirely in agreement
with them about the risk, but it was clear something had to be done to
help Edwardes and he suggested that Ross should seize the Nisa Gul
ravine and Buni on the road to Reshun while more troops were
hurried on to him.

Ross had immense confidence in his Sikhs, and he declined to wait.
Though Robertson never said so outright, it was clearly his view
that Ross, lacking campaign experience, could not conceive that the
meek-looking draggle-tailed tribesmen around him could suddenly
change into formidable warriors who would dare attack his splendidly
drilled and equipped company. He was adamant in his determination
to press on. At his wits' end how to stop him, Moberly even went so
far as to write an official letter, which he ceremoniously handed to
Ross, urging him not to leave the Nisa Gul ravine unprotected or to
go beyond Buni without a strong force. The note was handed back
with the cold remark that its proposals could not be entertained. Ross
was confident of success. But no one else was and as soon as he marched
out of the fort at Mastuj all the local notables fled with their families,
convinced that the British were doomed to destruction. Indeed, they
had been of this opinion for a long time and had only been stopped
from bolting earlier by the arrival of the Sikhs. Ross even refused to
make clear his intentions – probably because he didn't know them
himself – but as he took with him his men's baggage and a quantity of
hospital supplies, it seemed he intended marching all the way to
Chitral fort.

No sooner had he left than Moberly, now in command again, sent
to Gilgit for troops and guns. The following day news came from
Ross that he had found the villagers at Buni very helpful but that
Edwardes, as he had half-expected, had been involved in a skirmish at
Reshun. No guard had been left at the Nisa Gul ravine.

Approaching Reshun with every military precaution, Edwardes and
Fowler had been hampered by the length of their convoy and the
tailing out of their porters. Their total force consisted of Dhurm

Singh's forty riflemen and Fowler's twenty Bengal sappers and miners. As there were 150 porters, and at no point on the march could any two men walk abreast, their problem was to protect the strung-out baggage and ammunition in the event of attack.

As they were trailing through the Koragh defile, a narrow winding road with steep stony sides, a guide provided by Moberly informed Edwardes at the tail of the column that he had heard of severe fighting at Chitral and that the convoy was to be attacked. Edwardes promptly sent a message back to Moberly and hurried on to Fowler at the head of the column. Together they decided to push on to the safety of Reshun. The countryside was full of false rumours and everyone along the route so far had been helpful; most important of all, they still had no idea that the Chitralis were anything but friendly or that Umra Khan was the common enemy. Assuming that their reinforcements and ammunition might be badly needed at Chitral fort, they therefore saw no reason to retreat but they closed the column up to the best of their ability amd moved warily on to Reshun, which they entered at dusk on 6 March. Almost immediately they learned that not only had there been fighting at Chitral but that it was the Chitralis themselves who were the enemy.

Reshun was a large and attractive village of around two hundred families lying on a plateau in a valley between steep high slopes. The small fields, their soil as red as in South Devon or parts of Shropshire, and the blocks of drab houses surrounded by orchards and huge chenar trees, hung above the River Yarkun which flowed swiftly from the base of precipitous cliffs, while dozens of streams from the mountains flowed past the houses to irrigate the land before finding their way to the river at a point lower down.

Deciding to halt until they could get a message through to Mastuj and repair a damaged road ahead, Edwardes and Fowler, when it was suggested to them that they camp on the polo ground, sensed a sudden hostility in the air and chose instead a spot near the river where the steep banks prevented them from being surrounded.

Reshun was well known to the troops because routes on the frontier were always 'ticketed up' in advance in case they were ever needed.

This or that site was reported to have camping and wood for so many men, and such-and-such a village was reported to contain so many villagers who would be available as porters, so many goats, and so many chickens. In such a barren area where food was scarce, such foresight was necessary and often useful.[1] Anxious to test the attitude of the village, the next morning Edwardes – a strongly-built athletic officer and like Fowler as dashingly handsome as so many of the young men involved with the Chitral affair seemed to be – asked for porters. By 10 am 150 of them had assembled at the camp and fifty were signed on at once. It was only then that Edwardes let it be known that he was not yet moving on, and the headmen immediately protested that there was no food for them. Edwardes persisted and the camp was shifted to a cliff over the river where the bridge could be covered. Dhurm Singh and thirty men were left to guard the ammunition and build a sangar while Edwardes and Fowler set off with four local nobles, the remainder of the soldiers, and the fifty porters they had taken on, to repair the broken road out of the village; the only other route was very rough and the ladders on it precluded the use of animals or men with loads.

Fowler moved ahead on his pony looking for a ford, or the possibility of an ambush, and the others caught him up as he arrived at the entrance to a narrow defile commanded by a cliff on the far side of the river. As a good soldier, alive to the hostility that was now in the air and suspecting the intentions of the villagers who were trying to persuade him to push through the defile, Edwardes decided to wait until he had first made sure that the heights on his left were safe. It was a tenet with frontier forces that when moving forward the advance guard should always have with it a large number of men 'to picket the heights and hold the ground from which the enemy could bring fire to bear on the road below'. They had not enough men to reconnoitre in force, so Fowler was sent up the mountain with eight Kashmiri Gurkhas. Both he and Edwardes first searched the route with telescopes and field glasses and, seeing a solitary figure holding what seemed to be a rifle, assumed that he was merely one of the men responsible for breaking down the road.

The climb was difficult but eventually Fowler was high enough to see the top of the cliff on the opposite side of the river. There he saw several empty sangars and beyond them the next village, Parpish. Climbing further, he headed for the spot where he had seen the solitary figure and had almost reached it when a shot rang out, its echoes clattering and rolling among the slopes and gulleys of the defile.

Almost immediately two or three hundred men streamed out of Parpish, lined the cliffs opposite and began firing across the river. A naik, or corporal, was killed at once, but, snatching up his rifle, Fowler sheltered with his men behind rocks and was able to force back the men across the river. Bullets continued to spatter around them, kicking up the dust and whining away down the defile, and eventually Fowler was slightly wounded in the shoulder. Instinctively sensing a reverse, the enemy immediately relined the crest opposite and it soon became obvious from the way they were now shooting that they were also attacking Edwardes and that he was being driven back towards Reshun away from Fowler.

In danger of being cut off, Fowler realized that if he descended, the only route he could take would lead him into the teeth of the enemy fire. He decided to take the risk and he and his men scuttled down the slopes as fast as they could go under a hail of bullets from across the river. Men now also began to appear directly above them and great rocks began to bounce and thunder down the slopes, dislodging great cascades of soil, stones and shale. A bullet hit Fowler's boot, another went through a man's wrist and a third through another man's thigh, but no one was killed.

Regaining the flat ground by the river, they could see Edwardes being driven back and also an abandoned box of gun-cotton. The Gurkhas were beginning to lose their nerve by this time and it was clear they were going to have to race over a high spur that lay between them and Reshun. As they hurried along, Fowler's Gilgiti groom, weeping for the master he believed dead, saw him appear half a mile away and, without thinking of his own safety, ran back with Fowler's pony.

The man wounded in the wrist was bleeding profusely so he was bandaged and placed on the pony. Hurrying up the spur, breathless, as a group of Pathans who had now joined the Chitralis raced to intercept them, Fowler seized the pony's tail and gave his other hand to Edwardes. Despite Fowler's wounded shoulder they reached the top. The sepoys fought to keep the road clear but, as they crossed the summit, the breath harsh in their throats, a bullet lodged in the cantle of the pony's saddle while another mortally wounded a sapper. The man on the pony was lifted off and the dying man put in his place.

Going down the other side of the bluff, the pony moved more slowly than the men on foot and had to be driven along. Because it was impossible for the animal, they couldn't head for Dhurm Singh's sangar by a direct route and had to keep to the road where another party of the enemy now appeared.

No one was hit, and when the sangar was reached, they flung themselves, panting, under its shelter. They were overcrowded, however, and as the fire grew hotter, Fowler made more room by moving his sappers to the shelter of a nearby wall. By this time they had decided to make for a block of houses about 200 yards away. Dhurm Singh and twenty of the Gurkhas fixed bayonets and, led by Fowler, charged through the shower of bullets. The houses were cleared and occupied, the defenders disappearing through the windows into adjacent buildings. Rooms were searched, loopholes broken through and, after all available water jars had been filled, the nearby water channels were blocked up to provide more, only to be diverted by the Chitralis when they realized what was happening. Edwardes joined them from the sangar, which was becoming a hopeless position by this time as it had no head cover, and it was decided to fortify the houses and hold them instead.

Like most Chitrali houses, they were only eight or ten feet high with flat roofs, and opened into courtyards that were full of rubbish. Narrow alleys ran between them, with walls and trees affording good cover to the enemy sharpshooters. In front lay the polo ground, a four-foot wall with a gate, and beyond that the main village. Twenty yards to the right was a walled orchard that gave an effective screen for attackers, and near at hand were hovels, sheds and more walls which there was no time to destroy because a rush was expected at any moment. The sappers were brought in from behind their wall and in frantic haste everyone started to build up passages and construct parapets on the house tops. One end of the block of houses still remained in the hands of the Chitralis – though the connecting roofs were broken down – and from the hills as well as from the houses the fire increased and timbers from the demolished roofs and walls were hurriedly pushed up into fortifications.

As the sun set, the firing, which had been kept up against them from the moment the first trigger had been pulled, slackened a little. It was the month of Ramadhan when the Mohammedans had to fast between sunrise and sunset, and as they went off to cook their evening meal the opportunity was snatched to bring the wounded in from the sangar. The besiegers remained alert, however, and they had to make a hundred-yard dash through the firing. Among the wounded was Edwardes' fox terrier bitch, Biddy, who had been shot through the chest and was apparently dying. With them the rescuers also brought the ammunition containers and the officers' baggage. In the urgency to provide a cover for the defence they were all built at once into the sangars on the roofs, along with timbers, boxes and grain bins from the houses.

The sappers worked under constant sniping fire. Now that dusk had deepened into darkness and the attackers had finished their meal, they were expecting another rush. They were already dead tired but the Gurkhas were behaving very well. They had had no food or water all day, and by this time the enemy in one of the adjoining houses were trying to drive a hole through the wall. Though they were only five feet away, however, they were unable to do much damage.

Hardly had the sun set when the moon rose. Darkness would have helped because they could not work in an exposed position without being shot at and Edwardes and Fowler would have liked to set fire to some of the houses alongside. But wood to kindle the flames was unavailable and the blaze would in any case have thrown them up in silhouette to the attackers.

No attack was made, however, and at dawn the worn-out little garrison got some rest. During the night, the men, edgy with nerves, had continued to fire sporadically – often at imaginary targets – and two of the seriously injured had died. A little flour, rice and dhal and one or two chickens and a few eggs were discovered in the filthy and verminous houses, while the officers had a few tins of sausages and soup. All that could be collected was shared out with the little water they had conserved. The two Englishmen, aided by Dhurm Singh, did what they could for the injured, improvising bandages, crutches and splints; their sole antiseptic a weak solution of carbolic made from tooth powder.[2]

While Edwardes and Fowler were fighting for their lives at Reshun, Captain Ross had finally made up his mind what to do.

He had already decided to leave a small party at Buni and move ahead with porters to bring back the ammunition column when information arrived that the column was already in trouble and that the road from Buni was broken. He therefore divided his force and, leaving a small group behind to hold Buni as planned, marched out on 8 March with Lieutenant Jones, a native officer, ninety-three N.C.O.s and men and seventeen hospital attendants and servants, as well as a large number of porters without loads.

Everyone in the district knew he was coming and exactly how many men he had. It was impossible on the frontier for any human being to move without the inhabitants knowing all about it, and information flew across the rocky slopes as if it were carried on the wind. Every step Ross took was watched and, though he himself saw nothing, bright fanatical eyes peered from the heights and the dusty gulleys every inch of the way.

The headman of Buni was with Ross, but he was nervous because he felt certain the enemy was waiting for them. At midday they came to the village of Koragh but there wasn't a single soul there, nothing but a few scratching chickens and a smouldering fire. The silence in the stark hills round them was eerie and disturbing and the soldiers lifted their eyes uneasily, wondering what lay ahead. Then, on the slopes above them, men were seen climbing and making what appeared to be smoke signals.

Like the others at Chitral and Reshun, Ross decided these men were harmless villagers, but the headman and others pointed out that friendly villagers would hardly bolt without reason and that a very cautious advance should be made. At this the impetuous Ross grew annoyed and demanded to know why the headman was telling lies. The indignant hillman removed his head-dress and flung it at Ross's feet – the last form of entreaty of a Mohammedan – and said that if he were lying Ross should kill him. Incredibly, Ross still refused to believe him.

Reaching the Koragh defile, through which Edwardes and Fowler had passed not long before, the soldiers noted several newly-built but empty sangars close to the track, and men scattered over the hillsides. Even now Ross refused to believe there was any danger and, although it was a perfect place to stage an ambush, he made no attempt to reconnoitre the heights. Though Jones suggested it would be advisable to be 'more cautious', he was obsessed by his eagerness to press on and bring off a rescue that would make his reputation, and the party marched in all together.

The defile had been cut by the action of the river running through the cliffs and thunderous avalanches were always possible down the unstable slopes. At its lower end the pathway began to rise from the river above a group of caves and then zigzagged upwards, and as they reached this point the leading man of the advance guard was fired on from one of the sangars. Immediately, hundreds of men hidden on the hillsides appeared on the peaks and set the very slopes rattling down on the party in the defile.

With the sides rearing up at an angle of almost ninety degrees to 2000 feet, Ross had no chance. The men above could set virtually the whole cliffside moving, and stones, rocks and vast boulders began to hurtle and bounce into the ravine in blinding clouds of dust and loose shale, to send men flying, break bones and bring blood, before leaping on to the river bed below. Sheer terror threw the party into confusion as the shower of earth and stones came down on them, and what followed was a perfect example of what old frontier hands felt could always happen to a small party which allowed its guides to escape. Ross had put no guard on the porters and as the first shot was fired, they all dropped their loads and bolted.

With the local knowledge of these men, Ross might have escaped, but from the moment they vanished his only chance was to fight his way out of the defile at once and at any cost. At this moment when impetuosity and gallantry would have paid dividends, however, the impulsive and headstrong Ross did just the opposite. The enemy were only Reshun villagers and if he had pressed on he might just have forced a way through to Edwardes and Fowler. If he had headed back immediately with all his force he equally might just have escaped. What he did was to order back Jones with only ten men to seize the Koragh end of the defile, but the sangar by the road was now full of men and Jones' task was hopeless. The rocks were still rolling and bouncing about the defile, and by the time they had got within a hundred yards of the sangar Jones had only two sepoys left unwounded. He therefore sent word back to Ross who, instead of supporting him at once with the whole of his force, withdrew his men into two caves half full of water just below the path and close to the river.[3]

Jones joined him and they lay there all day. Making an attempt to get out after darkness, they seemed on the point of success when a new avalanche of stones forced them back again. That resolution of which Ross was capable should have driven him on to force his way through, whatever his casualties, before fresh enemies appeared, but instead he elected to wait. All the next day, 9 March, they lay in the caves, facing increasing numbers of Chitralis who had occupied a sangar on the slope opposite and kept up a galling fire against them as they tried to erect breastworks, often using the stones that were rolled down from above.

That night, short of the food which had been left behind in favour of baggage and hospital supplies, they tried again to escape. Once more they were thrown back by a 'torrent of rocks' and Ross decided instead to try to scale the hillside. They were within a few feet of safety when a small group of men in front of them fired, killing one of Ross's Sikhs, and then ran away. With their departure the road was clear, but Ross and his party did not realize it in the darkness and returned to the caves once more for another wretched day without food on 10 March.

It was at this late hour that Ross finally decided, after conferring with Jones, that he had to cut his way out, whatever the cost, and at 2 am on 11 March the party hurried back along their tracks up the defile. The villagers were ready for them, however, with their assortment of ancient weapons. Firing started and the boulders started bouncing about them. Ross himself behaved with great gallantry, charging a sangar on his own and killing four of its occupants with his revolver before he was partially stunned by a falling stone. As he staggered away, one of the old weapons exploded behind him and he fell, shot through the head. The party finally broke clear, but at a terrible cost, and only Jones and seventeen Sikhs reached the plain near Koragh where two charging groups of swordsmen melted away before their disciplined fire. Three more men were killed, however, and the remaining fourteen – ten of them, including Jones, badly wounded – stumbled into Buni at 6 am. They were all that was left of the whole force; many good rifles had fallen into the hands of the enemy, and Ross was dead.

Kipling's *Arithmetic on the Frontier* summed it up exactly:

> A scrimmage in a Border Station—
> A canter down some dark defile—
> Two thousand pounds of education
> Drops to a ten-rupee jezail—

An ominous absence of all news

13

The whole area of the frontier from Mastuj to Chitral and beyond was now ablaze. With Ross dead and Jones out of action, and Edwardes and Fowler hanging on grimly in Reshun, all hope of immediate relief for Robertson had disappeared.

From 8 March, after the attempt on the water tower, the days had been quiet at Chitral. Men seen among the trees close to the walls on the north-west had soon been driven away, and little else had happened. Sher Afzul seemed to be taking things easy in the hope that the supposedly hungry garrison would surrender and the fort would fall into his hands without fighting.

Captain Townshend reported that the Kashmiri troops were still depressed by the repulse of Campbell's sortie. He had the unthinking Victorian attitude to the coloured races, whom he treated with indifference or disdain. In Egypt he had been in the habit of saying that the most popular dish of the inhabitants was 'canal water, flavoured with the carcasses of animals which had died of bovine typhus with particles of cholera to act as bitters', and a favourite expression to describe their behaviour was 'in a miserable state of funk'. He had done well with native soldiers, nevertheless, but after the débâcle of 3 March, he felt the Kashmiris were 'very much shaken by their losses'.[1]

Because of this, like Robertson, he took the view that the defence of the fort should be passive and was unwilling to permit any offensive gestures which meant sallies beyond the walls. Lieutenant Harley was eager to organize fighting patrols, even offering to swim the river and surprise the enemy sangar opposite the waterway, but this would have meant employing the Sikhs who represented the hard core of the defence and risking another officer. Townshend wouldn't hear of it.

'The risk is too great . . .' he noted in his diary '. . . I mean to sit tight until we are relieved.' All the same, he was eager to get a man through the lines to Udny – especially after the attempt to fire the water tower – and Mir Hamza, a Chitrali of undoubted courage and loyalty, was prepared to try. Robertson would not allow it. One messenger a week, he felt, was enough, otherwise 'they would think we were excited'.

Sifat Bahadur had by now done wonders. The stables by the river had been loopholed to protect the waterway and both ends of the enclosure that contained them had been strengthened and pierced for rifle fire. While no one entirely believed the alarming stories they heard of Umra Khan's prowess at reducing forts, it was clear that when the enemy finally woke up they would press their attack against the water tower and the tunnel to the river. As the decision to protect them became firmer, the job was given to Sifat. Though the result was clumsy, the cover he erected served its purpose, in spite of the fact that the last two or three feet of the climb always remained exposed. The water-carriers could never be convinced of the risk they took as they paused there for breath. It wasn't until two of them had been shot dead that the rest began to halt just short of the top and then scramble up the slope and dodge into shelter.

In addition to roofing the tunnel the vigorous Sifat Bahadur also converted a mass of demolished buildings and passages facing the enemy-occupied area of flat marshy land near the river, into a simple enclosure which could easily be manned. By 10 March they were beginning to settle down to the business of the siege. At first the Sikhs, the only reliable force, had been set to guard the south wall because it was the weakest area but, as it became recognized that the north tower and the river parapet guarding the water supply were more important, they were transferred there. When an alarm was raised, Harley commanded the parapets occupied by, or near to, his men while Lieutenant Gurdon looked after those defended by the Kashmiris in the southern part of the fort. Townshend, the senior officer, placed himself at the head of the reserve which collected at the inner end of a broad passage leading from the great courtyard to the main gate. There they were sheltered from the firing and could move in any direction. On these occasions, Surgeon-Captain Whitchurch fell in with Townshend. He was without doubt the hardest-worked man in the fort, slaving all day in the stinking atmosphere of the hospital and at night falling in as a soldier, armed with a double-barrelled rifle, to repulse attacks.

By this time Robertson, with the help of Sifat and the reliable Wafadar – whose name appropriately meant 'faithful' – was occupied with protecting the defenders from reverse fire from the surrounding slopes by using doors taken off their hinges, carpets or canvas dodgers made from tents, to screen all firing positions, ladders and frequently used paths. Conserving their hardly-won ammunition, the Chitralis outside rarely fired when there was nothing to aim at. With one exception: curtains had been designed for the loopholes on the south wall and these were regularly shot at in the belief that there *must* be a man behind them.

Robertson's room looked out on to one of the small courts in the private part of the fort. During the day it was an armoury with rifles, packages of cartridges, and Chitrali swords stacked in the corners. At first alarms were sounded on bugles but after a while the men assembled in silence. One shot could set Robertson listening, more would make him put a foot from the bed where he lay, still miserably weak with his illness, and a heavy rattle of musketry would jerk him clean out. Then his servant would arrive with his coat and a lantern, while soft-shod feet made the nearby staircase creak and vibrate, and Sifat and the Gilgiti rajahs would appear with the servants and grooms, followed by Wafadar and another loyal Chitrali, to snatch up rifles and buckle on swords. During alarms this scratch force toured the drains along the south wall by which the enemy might enter, or moved to where anything was happening. Normally, however, they took up their position near Gurdon whose Kashmiris still could not be trusted.

On 10 March one of the Chitrali headmen left the fort to find out what had become of the body of General Baj Singh, the Kashmiri general who had been shot dead during the precipitate retreat on 3 March. A thoroughgoing rogue but the son of an illegitimate prince, this emissary was given a mount appropriate to his rank and a white flag was run up. When they saw him the besiegers cheered, imagining that as a headman he had been selected to negotiate a surrender for

Robertson. He was greeted effusively and he never returned; it was only afterwards that Robertson discovered he was also an expert military engineer whom he had unwittingly given to the enemy.

More letters were exchanged with Sher Afzul the following day. The notes seemed to suggest that he and Umra Khan had changed their tune and were prepared for peace, but when Robertson wrote to the effect that Sher Afzul should make his submission to the new young mehtar the only reply he got was a calm and dignified repetition of Sher Afzul's own terms.

The letter bearer, giving Robertson the first hints of what was happening outside, said that the British had suffered two disasters – one at Reshun, where sixty boxes of treasure and twenty loads of cartridges had been captured, and where ten survivors were still defending themselves in a fortified house; and one in which a British officer had been killed and sixty-two men crushed to death by rocks hurled down the cliffs, a bare dozen remaining alive to entrench themselves in a cave. The stories seemed so wild Robertson couldn't believe them. Unhappily, they were in essence only too true.

Not only Robertson was worried by the rumours. So was Lieutenant Moberly at Mastuj. The news that came in first was of the fighting at Reshun together with a note from Ross which seemed to make it clear that Edwardes was surrounded. The next information Moberly received was that Ross had detached forty sepoys under their officer to Buni and that Sher Afzul intended to seize the Nisa Gul ravine which Ross had so unwisely left unguarded.

Captain Bretherton returned on 10 March with a hundred Kashmiris from Ghizr but 'there was an ominous absence of all news' from the others during this and the next day, when it was noticed that not a single baggage porter was to be found in the area; an ominous sign which also meant that if any attempt at rescue were to be made the troops would have to carry their own baggage. On 12 March, news came that the Nisa Gul ravine was occupied by hostile tribesmen. Leaving Bretherton in command at Mastuj, Moberly took out a hundred men to see for himself. The ravine was empty.

The following day Bretherton went out but, owing to the destruction of the bridge at Sanogher, he couldn't cross the river. The next seventy-two hours were anxious. There was no news, not even rumours, and all attempts to find porters proved useless. On 14 March Colonel Phula, an energetic Kashmiri officer, arrived from Ghizr with sixty men, and on 16 March Moberly went out again with 150 men. Fifty of them were sent across the river by a ford – so that there was a party moving down both banks at the same time – but they were soon halted by a snow slide that blocked their route and had to cross back. The villagers were sufficiently impressed by the show of force, however, to start to restore the broken bridge.

A message sent on by Bretherton informed Moberly of the arrival at Mastuj of fifty Puniali levies who were being pushed on to Sanogher, and it was then that Moberly heard of the fighting at Koragh and of a wounded British officer and about forty soldiers at Buni. Next morning, 17 March, he recrossed the river where he learned that a hundred Hunza-Nagar levies were to reach Buni the following day. Late in the afternoon, he reached the village to find the wounded Lieutenant Jones and his few survivors, together with the men Ross had left behind – forty-six in all – who had fortified a house. They had debated whether to continue on to Mastuj but, because of the number of wounded, had decided against it. The fighting qualities they had shown in the break-out from the Koragh defile, however, had had a profound effect on the enemy and they had not once been attacked.

There was still no word of Edwardes and since it seemed his force had also been annihilated, Moberly was in a quandary. What should he do? Should he try to reach Reshun or was his first responsibility to make sure that Mastuj – the only secure post for any relief force heading for Chitral from Gilgit – was secure? His mind was made up for him when a message arrived at Buni from Lieutenant Gough at Ghizr on the other side of the Shandur Pass reporting that he was cut off from Gupis, the next stage back from Mastuj on the road to Gilgit, and was in need of help. With it came another message, this time from Gilgit, which indicated that no reinforcements had yet been sent from the south. With Phula and the wounded Jones, Moberly decided the only thing to do was return as fast as possible to Mastuj.

Right: Britain's attitude to Russia over Afghanistan. *Punch* cartoon of 1885

Below: Chitral fort from the river, showing the patch of sand, the water tower with the entrance to Campbell's covered way, and the thousands of wooden projections on the walls which could be used as handholds by the besiegers

OUR AFGHAN "BOUNDARY COMMISSION." JOHN BULL PUTS UP A NOTICE. (See p. 105.)

The bridge at Chitral and one of the guard towers. The building methods of both bridge and tower can clearly be seen

Amir-ul-Mulk with Sikh soldiers of the Chitral garrison

British officers of the garrison at Chitral

Above: In front, Surgeon-Major G. S. Robertson; behind, *l to r*, Lieutenant H. K. Harley, Lieutenant B. E. M. Gurdon, Captain C. V. F. Townshend

Above right: Captain C. P. Campbell

Right: Surgeon-Captain H. F. Whitchurch

Inside looking out. Chitral fort from top of gun tower showing river, north tower and top of water tower

Outside looking in. Chitral fort from river showing trees which had been allowed to grow over the walls and (foreground *l to r*) east tower, water tower (in front) and north tower; with gun tower and flag tower behind

Besiegers: Sher Afzul and his followers

Besieged: Shuja-ul-Mulk and his chief advisers. Wafadar is on the left wearing bandolier.
Futteh Ali Shah is on extreme right

Lieutenant J. S. Fowler (front left) and Lieutenant S. M. Edwardes (front centre) with the fox terrier, Biddy, and some of their command

The guns in the courtyard of Chitral fort below north tower. The two larger ones are those used by Townshend

The siege of Reshun. *Illustrated London News* artist's drawing showing the houses (centre) held by Edwardes and Fowler. Sketch by A. D. Greenhill Gardyne

The Eastern Relief Force

Above: Colonel J. G. Kelly and his officers. Back row, *l to r*: Peterson, Luard, Beynon; middle row: Browning-Smith, Kelly, Borradaile; front row: Moberly, Cobbe, Stewart

Right: Paris near Gakuch along which Stewart had to hurry his guns to join Kelly

His men, who had been on the march for forty-eight hours, were stupid with fatigue and sleeplessness, while Ross's Sikhs were still demoralized by the disaster in the Koragh defile, but as Edwardes and Fowler had noted, it was the month of daytime fasting for the Mohammedan tribesmen and Moberly decided to take advantage of the period after dusk when they would be eating. Telling the headmen at Buni that he intended to return the following day, he got his men secretly across the river as soon as it was dark and began his forlorn trudge home.

It was a difficult journey but crossing the river proved a wise move because they got a good start while the tribesmen were at their meal and, in addition, on the side of the river they had just left they saw the twinkling watch-fires of a considerable force waiting to ambush them at Awi.

Progress was slow with the men already exhausted, but Moberly had an unusual ability to transmit his own energy to his soldiers. Under his influence the burly Kashmiris even overcame their reputation for cowardice and slothfulness, volunteering to carry much of the Sikhs' ammuniton in addition to their own rather than see it destroyed. Only one man was lost, a Gurkha who had somehow managed to get drunk. Though Moberly hoisted him on to a pony, he fell off in the darkness and was cut to pieces by the long knives of the tribesmen following hot on the heels of the party. With the Puniali levies sent forward by Bretherton now holding the Nisa Gul ravine, Moberly plodded past and his little column stumbled into Mastuj after covering thirty-five miles in twenty-eight hours with little food and carrying excessive burdens. It was entirely due to Moberly's astuteness and ability that they had managed to slip through.

No wild firing

14

Despite the disconcerting but barely believed news that had come in about Reshun and the Koragh defile, life at Chitral was still not too difficult.

They had reached a period of full moon and Tirich Mir, the mountain to the north, flung up its 25,000 feet against a clear sky. With the moonlight the night-time alarms and the firing ceased, but with daylight there was always a sprinkling of bullets from across the river.

In the rooms under the fort Captain Townshend had discovered four ancient cannon, two of them 7-pounders made in 1839, together with eighty rounds of solid projectile, and he was now busy constructing a position for them on the south of Sifat's enclosure. The guns were in good order and on 12 March, it was decided to try a shot with one of them. By mistake, however, the detachment told off for the duty carried the gun not to the west side of the fort but to the garden on the east and, being in the open, they had let off only a couple of rounds when firing started and a man was wounded.

A week later – about the time when Lieutenant Moberly was returning to Mastuj – another attempt was made to use the gun through an aperture knocked during darkness in the west wall of Sifat's enclosure. Daylight revealed a tree in the way and another hole had to be made. The shot hit the top of the nearest enemy sangar but apparently without much damage, so Townshend decided that the guns were useless and from then on they were used merely for decoration in the yard. Perhaps it was as well, because Wafadar bragged that when salutes had been fired in Robertson's honour in the past 'not more than three or four men had to retire to hospital on each occasion with burns'.

Robertson's window opened towards the south. Beneath him the mehtar's treasure was stored while on one side of him was a dark room occupied by Townshend and Gurdon whose only window was a ventilation hole near the ceiling, and on the other a chapel occupied by Harley, with nearby a durbar hall they used for taking baths. It had a long casement window that was often hit by enemy marksmen but behind a barricade of Chitrali saddles, old boxes and carpets, they felt quite safe. Alongside this hall was the ante-room which had been a favourite place for the mehtars of Chitral to commit their murders, and it was here that Afzul-ul-Mulk had had Shah-ul-Mulk, Wazir and Bairam killed, listening outside to the sickening sound of them being hacked to pieces.

These rooms were reached by a long passage guarded by a sentry who never failed to challenge, so that on lively nights it was possible to be hailed a dozen times by the sentry's exuberant 'Hukm dar?' Robertson was happy to accept the challenging as part of military discipline but he also enjoyed playing games and rarely gave the right reply to the password, shouting 'Colorado' when he should have shouted 'Timbuktoo', and vice versa, without ever being stopped.

Lieutenant Harley's quarters had at first been on a verandah but rain and bullets had driven him to the chapel. He enjoyed singing at the top of his voice and, though his songs were often churlishly received by men living in too close proximity to each other, they would have been badly missed. Possessed of unquenchable good spirits, he was always willing even after an all-night watch, to talk instead of going to sleep if there were someone willing to listen.

Food was rough. Mostly it was tinned beef covered by a great deal of mustard, of which there was a plentiful supply. There was also plenty of pea flour for dhal so that every day the officers were able to have pea soup for dinner. Shuja-ul-Mulk handed over a few ornamental birds his brother Nizam had collected, and there was also bread – half flour and half grit – and a little rice. Even this simple diet couldn't be eaten by Robertson who was being half-starved by Surgeon-Captain Whitchurch on a milk diet and small doses of brandy. In addition to his other duties, Whitchurch also superintended the food.

It was becoming clear by this time that the sufferings to be borne during a siege weren't measured merely in terms of killed or wounded, or even by semi-starvation or sickness. Other miseries included the depressing cheerlessness of the fort, anxiety, confinement, bad sanitation, overcrowding – and smells! Five hundred-odd people cooped up in a space eighty yards square created enough effluvia to upset the stomach of even the strongest, but fortunately Robertson had turned down a suggestion that latrines should be dug in the courtyard and they were all near the stables outside the main wall by the river. Nevertheless the smell that came from this area was frightful and the liquid sewage had a habit of flowing back into a large room which served not only as a public thoroughfare but also as a guardhouse. Sifat finally dug a channel to carry it away, but such were the slopes of the cliff it all drained into the covered passage to the river and the rocky basin where the buckets and water skins were filled.

Townshend's diary at this time carried the following entry: 'The British Agent desires me to let off thirty rounds a day from the towers on to Sher Afzul's house.' This was less to hit Sher Afzul than to let *him* also experience the discomfort of sniping, and on 13 March, since Sifat and his men invariably wasted cartridges in an alarm, to keep them busy they were given some old Enfields. It was hoped that the Chitralis, noticing the different bullets landing among them, would assume that the garrison were running short not only of food but also of Snider and Martini-Henry ammunition.

That night, following a bright day, the darkness was deep and one or two Chitralis were sent round outside the walls to see if there were any signs of mining. They had just returned when there was an outburst of firing from the Sikhs near the north tower. Wild cries were heard from the garden, where a bugle sounded the British call for the charge, and Gurdon heard a voice cheering men on to assault the east tower.

The garrison was ready, however. During the Hunza-Nagar Expedition in 1891, the British had been greeted with fireballs which had lit up the scene during night movements, and Robertson had learned that they were made from a type of pine wood which blazed quickly and brightly from the turpentine it contained. Since much of the fort was constructed of this wood, there was a lot of it inside the walls and Sifat had made bags of canvas about a foot in diameter and stuffed them with pine chips and straw saturated with kerosene. One of these fireballs was thrown down, and for nearly half an hour blazed so brilliantly the garrison was able to reply to the firing with volleys that echoed and re-echoed through the ancient walls. The enemy had been working on a sangar 150 yards upstream on the same side of the river as the fort, and it was this noise which had alerted the Sikhs. A feint had then been made against the east tower to hide what was going on, with the idea of its being developed if the garrison was caught napping.

On two successive nights, enemy sangars were built. Gurdon was eager to lead a sortie against them, but another reverse like that of 3 March couldn't be risked because, although there were one or two fine Kashmiri officers and men, on the whole the 4th Ragunaths were of little use and they daren't chance losing another British officer.

On the morning of 14 March, another new sangar was pointed out by the sharp-eyed Wafadar and it was decided that the stables facing it should be fortified. The walls were so old and crumbling, however, that as the new loopholes were made, they enlarged themselves unexpectedly as mud and bricks and rubble fell out, and the enemy marksmen were deadly. On one occasion a man was about to fill up an embarrassingly large hole with a stone when a bullet from across the river whizzed between the stone and his face. As he moved forward again, the stone was hit smack in the centre. Although the water tower was now felt to be safe from attacks, it was decided that the covered waterway was so important twelve Sikhs should be stationed in it every evening. The fortified stables were given to a section of the Kashmir Rifles, though the stench from the latrines was so appalling it was decided they must be changed every day. By this time, under the instructions of the British officers, the Kashmiris were beginning to recover their nerve and Townshend's military diary reported, 'Ragunaths steadier and better in hand last night – no wild firing. British Agent pleased with them.' Even so, they were restricted to volleys because they were quite capable of loosing off great quantities of ammunition in their excitement. There was another reason: the ancient weapons they used, with their worn rifling, had to be conserved as much as possible because with every shot they fired they became markedly less accurate.[1]

Quite apart from this, it was also always important to avoid fighting whenever possible and when a flag of truce appeared in the evening towards dark carried by an old woman, the garrison was glad to accept it. The old woman mumbled that Sher Afzul would guarantee a safe journey to Gilgit of all troops and stores – if only they would go and the government of India would accept him as mehtar. The old woman also mentioned that the people of Yaghistan had risen against the British and that even in Gilgit and Punial the drums of revolt were being heard.

She was sent away without reply and during the night there was a series of alarms. Fireballs were thrown out and the Pathan yells in the garden added to the chaos in the darkness. Much of the garrison's firing was probably directed at animals which had been turned out during the afternoon because the stocks of hay and straw inside the walls were almost finished. Only eight ponies were kept in case they were needed for food and those which had been pushed out lingered near the walls where several were killed – if nothing else, Robertson thought dryly, a sign that the shooting of the Kashmiris was improving.

The following morning it was seen that the threatening sangars had been improved but there was no shooting. The weather had grown colder and, as the sky took on the colour of ashes, rain began and fell without ceasing so that they took advantage of the calm the downpour brought to convert the end of Campbell's covered waterway into a secure little fort. The idea had been suggested by Sifat, who had a quick eye for a strongpoint, but as his men laboured, the besiegers could also be heard at work constructing yet another sangar in the garden. In the afternoon, the rain changed to sleet and by evening the ground was covered with four inches of snow.

Further letters arrived from Sher Afzul, reiterating his desire for peace but insisting on his conditions being agreed to, and advising the Chitrali nobles in the fort to leave at once and submit to him. The letters depressed Townshend who, with Gurdon, had by this time reached the gloomy conclusion that they were 'in a very serious position' and that relief was doubtful, due to a general lack of transport, supplies and troops in the Gilgit area, and because more than likely Yasin, Ghizr and Mastuj had also risen or were about to. Their only hope seemed to be a column from Peshawar to the south. 'What on earth Mr Udny is doing one cannot even conjecture,' Townshend wrote in his diary. In fact, Udny had been trying to get a message into the fort with Kafiri messengers but none had got through.

In Sher Afzul's communication was also a note to the effect that a letter had been received from a British officer prisoner, describing the capture of British-led troops at Reshun, Buni and Mastuj, and inviting Robertson to send for it. Robertson was inclined to disbelieve the story because it was normal Chitrali diplomacy to make extravagant claims in an extravagant manner, and to continue to make them in exactly the same form, even though they were rejected twenty times over. He therefore replied asking simply if his original letter suggesting Sher Afzul should come to the fort had been received.

Bright skies and six inches of snow greeted the garrison the following day. The guards were wretched and blue with the cold and wet of the night but hardly a shot had been fired for twenty-four hours, even during darkness. During the afternoon, a man with a white flag appeared bringing two letters, one from Sher Afzul and one said to be from Chitrali headmen demanding Sher Afzul as mehtar. Both were of extraordinary length. Sher Afzul claimed he had received Robertson's first letter but considered the suggestion that he should come to the fort improper to a man of his standing.

The packet also enclosed another letter. It was from Lieutenant Edwardes and was dated Reshun, 13 March. Written in a mixture of French and English, it described what had happened to him and his party up to that date and it was enough to make Robertson's heart stand still.

Inside the hurriedly fortified houses in Reshun, Lieutenant Edwardes' little party had taken stock of their casualties. One man had been hit in the face and there was another with a wound in the groin for whom they could do nothing. Biddy, Edwardes' terrier, was also howling and squealing with pain and quite helpless. They were all plagued by the fleas and bugs with which the houses were infested while their water was growing desperately short.

As daylight had increased on 8 March they had waited for the next assault on their fragile fortress, but the villagers and the Pathans who had joined them seemed to have decided to conserve their ammunition and the day was quiet in a sweltering heat. They were surrounded by hundreds of enemies, many of them armed with Sniders and Martini-Henrys, and to increase their anxieties the memory of the Mutiny was less than forty years old. That had been a traumatic experience, with British soldiers and their families hounded like criminals out of their secure lives to die of thirst, heat and disease, and ever since, British officers and been inclined to look over their shoulders at their native troops and wonder which of them were disloyal enough to drive a bullet through their backs.[1]

The men in the little fortification remained steady, however, and despite the firing that went on all day from the sangars the enemy had built on the slopes and round the houses, there were no complaints. The fortifications were strengthened wherever possible, and after dark Lieutenant Fowler slipped out with a small party to bring in what baggage was left in the sangar by the river. Water was also needed by this time, and on his return he went out again with two great jars lashed to poles and carried by twelve men and a water-carrier. Edwardes watched in silence as they left, his eyes moving swiftly over the silent polo ground in front and the dark buildings about him. Fowler had not gone more than a few yards when several of the men with Edwardes, tense and unnerved by their experiences, fired at shadows. They were checked at once and Fowler's party, who had flung themselves down at the shots, scrambled to their feet and continued, with Fowler and four men acting as guards while the others scrambled down to the river and filled the jars. A second journey was made and, emboldened by their success, they even ventured a third using the pony. By the time the moon rose they were well off for water.

By this time the exhausted soldiers were falling asleep on their feet, and, although they were doubled, it was difficult to keep the sentries awake. Just before daylight digging was heard on the polo ground and a Gurkha havildar and three men were sent out to investigate. Almost at once firing broke out and they bolted back in a panic, one of them with a cut hand, more than likely caused by his own bayonet.

The roof fortifications were in two sections, one defended by Edwardes and the Kashmiri Gurkhas, the other by Fowler with his Bengal sappers, and immediately before dawn in a dead aching silence, Fowler head Edwardes shout:

'Present! Fire!'

Edwardes had seen men creeping forward, and at his cry the shadows came to life and at once the silence was split by Pathan screams, war cries, drums and the rattle of musketry as a ferocious assault was launched from the polo ground, the garden wall and the adjoining houses, the ragged attackers pouring over the stones and through the trees. The crash of volleys filled the crowded rooms as the charge was stopped in its tracks. As the Chitralis and Pathans retreated, dragging their wounded with them, the defenders pulled aside their own injured and looked to their weapons in readiness for the next assault. It came almost immediately and the houses were filled with smoke and the cries of wounded men. Every time the attackers tried to advance they were driven back, Edwardes' party firing sometimes from a distance of only twenty yards. As the assault finally died away, the Pathans crouched behind the walls, beating drums, howling, cursing and taunting the besieged men throughout the rest of the night. Edwardes, however, had lost four more killed and wounded, so that only thirty-four men were now left of the sixty who had first marched into the village.

Drumming and shouting continued all the next day and the weary little garrison – filthy with dirt, smoke and sweat – prepared again for the hours of darkness. But the Pathans had lost too many men, and the night was quiet as the besieged men stared through their loopholes, their nerves stretched, their eyes smarting with the strain. The next day was also quiet, though continual sniping across the polo ground worried them. The hot weather made it necessary to get rid of the six dead Gurkhas. They were placed in a shed alongside the house and surrounded with wood and straw, which was then ignited, so that the surviving Hindus had the satisfaction of seeing the bodies of their friends disposed of in the orthodox manner. During the day distant firing brought their heads up in the hope of relief, but nothing happened; the sound was undoubtedly that of Ross's attempt to escape from the Koragh defile.

With a late moon they could expect a few hours' darkness that night. With little water left and enemy watch fires on the cliff opposite, Edwardes, Fowler and Dhurm Singh decided on a sortie. Edwardes felt he ought to lead but it was decided he didn't know the ground well enough, and Fowler – a long lithe Irishman who was a good rider and a noted sportsman – once more reached for a rifle and bayonet.

Their hearts thumping, the little party crept out one after another, to gather in the shadows and head in a wide sweep towards the fires. Eventually they came on twenty men in a hollow cooking round a big blaze with only one careless sentry. Just as Fowler gave the order to attack the sentry heard them and Fowler had to jump for him. Missing his footing, he fell heavily, and his men, rushing to the edge of the hollow, poured a volley over him, killing most of the tribesmen.

Immediately, from another sangar just ahead, the tribesmen began shooting wildly in the wrong direction, and Fowler and his men rushed in from the flank and rear with the bayonet. Very few of the tribesmen escaped. As he was withdrawing, however, Fowler heard firing and drumming behind them. Realizing Edwardes was under attack again, he had to leave all the weapons he had captured and hurry back to his assistance. By the time his party arrived the assault was almost over and the only injury Fowler's men had sustained was a sprained thumb suffered by Fowler himself when he fell.

Hunger and thirst increased on 11 March, by which time they knew the food could not last much longer. An attempt to get water by digging a well in one of the houses was made, but twelve feet down solid rock was reached and the besieged men looked at each other despairingly. Fowler and Edwardes were also worried about the ammunition boxes they had been guarding, and several times they discussed destroying some of them to prevent them falling into the hands of the Pathans. In the hurry of improvising their defences on the first night, however, they had been compelled to build the boxes into a rude parapet and these had since been covered with kit-bags, beams, bricks, and debris, so that it was virtually impossible to get them out again. The nights remained brightly moonlit and any noise immediately drew the enemy's fire. Guessing that the ammunition was desperately needed by Robertson at Chitral and knowing nothing of the disaster in the Koragh, they still expected to be relieved by Ross, and so they decided to hang on to it as long as they could.

By now the enemy had built a fortification in a plane tree level with the roof position. Its occupants were driven out again and again by rifle fire, but they always returned. That evening it was decided that another attempt had to be made to get water. Fowler again carried it out successfully, though he suffered an agonizing few minutes as his parched soldiers ignored the danger in their desperation and drank at the river before filling their containers. On their way back they took a wrong turning and almost walked into the arms of the besiegers.

They had hardly settled back in their positions when a shed in front of the fortified house was set on fire and some of the gun-cotton abandoned in the fight on 7 March was thrown on to the flames to make them flare up in a bright glare. Heavy rain fell on 12 March and was carefully collected. Hardly a shot was fired on this day but by now Edwardes and Fowler had given up all hope of rescue and had decided to fight it out to the end. On the morning of 13 March, however, a huge Pathan carrying a white flag and shouting 'Cease fire!' appeared. A message was passed to Edwardes to say that Sher Afzul's foster brother, Muhammed Isa, had arrived from Chitral with two other chiefs, Yadgar Beg and his nephew, Muhammed

Afzul Beg, to put an end to the fighting, and was anxious to speak
with the British officers.

Edwardes went out to meet him, waiting at a gap in the wall of the
polo ground where he could remain in full view of his own men.
He was hardly able to believe he was still alive and thankfully breathed
in the fresh air. Surrounded by orchards and the high slopes of the
mountains, Reshun was a very beautiful village, and Chitrali lovers
singing of the ripeness of their sweethearts' lips would compare them
to the 'beauty of the red Reshun soil'. To Edwardes, after the awful
turmoil of the close fighting in the fortified houses and the deaths of
his men, it had never looked more attractive.

Nevertheless, he was not blind to the possibility of treachery, and
as he went forward, Fowler took the precaution of covering Muhammed Isa with his rifle. Edwardes returned with the news that
negotiations were in progress at Chitral between Umra Khan and
Robertson and that Umra Khan was to be given the mehtarship.
Refusing to budge without orders from Robertson, however, he
had suggested an armistice during which his men were to be pro-
visioned and allowed to collect water. Muhammed Isa had agreed
with a great show of friendliness and several men went to fill water
bags at a watercourse beyond the polo ground. They returned to say
that the village was packed with Pathans and Chitralis, all of them
bristling with weapons.

A few supplies including a sheep were sent in before dark and
Edwardes was allowed to send a letter to Robertson at Chitral, but
he and Fowler did not allow their men to relax. Rain, which fell again
during the night and on 14 March, was collected. Fowler's pony had
its first drink for six days, from a puddle which had gathered. The
wounded were given mutton soup and they were all able to get a
little of the rest for which they were now growing desperate. By this
time, the terrier, Biddy, was little more than a skeleton but was
actually beginning to crawl about after Edwardes.

In the afternoon, accompanied by Yadgar Beg – a glib rogue with
a persuasive tongue as Robertson had found at Chitral – Muhammed
Isa again met Edwardes. From what he said it seemed now as if
Robertson were in control again at Chitral. The belief was strengthened
because both Edwardes and Fowler knew that one determined charge

by the enemy would easily overwhelm their little garrison, and they couldn't imagine why otherwise Muhammed Isa should bother to parley.

By this time their position looked as if it had been hit by a hurricane. Trees had been sliced and boughs splintered by the storm of fire, branches littered the ground or hung down half-severed, and the mud walls into which the sepoys were digging to improve the fortification were full of lead bullets. No one was allowed to approach the fortification and though a little food was again sent in, it was not enough; even if Muhammed Isa had wished to send more, there was very little left in the barren district because of the number of men now gathered there.

On the night of 14-15 March, snow fell to a depth of about an inch but when the ground had dried the next day, Muhammed Isa invited the British officers to tea and challenged them to a game of polo in honour of peace having been made. Edwardes declined but Muhammed Isa persisted, asking them at least to watch and saying he was still anxious to meet Fowler. In the end, conferring with Dhurm Singh, the Gurkha subadar, they decided it might be wiser to accept. The polo players could still be directly covered by the sepoys on the roof, but they also stipulated that all spectators were be to moved to the opposite side of the polo ground. Muhammed Isa and Yadgar Beg accordingly drove everyone away and, after carefully instructing their men, Edwardes and Fowler went out. They were given a charpoy or bedstead to sit on, and moved this well into the open so as not to be hidden from Dhurm Singh and the garrison. Muhammed Isa joined the game and Yadgar Beg sat between them.

Muhammed Isa seemed anxious not to renew the fighting, and Fowler recognized his pony as one he had last seen Lieutenant Gurdon riding. He had been told that a British officer had been mortally wounded at Chitral and could now only assume it was Gurdon. The truth was that the pony had been seized when Gurdon's groom was killed in the sortie of 3 March, but Muhammed Isa was quick to claim that he had killed Gurdon with a tulwar. As a result, it was Gurdon's name instead of Baird's which eventually found its way to Simla and led to his family in England being mistakenly notified of his death.

The polo game started – 'The polo was very poor,' Edwardes

thought[2] – but the villagers wanted to watch, too, and the numbers increased until there was an enormous crowd. Then, as the game finished, tea was served and the British officers, who had risen, were politely asked if the dancing by the defeated side – a normal courtesy after a game – might begin. They agreed but failed to notice that meanwhile their seat had been moved a little. As the dancing grew wilder, Fowler noticed more men climbing the wall to the polo ground and surrounding the dancers, and he jumped up, saying it was time to go. As he did so Muhammed Isa, a fat powerful man who was now sitting between them, threw his arms round them and they were promptly seized by tribesmen and flung down behind a wall where they were hidden from their men. The alert Dhurm Singh had not missed the move, however, and a volley rang out.

Immediately a rush was made against the fortified houses and, as the firing flared up, Edwardes and Fowler were dragged away trussed like chickens; the big Pathan who had first begun the negotiations for a truce demanding to know where the money they had carried was hidden.

'Go the the devil,' Fowler snapped back, and immediately their boots and stockings were dragged off and the brass buttons cut from their uniforms in the belief that they were gold. The firing against the houses had increased tremendously by now but Dhurm Singh's reply was equally fierce. As the attack persisted, accompanied by shrieks and the waving of banners, the sheer weight of the Pathans' fusillade began to take effect and the return fire from the fortification began to slacken. Finally, exhausted Gurkhas started to emerge through the rolling clouds of smoke, staggering and carrying dead and wounded, while the attackers surged forward with a howl of triumph under Umra Khan's white banner with its bloody hand emblem. The gallant Dhurm Singh, who had behaved so splendidly throughout the whole of the operations, continued to fight like a lion until the final attack swept over him and he was overwhelmed and cut down. Only a dozen men were made prisoners. Two of them had shot themselves to avoid capture.

As the hacked and bleeding bodies were dragged out, the howling villagers swept through the now ghastly block of houses, brandishing captured weapons and throwing out clothing and equipment. As cigarettes and cigars and personal belongings were carelessly tossed about, out of bravado Fowler asked for a cigarette. One was placed between his lips and lit and, though he had 'never felt less inclined to smoke in his life', he considered it was the only way with his arms tied he could show his defiance.

As the yells of triumph died, the two officers were flung into a filthy hut where the guards constantly jerked at the ropes that tied their elbows together to make sure they were secure. The following morning they were told by Muhammed Isa that they were to be separated and said good-bye, expecting never to see each other again. Fowler, with a rope tied to each arm, was marched off by two Chitralis and two Pathans towards the river, while Edwardes was led to the polo ground. Both river and polo ground were favourite killing places and both officers fully expected to die. As they parted, Edwardes whispered to his Chitrali guard to give him a few moments' warning before the last blinding passage to death. The guard glanced round, then, stooping as if by accident, pressed his fingers, wishing him luck. It was not, however, to execution that Edwardes was being led but to another extraordinary game of polo where, sitting alongside Muhammed Isa, he was forced to stare across the polo ground at the battered and bloodstained fortification he had just lost, and the precious boxes of ammunition he had been unable to destroy.

An outbreak of firing came as a relief 16

So far, cocooned in their prosperity, concerned with the affairs of the royal family, the Church, Parliament and the nobility, the newspaper and magazine readers in England had not had a single hint that anything untoward was happening on the frontier.

It took a long time for news to travel from the north, of course, and the newspapers in Calcutta had only been able to report that, though something was stirring, 'the news continues to be scanty'.

There was little alarm in India itself, and in London the people were even less moved by the information. They had problems of their own. There had been blizzards and a spate of bitter winter weather which had lasted from early February, bringing pack ice to the Thames. Preoccupied with keeping warm, they were hardly aware of the problems of India, and the small affair in mountain-locked Chitral was easily overlooked.

The first hint that something was badly wrong came from a report by Reuters' correspondent on 9 March. Under the heading 'Unrest At Chitral', he announced, 'A crisis is expected . . . Fighting is considered inevitable.' Despite this 'inevitability', no one took much notice. Even on 12 March, after Chitral had already been besieged for nine days, it was still being maintained that the government of India felt no anxiety. It was noticeable, however, that *The Times* of London had been quick to publish a report from St Petersburg that the *Novoe Vremya* had been asserting Russia's rights to the possession of the Pamir plateau as far as the Hindu Kush.

The first real indication that all was not well came on 15 March in the news that an ultimatum had been sent to Umra Khan who had already been warned – in 1891, 1893 and 1894 – to keep his hands off

Chitral. The first hard facts appeared on 17 March, with the information that an expedition was being raised to put things straight.

By this time Robertson and his men had been tightly shut up for a fortnight. The only forces in a position to save them had been wiped out themselves, while Mastuj, through which any reinforcements from Gilgit would have to pass, was so surrounded by enemies the garrison there could make no move except for their own protection.

On his return to Mastuj from Buni, Lieutenant Moberly had had no time to sit back and recover his breath because a reconnaissance up the Laspur valley the following day had run into a force of tribesmen near Chakalwat. Expecting him to attack, they had immediately climbed the cliffs to points where they could set the rocks rolling but there had been no advance and the only casualties had been a number of Chitralis who had slipped and fallen.[1]

The skirmish had been an indication of the importance of holding Mastuj, however, and Moberly had at once begun to set the old fort in order for a siege. Trees were cut down, abbatis constructed, walls strengthened and loopholed, and on 21 March, Kashmiri recruits were given rifle instruction. The result was 'not encouraging'.

On the edge of a sloping plain, Mastuj was a shabby uncomfortable place even without a ring of tribesmen sitting outside waiting to slit the throats of the defenders, and Algernon Durand had thought it the draughtiest place he knew. At the junction of three large valleys, there was 'always a wind, generally a gale', and the fort was in a dreadfully dilapidated condition. It was covered with dust from mountain avalanches, and the earthquake some years before had so shaken the walls they were almost in a state of collapse.

With Moberly thus in no position to send aid, and Robertson still waiting for the relief he had firmly expected, Lieutenant Edwardes' letter arriving from Sher Afzul under a white flag had had a depressing effect on the garrison at Chitral. According to Captain Townshend, Robertson 'appeared thunderstruck'.

He was in a terrible dilemma. He had had no intention of giving an inch, but now he had to take into consideration the lives of Edwardes and Fowler whom he believed to be still at Reshun. Edwardes' letter,

E

dated 13 March, had been written before Muhammed Isa's treachery and the butchery that had followed, and indicated only that Edwardes had come to the conclusion that the forces surrounding him were so powerful he had no choice but to parley. It knocked the props from Robertson's intended defiance and, in an attempt to help the men he thought to be still holding out in Reshun, he sent a letter to Sher Afzul proposing a three-day armistice. The parley would begin the next day with Robertson's Indian head clerk, Amir Ali, acting on his behalf.

A white flag, the prearranged answer, was raised over the old mission house and the fort ran up its own in reply. Throughout a sleepless night, Robertson tried to think up some means of getting a letter to Edwardes. He was convinced – rightly as it had already turned out – that treachery was intended at Reshun and his only hope lay in getting a warning to the two British officers who, he felt, were new to the double-dealing of the frontier chiefs.

The darkness seemed interminable and even when the first light of a new day began to fill the dusty old fort, it seemed ages before Amir Ali reported to be briefed. His chief task was to get permission for a letter to be sent to Edwardes, something which would require every ounce of tact he possessed.

A distinct air of excitement was noticeable inside the fort at the thought that the negotiations might bring peace, but Robertson was still low in spirits and less sanguine. To Captain Campbell he said he would do almost anything to save Fowler and Edwardes, but that to make a sortie from the fort would mean their all being butchered.

The man who came to escort Amir Ali to Sher Afzul turned out to be none other than the defecting spy who had been replaced by the incendiarist of the water tower, now terrified out of his wits lest Robertson decided to detain and punish him for his earlier treachery. Amir Ali followed him out of the fort, however, armed with three points he must stick to in dealing with the enemy. First, the truce could not last any longer unless flour and sheep were supplied to the garrison. Second, that the road to Mastuj should be opened for letters. Third, nobody should approach the walls of the fort. There was also a fourth point – on which he might give way – that a neutral zone should be worked out.

He was led through the bazaar-serai – now strongly fortified and full of Pathans armed with Martini-Henrys – to the mission house where he was received by two princes, escorted by about two hundred Jandolis. Two khans, relatives of Umra Khan, were sent for and when they arrived they had thirty or forty riflemen in front and a similar number behind, so that the durbar room was packed with men carrying loaded rifles. Despite the danger and the obvious tension, Amir Ali kept his head. Sher Afzul seemed nervous. By this time he was virtually the prisoner of Umra Khan who was not in the town of Chitral at all and never had been. The two khans – Abdul Majid Khan of Sheena, his first cousin, and Abdul Ghani Khan of Shahi – were his emissaries and, in effect, Sher Afzul's guards and advisers. Umra Khan himself was still at Kila Drosh, preparing to head back to his own Jandol after learning of the government of India's reaction to his latest aggression, because he was anxious to organize opposition to any moves made against him from the south.

To Amir Ali, Sher Afzul said he had nothing to add to his letters, and that he wished for peace, but only on his own terms. In reply, Amir Ali doggedly put Robertson's points, all of which were peremptorily refused. Then Majid Khan, speaking on behalf of Umra Khan, declared they would have no truce, not even if troops arrived from Mastuj. Like everyone else he guaranteed the garrison's safety if they would only leave and return to Gilgit. By pushing into Chitral, he said, the government of India had antagonized Bajour, of which Jandol was a part, and all the Bajouris were prepared to fight. Sher Afzul endeavoured to interrupt the young khan but, silenced with a gesture, he meekly confirmed what had been said. It was clear he was not a free agent.

When Amir Ali returned, Robertson wrote a letter demanding guarantees and hostages before he moved from the fort and again asking permission to send a letter to Edwardes. The answer stated that the negotiations would be passed on to Umra Khan and that until his views were known there had better be no more fighting. There was clearly no hope of getting a letter through to Edwardes.

The garrison were only too glad of the extra days of truce and to be able to bring in wood and walk about without being fired at. Since Futteh Ali Shah's house nearby appeared to be in process of fortification, they took the opportunity to fit bullet-proof covers to the towers and improvise shelters for the men on the walls with beams from the garden, packing cases and boxes filled with earth and firewood. Eventually the tribesmen threatened to fire if they didn't stop. They didn't stop but nothing happened.

Neglected for years, the fort was desperately in need of strengthening. The gun tower, at the south-east corner, was considered a work of art by the Chitralis but the concussion from even one round of one of the small 7-pounders 'would probably have split the walls wide open if it didn't bring them down altogether'. It contained more of the pine timber than any other tower, but it was solid rubble to the first floor where a long inside ladder led to the top compartment, which was reached – not without difficulty – through a manhole.

The flag tower at the south-west corner was even higher, roughly seventy feet. Here the top was reached by a long outside ladder in full view of the enemy, so that the Sikhs on the top platform could only be relieved after dark. Both the west and south aspects of the fort were badly covered, the flag and gun towers projecting only a short distance from the walls. The garden, or south-east, side was better protected, being covered from a large hole which had been cut in the wall of the gun tower which enabled fire to be directed towards the garden door. The hole was covered during the day by a large Morababad tea tray and when this was removed in the evening no lights were permitted.

The top of the gun tower had a little gallery like a 'stunted sentry box' overlooking the summer-house, and this was now strengthened with planks and a slit was cut facing the flag tower so that a rifleman could cover the south wall. For purposes of identification this contrivance was called the 'machicoulis gallery' though, as Robertson pointed out, they forgot the machicolation through which the foot of the tower could have been seen and protected. The garden, however, could be watched from an unblocked window frame on the eastern side. A well was also started near the hospital on the advice of the Chitralis who believed that water had been found there in earlier days, and damp soil brought cheers. Underneath, however, the earth was bone dry again.

Up to the time of the truce, nothing outside the fort had been seen moving and only an occasional puff of smoke indicated the position of an enemy marksman so that within a radius of 700 yards there was stillness and the quietness of death. For hours not a sound had broken the silence because inside, apart from the sentries, everyone was getting as much rest as they could.[2] Sometimes, the unnatural silence had become so oppressive that 'an outbreak of firing came as a relief', but now, with the armistice, cattle and goats were allowed to graze near the fort.

During the afternoon of 18 March, a soldierly-looking man approached the fort and saluted the British officer on duty in military fashion. He said he had been a sergeant in the 5th Punjabs but was now an officer of Umra Khan's regular troops. No one felt any surprise at his switch of loyalties because it was known that the skill of the besiegers lay in the fact that many such men were among them. At least a dozen famous regiments had their representatives outside, all of them proud of their military knowledge and eager to use it to murder their former comrades inside!

The old soldier was friendly enough, however, and stood at attention all the time he was talking. He lied freely to cheer the garrison up, insisting that Sher Afzul was short of ammunition and on the point of marching away. As usual, Robertson's clerks went through the farcical procedure of trying to bribe him to bring food on the grounds that they were hungry. By this time, even the garrison was beginning to believe them.

Certainly they were far from happy. Bad sanitation, stone dust mixed with flour, and exposure to the snow, had brought fever and dysentery. There was no milk for the sick or much in the way of help for Surgeon-Captain Whitchurch. Since the medical supplies had been left outside the fort during the precipitate retreat on 3 March, the only chloroform on which he could call was the small amount in his own panniers.

After dark it rained heavily, drenching the sentries listening wretchedly to the tribesmen outside drumming and cheering on their dancing boys round their blazing fires until long after midnight. On 19 March, however, the rain stopped, and the penultimate goose was killed. That day more letters were delivered, this time by the two Jandoli envoys, Majid Khan and Abdul Ghani Khan, including one they had written themselves. This was 'solicitous' about Robertson's health, but repeated the demand that he should withdraw; this time south to Peshawar. Robertson wrote back politely that he didn't think 'the present a good opportunity to visit Jandol and Swat'.

It was all rather ridiculous but it had always been part of frontier manners to be fulsome whether dealing with treachery or trivialities,[3] and a sharper and unexpected note was introduced by Sher Afzul's letter which, in the same vein and heavily larded with the same formal and farcical courtesy, bitterly reproached Robertson for his lack of confidence in him. It went on to explain that no letter had been allowed to go to Edwardes because, during the truce at Reshun, both Sher Afzul and the Jandoli khans had sent instructions as to how their troops should behave, but that the truce had been broken before the instructions had arrived. The sting was in the tail which contained the information that in any case the matter had now become entirely academic since the fight at Reshun was over and the two British officers and a number of their sepoys were at that moment heading towards Chitral as prisoners.

The defeat of the little garrison at Reshun tied Robertson's hands even more. The information that the two officers were now in the region of the fort, however, produced a measure of grim excitement and every eye in the place was turned towards the valley for a view of the captured men.

All day, small groups of Pathans and Chitralis had been seen moving towards them, many of them wounded and struggling along on foot or on ponies. With them they carried seven or eight corpses, and since to carry these from Reshun – a matter of twenty to thirty miles – indicated that the dead men were chieftains, Robertson could only conclude that Edwardes and Fowler had put up a fierce resistance.

The Chitralis in the fort were certain that the fight had gone badly for their fellow-countrymen. And in that curious way in which outside news somehow always managed to reach them it was also reported that the two Jandoli khans were anxious to make terms for themselves, while a message from Shuja-ul-Mulk's mother outside the fort said – wrongly – that the Chitralis had been beaten in a fight

on the road from Mastuj and that on no account must Robertson
abandon the fort.

On 20 March, new information indicated that Edwardes and Fowler
were being brought to Sher Afzul and that ponies were being sent
to meet them. Once again, the demands that Robertson should leave
were reiterated and, eager to keep the truce going, he sent a whole
list of complicated and impossible qualifications. He was really
bartering for the release of the two officers and even expressed himself
willing under certain conditions to retire to Mastuj, knowing his
terms would never be agreed to. Had they been, he was ready to
retaliate with a new demand that Sher Afzul and the two Jandoli
khans should offer themselves as hostages for everyone's safety,
knowing perfectly well that they wouldn't.

That afternoon, a crowd about a hundred strong, following another
procession of corpses, approached with two riderless ponies. Immediately, armed men flocked into the sangars between the fort and
the roadway in case a sortie to rescue the prisoners was contemplated.
Everyone in the fort was trying to spot Edwardes and Fowler. They
were not seen but Amir Ali, led out by the ex-sergeant of the 5th
Punjabs, was allowed to meet them. He took with him presents of
money for the khans and tobacco, pipes, underclothing, tea, sugar,
knives, forks and plates for the two officers. They appeared to be in
good health but had been stripped of everything but what they wore.
The story they passed on was a grim one.

Still surprised he was alive, Lieutenant Fowler had barely left
Reshun when his Pathan and Chitrali guards had quarrelled about
whether he was to be taken to Umra Khan or Sher Afzul and had
threateningly opened the breeches of their rifles to each other to
show they were loaded. The road had been bad even for Chitral, and
Fowler was limping along in the soft leather boots he had been given
to replace the ones he'd had stolen. He had been determined not to
hurry, but the guards had not seemed to mind and soon afterwards
Lieutenant Edwardes had appeared. The man who had pressed his
hand near the polo ground had also allowed Biddy to crawl after
them and this man now untied Fowler.

At the next village when a group of Pathans approached, the Chitrali
pushed the two officers into a house and barricaded it with the help of

a villager. Quarrelling was heard outside but eventually the leader of the Pathans was allowed to enter with a priest. In spite of his villainous appearance, the Pathan was not unfriendly. Like so many of Umra Khan's men he had onced soldiered with a British-Indian regiment, and knew enough Hindustani to converse. From him they learned at last what had happened to the relief they had expected from Ross.

They discovered that twenty or thirty of Ross's Sikhs who had failed to follow Jones to safety had fallen back again to the caves in the defile and had defended themselves there for a week. Though enemy sangars were built even over the mouths of the caves, they had continued to hang on without food or water, sustained by the opium they habitually carried.[4]

But then the three Chitrali chiefs, whose treachery had by now led to the capture of Edwardes and Fowler at Reshun, turned their vicious attention on them. The Sikhs had been promised their lives in return for surrender but when the emaciated men had stumbled out, those unable to walk were at once butchered and the remainder were shut up in a house at Kalak where next morning the three chiefs had them brought out one at a time and hacked to death. Only one man escaped.

Next day the river was recrossed and the journey continued, but with endless problems over billeting. Though curious to see the Englishmen, no villager was eager to have their large company of guards quartered on him, and this always led to some wretched family being kicked out and its home appropriated, while the armed men surrounded the place and even swirled on to the roof to watch the Englishmen through the smoke-hole.

On 19 March, orders came for them to be taken to Sher Afzul and, though ponies were provided for them, they were of little use because the hanging roads of the Baitari cliffs had been destroyed to stop Robertson retreating. As the besieged fort at Chitral came into view they were taken over by the Pathans. From this point they were better treated and their jemadar and eleven sepoys reappeared unharmed.

Two of the sepoys were allowed to cook for the officers, but there was still great difficulty in obtaining food for them because all the grain in the district had been carried into the fort by Lieutenant

Gurdon or Futteh Ali Shah or else eaten by Sher Afzul's men. And when they traversed the scene of Campbell's retreat on 3 March, still dotted with dreadful masses of corruption where men had been cut down, they began to suspect that their chances of ever reaching safety again had grown even slimmer.

As the two officers were led away, Amir Ali noticed a marked difference in the attitude of the two Jandoli khans. Under the influence of the bribes he had brought, they were noticeably more friendly and began to ask for watches, revolvers and cartridges, while several of their followers whispered that they – the followers – were eager to serve Robertson. This, Amir Ali knew, 'really only meant that they wanted presents too'.

As Robertson had expected, nothing came of the meeting, nothing beyond a heartbreaking awareness for Edwardes and Fowler that their hopes of regaining their freedom were dead. To them the fort presented a curiously dishevelled appearance because the shelters that had been erected to protect the garrison from reverse fire were without uniformity and the walls were covered with rough wooden frames and boxes of earth.

At least they were not now being ill-treated, and were even given tea and cakes by Sher Afzul who was sitting surrounded by his escort with a loaded rifle in his lap. He complained that the war was none of his doing and seemed anxious to be friendly. Fowler even got his boots back, but no move was made to release them.

The meeting had not raised the spirits of the garrison either. From Amir Ali, they had learned for the first time how severe the reverse at Reshun had been. 'Only twelve sepoys remain out of a total of sixty,' the shocked Townshend noted in his diary. 'Could any situation be more serious than this?'

The interminable and faintly ridiculous correspondence between Robertson and Sher Afzul recommenced, quite pointlessly, on 21 March. Amir Ali was allowed to see the prisoners again, and Edwardes managed to pass over a letter asking to see Gurdon who was promised safe conduct. By now, however, the garrison was at its lowest ebb and not inclined to be trustful. The ground was saturated with rain water and sewage which would not drain away, and Robertson's illness was at its worst. They had also now been cooped up for three weeks, and Townshend was at last facing the stark and unpalatable truth that the Kashmiris were of no value whatsoever. Almost with the relish of a man who could say 'I told you so,' he wrote in his diary, 'I am sorry to say that the men of the Rifles are now pretty well useless. Their officers appear helpless and give no orders. One cannot trust them to do anything. I have to get Gurdon or Harley or myself to superintend the smallest duty. As for the N.C.O.s – words fail me to describe them! The men are dirty and slovenly and do not obey orders with alacrity. The fact is, they are . . . decidedly "not for it" any longer.'[5]

By this time he was bitterly calling Chitral 'the damned fort'. He had taken a liking to little Shuja – 'I see him every day,' he wrote, 'and we have long and friendly conversations' – but when he had to mount a guard over the Chitralis' quarters the women irritated him intensely. Despite his undoubted fondness for the ladies,[6] he didn't enjoy having them on the frontier, and even at Gilgit he had been furiously indignant when the transport official had brought his wife to live there.

'I call it turning the place into a regular Punch and Judy show,' he had written. 'Gilgit will be getting quite suburban, and lines of dubious-looking lingeries hung out to dry like you see in the outskirts of London.' The women in the fort were the wives and daughters of the Chitralis and lived in a large room close to the officers' mess where their laughter and whispering could be constantly heard. 'It is rather a nuisance to be a witness of their *vie intime*,' Townshend complained petulantly. Without knowing the details, he also condemned Edwardes and Fowler for allowing themselves to be captured, taking the view that the Pathans' double-dealing was only what one would have expected. 'Such a stupid affair has never been heard!' he wrote furiously. 'How will these officers explain the fact that they left their sepoys, and quitted the post where they had been barricaded and besieged for six days, to see a game of polo at the invitation of the enemy?'[7]

The next day more letters arrived, promising safety to any British officer who wished to talk with Edwardes and Fowler. Among them was a note for Whitchurch from Fowler, giving the numbers of their party and more grim details of the fight at Reshun. It was clear by now that the enemy believed the garrison to be desperate for food. This pleased Robertson, though the garrison as a whole remained far from happy because the besiegers had captured a large number of rifles at Reshun and all the ammunition and gun-cotton ordered up from Gilgit; worst of all, some of the men who had been taken prisoner knew how to use the explosive.

Once again Amir Ali was sent out, this time with watches and revolvers as bribes for the two khans. Getting them on one side, he managed to whisper that if they could slip Edwardes and Fowler into the fort they would be well rewarded. Although they were clearly tempted, they hadn't the courage to make the move, and when Sher Afzul arrived the discussion had to stop.

The arguing over terms started again. Threats were made to reduce the fort, and Amir Ali was asked sarcastically what hope there could be and how could the garrison ever expect reinforcements to cross the Shandur Pass at that time of the year. His reply was bold and indicated a flash of genius. 'The pass,' he said, 'will be worked into a plain by the thousands of men tramping over it from Gilgit.'

It stopped the argument dead.

No one really wanted the discussion to halt entirely, however, the chiefs because they were still hoping to persuade the garrison to leave without a fight and the British because it was important to keep the truce going. So when Amir Ali returned, he brought with him Sher Afzul's Hindu diwan to carry on the arguments inside the fort. From him it became clear that despite the hostility for the British among the men outside, there was a great deal of treachery going on among themselves too, and from him also came the first glimmering of good news since the siege began.

He tried hard to be forceful and persuasive but his urgency made Robertson suspicious. His own demands became firmer and, as the diwan's anger increased, Robertson's questions grew more probing until in an unguarded moment the diwan let slip something which only served to strengthen Robertson's resolve.

Help had at last been assembled in the south and British-led troops were finally on the way.

There is an excellent road

On 25 March, Edwardes and Fowler finally reached the verminous fort of Kila Drosh, near the southern border of Chitral, where Umra Khan was waiting. They found him an intelligent, pious man who, though easily ruffled and obviously angered by British arrogance, gave them hope with his spotless garb and good manners.

Their journey had been a terrible one and they had several times been half-frozen and soaked to the skin, but Umra Khan clearly tried to make up for their ordeal. Their habit of eating with a knife and fork intrigued his followers but he was always careful to see they were not molested, giving them a great deal of freedom and improved conditions of living. He loved hawking and allowed them to walk alongside his horse. He was never armed and appeared anxious to respect their religion, saying to them two days later as they crossed the Lowarai Pass into Dir, 'If you want a quiet time in which to say your prayers, you can say them in a corner of the mosque when I say mine.'

The march over the pass during a blizzard was another terrible ordeal. By this time Edwardes was growing weak and suffered a great deal from the cold, but he and Fowler gained some protection from the awful weather by persuading their guards to acquire Chitrali robes for them. Biddy was still with them, a miserable object though somehow struggling along, but one of their sepoys died, while another could hardly be induced to press on. However, they gained a little satisfaction from the fact that the Pathan who had stolen Fowler's boots and been wounded in the final attack on Dhurm Singh at Reshun, also died near the summit.

Once over the pass they were in a savage and unruly country where everyone crowded into the local fort at dusk and even the heavily-laden porters carried guns. Here they met Mahomed Shah, one of Umra Khan's brothers, who was dressed in a brilliantly-laced military frock coat and Russian boots which were clearly too tight for comfort. He carried a 20-bore gun, a 12-bore rifle, and a Winchester repeater given to him by Amir-ul-Mulk.

On 30 March, they reached the fort at Barwar at the upper end of the Jandol valley, the hereditary home of Umra Khan where he had carried out the picturesque and dramatic murder of his elder brother. Here the two officers were able to cook, wash and repair their clothes and Fowler also managed to acquire a club which made him feel much better. It was here also that they first heard that moves 'to restore British prestige'[1] had at last been put on foot.

To quote General Bindon Blood: with these moves – the first hint of which Sher Afzul's diwan had dropped to Robertson – 'the fun began'.

The prestige of the sirkar, that indefinable but infinitely important moral ascendancy of the British in the east, was at stake; anything in the nature of a reverse in Chitral would be certain to have far-reaching effects along the frontiers, and, alarmed at last, the government of India had mobilized a whole division of troops at Peshawar. Camels had been hired a week earlier, when the first hard news of Robertson's plight had reached them, but no one would say why and the Indian press had grown curious. After a council meeting at Calcutta, however, the reasons were finally made known and Major-General Sir Robert Cunliffe Low, in command of the Lucknow District, received instructions to be prepared to march on Chitral from Nowshera on the Kabul river, north-east of Peshawar.

The government had been driven to the decision by the uproar that the news from Chitral had stirred up. It was not long before that General Sir Frederick Roberts had carried out his expedition to Kabul and Kandahar to avenge the murder of Sir Louis Cavagnari. Like those names, Chitral, as it finally flashed across the electric telegraphs, had the sound of drama that was much to the taste of the British in their staid homes in India. Somewhere in the mountains to the north, a few young British soldiers were holding thousands of savage tribes-men at bay and they must be rescued.

As the affair became public property for the first time, it grew so inflated that in India there was even talk of a 'serious military reverse'. This was a gross exaggeration, of course, but in 1895 Britain was at the height of her power and any resistance to the word of the Empire was capable of rousing the proud Victorians to fury. They were highly jealous of what they considered, with no very good reason, their reputation as soldiers and it was to everybody's delight that news of the First Division's mobilization came on 19 March. This force was not to be encumbered with a heavy baggage train. It would be light and swift-moving, every officer being limited to forty pounds and every man to ten. No tents were to be taken, despite the snow and ice of the passes that had to be faced, but 28,000 pack animals had to be collected nevertheless, and it was no easy job. Because of the cost of maintaining it in peacetime, the army in India as a whole had very little organized transport. Only a few mules and mule carts were kept at the larger up-country stations, so that when the orders to hire went out, tens of thousands of animals, 'hastily impressed, dishonestly purchased', and often without attendants and gear, were pushed to the bases.

There were other problems, too, because the Indian army had never learned to travel without the dozens of camp followers that were considered essential to cut forage, carry water, cook and act as servants. Fodder was brought in, however, as the troops gathered from all along the frontier and a newly-built single-track railway helped. Unfortunately, as there was no properly prepared railhead with the necessary installations and depots, the organization still remained rather confused.

The news of this division, when it reached Barwar, immediately put Fowler and Edwardes in danger of their lives again. Suddenly afraid, the tribesmen grew angry and sullen, and there was even worse news to come, because it now seemed as if half the might of the British Empire was being concentrated for the expedition. The division was to consist of three infantry brigades and was to be 15,000 strong which, even considering the numbers of tribesmen it was to oppose, was huge. The dictum on the frontier had always been that it was best to employ no larger a force than was absolutely necessary, and this one looked like a sledge-hammer to crack a nut.[2]

The First Brigade consisted of the 1st King's Royal Rifles, the 1st Bedfordshires, the 15th Sikhs and the 37th Dogras; the Second Brigade of the 1st Gordon Highlanders, the 2nd King's Own Scottish Borderers, the 4th Sikhs and the Guides Infantry; and the Third Brigade of the 2nd Seaforths, the 1st East Kents, the 25th Bengal Infantry, and the 2nd Battalion of the 4th Gurkhas. Divisional troops also included the Guides cavalry, the 11th Bengal Lancers, the 13th Bengal Infantry, the 23rd Pioneers, Nos 3 and 8 Mountain batteries, the Hazara Mountain Battery and Nos 1, 4 and 6 Companies of the Bengal Sappers and Miners whose ranks also included a photographic section under a certain Sergeant Mayo, which was to produce a series of excellent pictures for the world's later delectation. The lines of communication troops consisted of the 1st East Lancashires, the 29th and 30th Bengal Infantry, and the 2nd Derajat Mountain Battery of four guns. With the reserves that were also made available, it was a colossal force to crush one restless chief.

The commander, Major-General Low, had been over forty years in the east. At the siege of Delhi, during the Mutiny, he had been aide-de-camp to Sir Archdale Wilson, the commander of the attacking British forces, and he had also been present at the second siege of Lucknow. He had since seen several small frontier fights and had won his spurs in Afghanistan where, by taking charge of the transport and converting it from the least to the most efficient portion of Sir Frederick Roberts' force, he had made Roberts' march on Kandahar possible. From Afghanistan he had gone to Burma as leader of the Mandalay Brigade. His subordinates were equally skilful and experienced.

Brigadier-General Alastair Angus Airlie Kinloch, commanding the First Brigade, had been mentioned in despatches for his service during the Afghan campaign of 1870–77. On his staff he had no less than the Hon. Fred Roberts, the son of the great man himself, who would later emulate his father by winning the V.C. Brigadier-General Henry Gordon Waterfield, commanding the Second Brigade, was an Indian Staff Corps officer who had distinguished himself in the Hazara Expedition of 1888. He was known to his men as the Bear. In command of the Third Brigade was Brigadier-General William Forbes Gatacre – who had been deputy adjutant and quartermaster-general with the Hazara Expedition and had later served in Burma. Gatacre was considered the man to watch because his exploits, 'based on an almost superhuman energy and power of endurance', were expected one day to 'become fabulous'.[3] He was the sort of man who, after making a record, set out to break it as a point of honour. A believer in keeping his men fit 'with plenty of work and very little rum', there was little wonder he was known to them as 'Back-Acher'. He was a lean long-faced buzz-saw of a man, nagging, fretting, interfering, adjusting, always active and always trying to do everything himself, on his feet at dawn and never stopping until he went to bed. Later subordinates called him 'impossible' and his addresses to his troops before battle were stigmatized as 'twaddle'. Though the men respected him for his efforts on their behalf, his officers constantly resented the way he did everyone else's work and was unable to let them get on with their jobs.[4]

Colonel A. G. Hammond, V.C., commanding the Corps of Guides, was another frontier soldier of distinction who had served in three campaigns as well as in the Afghan War and had commanded a brigade against the Hazaras. Under him in command of the Guides infantry was Colonel F. D. Battye, considered to be one of the most gifted and experienced officers in the Indian Army. Distinguishing himself in the fighting of 1879 and 1880, he came of an old military family and had no fewer than seven relations on the army list. Unfortunately, it was also an unlucky family that seemed to lose a son in every frontier skirmish that took place.

As chief of staff Low had Brigadier-General Bindon Blood, a handsome and lively scion of an ancient Irish family. The assistant adjutant-general and quartermaster-general on the lines of communication was Colonel Ian Standish Monteith Hamilton, a Gordon Highlander who had already distinguished himself on the frontier, in South Africa where he had had one arm permanently disabled at Majuba, on the Nile expedition and in Burma.

Supply was a job no one liked – 'I don't like this Carter Paterson business', one officer said – but in Hamilton, Low had picked not only a good soldier but a good organizer. Later a friend of Churchill, he was a wit and a writer of distinction. Looking at the numbers he would have to supply, he seemed to feel there were almost too many of them. The relief force, he wrote later, had to be fed, watered and ammunitioned 'over pathless mountains, bridgeless rivers and snow-bound passes swarming with hostile tribesmen. Thousands of animals, donkeys, mules, bullocks, camels had to be kept on the move . . . and . . . life was a never-ending struggle to extemporize methods of coping with bandits, fire and flood, and it was all I could do to keep my hair on my head or my head above water.'

As the regiments tramped into the crowded dusty camps, the government announced that the division would advance on 1 April if no word had been received by then that Umra Khan had vacated Chitral. The following day it issued a proclamation to the people of Swat and Bajour 'who do not side with Umra Khan'. The sole object of the expedition, the proclamation said, was to put an end to unlawful aggression on Chitral territory and the government had no intention of permanently occupying territory or interfering with the independence of the tribes; acts of hostility would be scrupulously avoided so long as the tribesmen refrained from attacking or impeding the march, while all supplies and transport would be paid for.

Winston Churchill, at that time a brand-new lieutenant in the army with an ambition to enter Parliament, shrewdly suspected that the Liberal Government had suddenly got cold feet. They had never liked the 'Forward Policy', which had been the aim of successive administrations, and after years of pursuing a single strategy towards the north he felt they had caused the proclamation to be issued to soothe their supporters by appearing to localize the disturbances and disclaiming any further acquisition of territory.

It was probably also to appease those European countries who were working themselves up into a rage with their envy of Britain's power. On the first outbreak of fighting, the cables had carried the news to Europe and jealous statesmen there thought they saw the beginning of the decline and fall of the Empire, so that a positive welter of jealousy broke out, while in France the anglophobia which was said to be 'rampant'[5] changed to actual pleasure when, on the same day as the proclamation, the news of Ross's disaster arrived.

On 22 March, in the House of Lords, Lord Reay made appropriate noises about the government's preparedness and the division's readiness to advance. In Calcutta, the correspondents, jumping the gun a little, announced that 'stern fighting' was ahead.

Another story stated that 300 of Umra Khan's warriors were in the town of Chitral while Sher Afzul had got into the fort with his men and had sent the greater part of the treasure he had captured there to Umra Khan as a sign of his friendship.[6]

The people in the safe areas to the south seemed to be going through the same emotions of fury and indignation that had motivated them during the Mutiny, but, as Younghusband said, the news of Ross's disaster had 'altered the situation' quite considerably. Chitralis and Pathans had actually fired on British troops going about their lawful business and it was perhaps the arrival of this information that finally decided the government that actions might speak louder than words.

India was growing concerned, and *The Times* correspondent in Calcutta gave vent to the age-old worry. Pointing out that the Dorah Pass led straight through the mountains to the disputed territory bordering Russian-owned Bokhara, he sounded an ominous note: 'It is through the Dorah Pass that the Russians would move on India.' That old bogey-man had not been mentioned before but everyone was aware of Chitral's position astride the shortest route to the Punjab from Afghanistan and the Russian territory of the Oxus. It began to look as if the real reason for Sir Robert Low's vast force was less to crack the unorganized opposition of a few thousand ill-armed tribesmen than to let the Russians know what would face an attempt on India.

A route north was sought. *The Times* knew of one, of course. 'There is an excellent road . . . from Peshawar through the Bajour country of Umra Khan,' it reported, but though the road undoubtedly existed, it was suddenly realized that no one had ever travelled along it before and that a lot of the country it traversed was unexplored. All Low knew was that there were three passes into the valley of the River Swat – the Mora, the Shahkot and the Malakand – all of which were around 3500 feet high and very difficult for pack animals. Altogether four high ranges and three difficult rivers, in addition to mountain torrents, had to be crossed; and once all these barriers had been overcome, he would still be advancing into Dir where the inhabitants were Yusufzais who 'regarded themselves – and indeed were regarded – as the truest and finest exponents of the Afghan way of life, in bravery in war, in dignity in council, in the use of a clear and undefined . . . tongue'. As they had shown in the Ambela campaign not long before, they were willing to resist fiercely 'the violation of their purdah'.[7]

The Pathans were skilful fighters and, since they could disperse just as quickly as they could gather, the problem was going to be how to bring them to battle. But the only information so far available was that the Mora Pass was reported held by hostile tribesmen and that the other two might be heavily defended as well. The Swati and Bajouri tribesmen had sent back a dusty answer to the request for undisputed passage through their territory. They obviously intended to contest Low's thrust north. When later reports began to indicate that *all* three passes were indeed heavily guarded, and especially the Shahkot, Low had no alternative but to feint against this pass and the Mora and then launch a full-scale attack through the Malakand. Winston Churchill, who had his baptism of fire there soon afterwards, described the Malakand as 'a great cup of which the rim is broken into numerous clefts and jagged points'. It was a very strong position because it was impossible to concentrate troops at the bottom of 'the cup', while those who *could* be pushed in were in full view from the surrounding heights.

It wasn't a healthy prospect and the government of India grew worried in case the terrain and the hostile tribesmen – even the size of his force – might delay Low too long. Every day – even every hour – was important and, somewhat alarmed, they decided to mount a second column from Gilgit.

'Colonel Kelly, commanding the 32nd Pioneers at Bunji,' it was announced, 'has been put in command of the military operations in the Gilgit quarter.' Since it would not be possible to send reinforcements in his direction before June, it was also decided that Kelly had better do the best he could with what he had to hand.

Bunji was about forty miles to the east of Gilgit, and Gilgit was over 200 miles to the east of Chitral. The road was mountainous all the way, and over the Shandur Pass it climbed to 12,400 feet through a terrain where the snow would be deep until June. There were also defiles, like the one at Koragh where Ross had come to grief, which could provide excellent defensive positions for the tribesmen who were by now known to be gathering round Moberly at Mastuj.

To Kelly, a long-nosed Irishman, this was the opportunity he had been waiting for all his life. Until 22 March, when his orders arrived, it had seemed that the authorities had lost sight of him. Commissioned in a Western Indian regiment at the age of twenty, he had transferred to the 94th Foot and then to the Bengal Staff Corps towards the end of the Mutiny. Since then he had spent long periods as a lieutenant and a captain, and though he had served in the Hazara and Miranzai campaigns of 1891, he had been in command of the 32nd Pioneers for only three years. His present position was an odd one because he was only in the area at all as a result of an earlier decision to stiffen the Kashmiri troops at Gilgit, the few Afridi Irregulars and Robertson's escort of Sikhs. With the government's usual parsimony, it had also been decided to economize by using reinforcements who could mend the roads, and so Kelly's Pioneers had been sent.

The regiment's ranks contained artisans and even cabinet makers, as well as men skilled at making roads, for which they drew extra pay. They were largely low-caste Sikhs, short and sturdy in stature, with coarse features and dark complexions in contrast to the more stately high-caste Sikhs who avoided them like the plague. Known as Masbi Sikhs, they were good fighters, and in addition to his ordinary equipment each man carried a pick or a shovel. Because British officers were supposed only to be seconded to the Kashmiri troops, Kelly, in effect, was simply in charge of his regiment with orders to take over full command in the event of hostilities.

He didn't hesitate. His instructions were to co-operate with Low's force but, with something like 200 miles of mountainous country between them, this was impossible. However, he had 400 men, and half this number were ordered off at once to Gupis under Captain Harry Benn Borradaile and two subalterns, Lieutenants H. Bethune and A. S. Cobbe. They left on 23 March, the day Moberly finally came under siege at Mastuj. The rest of Kelly's force waited at Bunji until a half-battery of Kashmiri mule mountain artillery arrived from Nomal, eighteen miles away. This artillery – two 7-pounder mountain guns – followed a day later. These small guns could be carried on the backs of mules or even, if necessary, by men. The wheels, carriage and barrel were all detachable, and experienced gunners could unload and assemble them in an incredibly short time. Because they could go anywhere a mule could go, they could be fought from any piece of flat land available. The gunners were Mian Dogras to a man, members of the proudest of clans. Except for transport animals and – an all-important necessity when operating at the heights that existed in Chitral – sunglasses, they were well equipped and were commanded by a tall burly dedicated lieutenant of the Royal Artillery – Irish despite his name, Cosmo Gordon Stewart – who had worked them up to a high pitch of skill.

All Kelly's officers were, like himself, men with a wide knowledge of the frontier. Even so, it was still a pitifully small force and the route they would have to take would make tremendous demands on them.

It was no time to weigh the odds, however, and, small as it was, the little force wasted no time. Indeed, anticipating the summons, Kelly had been ready for days. They were not all so fortunate, and Captain Luard, the Gilgit agency surgeon, because his equipment was at Gupis, had to set off in a Norfolk suit and a high celluloid collar.

They marched out of Bunji towards Gilgit, accompanied by servants, camp followers, what porters they could collect and the usual tribe of pet dogs. They were in a grim mood because they had just learned from Mastuj how Ross and forty-six of his sepoys had died. The job of column staff officer was filled at the last moment by Lieutenant Beynon of the Gurkhas who, suspecting something was in the wind, had had his kit packed for some time. With them to record the events for *The Times* was Francis Edward Younghusband, the former agent at Gilgit, whose brother, George John, was with Low for the same reason.[8]

As they left Gilgit a sudden downpour that turned the road into a quagmire managed to continue for two whole days and, since they were marching without tents and with very little baggage, in their wet clothes they were silent at a prospect of chilly bivouacs in shelters run up from waterproof capes.

It was only a foretaste of the hardships they were to endure.

Illegal, to fight without the Union Jack

While the governments in London and India were working themselves up into a lather of excitement, in Chitral Robertson was still doggedly pursuing his policy of 'jaw, not war'.

Learning what he had about the chances of relief, he had tried to keep the truce going as long as possible, but as he had finally run out of excuses, Sher Afzul's diwan had begun to show signs of irritation and on 23 March, making no bones about his growing anger, he had laid the matter squarely before Robertson.

'Supposing Umra Khan's conditions are not agreed to?' he demanded sharply. 'What is to prevent us from taking the two British officers down to the river and killing them?'

With his new hope of relief, Robertson could afford to return shortness with shortness. 'What prevents me, Diwan Sahib,' he retorted, 'from ordering *you* now into the courtyard to be shot?'

The diwan 'turned a shade grey' and changed his tune and, because he wanted a bribe, promised to look after Edwardes and Fowler. At dusk Sher Afzul hauled down his white flag, and the garrison hitched at their belts and reached for their weapons as their own followed soon afterwards. Robertson had managed to hold up hostilities for six whole days. The fact that the truce was ended was made very clear almost immediately. Even during the truce, Wafadar had continually begged the white officers not to allow themselves to be seen on the west wall where they could be hit, and that night hostilities reopened with an act of treachery.

On the frontier nobody was ever taken on trust. Although the two Jandoli princes, Majid Khan and Abdul Ghani Khan, had been sent by their kinsman Umra Khan to keep an eye on Sher Afzul,

Umra had also appointed a spy called Gulwali to watch *them*. This man had managed to get word to Wafadar that Umra wanted only peace and forgiveness and that it was the two young khans who were for war. In the tangle of lies, half-truths and more-than-truths it was becoming impossible to know who really wanted what. Since Gulwali seemed willing to talk, arrangements were made for him to meet Robertson secretly after dark. When, however, Lieutenant Gurdon's Chitrali servant was sent out to lead him in, he found an ambush had been prepared at the rendezvous with men waiting to seize him. Keeping his head, he tore free and courageously shouted to the soldiers on the gun tower to disregard him and fire. He was not hit, and as his attackers dived for cover he managed to escape.

For the next two nights it rained hard. 'Incessant rain,' Captain Townshend noted in his diary, and 'Rain falls in sheets', and since the tops of the fort's walls were constructed only of mud and stones, they had to be covered with tarpaulins to prevent them melting away. 'Everything in the fort is soaked,' Townshend reported sourly. 'Mud, stinks, dirt! All the result of the incessant rain! Our tobacco is all finished and cheroots only exist in the imagination! No whisky! No liqueurs! Nothing!'

Since Sifat's enclosure was imperfectly loopholed, the area outside the west wall had had to be left unguarded at night so it was now decided to make an attempt to illuminate it during the hours of darkness with a large bonfire. A great stack of logs was built and set alight but since, not unnaturally, there were no volunteers to risk their necks to tend the blaze, it failed to last the night.

The rain kept coming down, in ceaseless torrents now, and was heavy enough to carry away a large part of the parapet of the west wall. Everyone was wet through and miserable, while the exposed sentries and water-carriers were in a dreadful condition, and rum or tea, according to taste and religion, was given them as they came off duty. Excitement was caused during the morning when someone reported hearing a distant gun, but it was never heard again and the excitement soon died away. Now that the truce had ended, regular sniping started again and, though no one was seriously hurt, one of the flying bullets went through the turban of Lieutenant Harley's orderly, nicking his scalp. He was not much troubled by the wound but was furious at the damage done to his headgear.

With the enemy so active, for a change there was no communication from Sher Afzul, and the Chitralis in the fort were beginning to believe Robertson should have accepted the terms that had been offered. Even the faithful Wafadar was reproachful and seemed to feel the rules of the game were not being followed. When a garrison found itself helpless, he said, it was normal in Chitral to capitulate.

The heavy rain continued for three days. No one could get dry in the cheerless fort before being drenched again and the cold wind, blowing on their saturated clothes, chilled to blueness men who were already suffering from fever and dysentery. As the third week of the siege ended, the garrison was as miserable as the besiegers could have wished.

Despite the misery, it had not escaped Robertson's notice that however much discomfort the rain caused, at least it saturated the fort itself and saved them from the danger of the place being set on fire, a constant worry that had caused them to order the water-carriers to sleep with their water skins full and to organize nightly patrols. It also stirred the superstitious among the Chitralis, and one morning Robertson noticed a small paper flag stuck in a roof. This was followed by other small banners, which he learned had been placed there on the instruction of Shuja-ul-Mulk who had noticed the wretched condition of the garrison. One of the plausible rascals in his train had persuaded him that verses from the Koran written on slips of paper placed in cleft sticks stuck into the muddy roofs and walls would be an appeasement to the gods. 'What can *your* religion show to rival this?' he delightedly asked Robertson when the rain stopped.

On 26 March, a last attempt was made to use one of the 7-pounders but, when it was brought out once more, one of the Sikhs was immediately killed by the bullets it provoked and the attempt was abandoned. After the proper rites, the body was carried down the covered waterway and thrust out into the river.

Though still confined to his dark little dungeon of a bedroom,

Captain Campbell continued to play a surprisingly large part in the defence of the fort. He was always available for advice, and his knowledge of the tribal languages enabled him to keep his ear close to the ground. His orderly, Duffadar Mohamed, an exceptionally handsome trooper of his own regiment, the Central India Horse, brought him the rumours and the garrison chatter to chew over and, because he was popular with the Indians, he was always receiving visitors from whom he now learned that a night attack might be made at any moment. The annual Mohammedan fast of Ramadhan – a period when Mohammedans were considered to be exceptionally fanatical – was coming to an end, and it was also said there would be a determined charge across the stretch of sand on the north-west corner in broad daylight against the covered way to the river.

The excitement intensified after dark when a man outside, after shouting to one of the Chitrali servants by name, asked the guards not to shoot as he had a letter for Robertson. Lieutenant Gurdon hurried to the tower with the Chitrali servant but when they could get no answer to their enquiries it was decided to keep the garrison on its toes in case the approach was part of the preparations for some 'devilry'.

On the last day of Ramadhan the garrison prepared itself again for the attack but not a single enemy was seen; the vicious and bloody fighting at Reshun had shaken the nerve of Umra Khan.

28 March was the Mohammedan festival of Id, but little happened until just before sunset when more letters arrived. They had been sent from Kila Drosh, to the south en route to Dir – one from Edwardes, one from Umra Khan and one from Fowler. For once, Umra Khan's letter was decipherable and dealt with his plans for the two Britishers: 'I told them,' it said, 'they were at liberty to choose [whether] . . . to go to the colonel [Robertson] at Chitral; . . . to go to Jandol; . . . [or] to remain at Drosh. . . . Both the Englishmen said they would go to the colonel at Chitral, if their sepoys were also released with them. I told them that their sepoys would not . . . be allowed to . . . go. . . . I have detained the sepoys because they are Musalmans, all Mohammedans being brethren.' Edwardes' letter gave the full melancholy details of the tragedy of Reshun and confirmed Umra Khan's offer, while Fowler's confined itself to a bland request to Campbell to

take care of the pony stolen from him at Reshun – if he ever got the chance.

No one was very impressed by Umra Khan's apparent willingness to release his captives and Robertson considered the offer was merely one of the cruel jokes the frontier tribes enjoyed playing; the two Englishmen would never have been allowed to go free because of their high bargaining value as hostages. In this he was dead right and when the suggestion had been put to Edwardes and Fowler, they had all, including Umra Khan, burst out laughing.

On this day the garrison raised its own flag. Robertson had lamented that he had not got his British agent's flag and had even begun to grow superstitious about it, feeling its absence brought bad luck. 'It seemed almost improper,' he thought, 'not to say illegal, to fight without the Union Jack over our heads.'

Harley at once produced one of his Sikhs who was a good needleman and Shuja-ul-Mulk provided red cloth. A blue turban and white cotton material were also contributed while Surgeon-Captain Whitchurch possessed a tobacco tin with a picture of the Union Jack on it. With everybody giving advice, the Sikh started work with scissors, needle and thread. 'The width of the stripes and their other proportions were earnestly debated,' Robertson recorded. 'The pole and everything connected with it were also anxiously discussed. When the flag was finished a day later and brought for final inspection, we found it admirable in every way except that its contriver had sought to improve our national ensign by sewing in the middle a crescent and crossed swords cut out of the white stuff.'

With the crescent and swords removed, the flag was eventually hoisted – at night, so that no one should be hit, an occurrence which might have been regarded by the superstitious sepoys as a bad omen. At dawn the next day, as they saluted or raised their caps to the flag, they all wore a smile of confidence, though critical eyes noticed that the white diagonal stripes were all of the same width. The flag could never be flown upside-down as a signal of distress – something which might well before long become necessary.

It was the constant concern of the men in the fort to strengthen the defences and provide new ones, and each night every spare pair of hands was occupied in building work. At the same time, Robertson remembered his promise to the dying Baird not to forget Whitchurch and, in compliance with official army regulations, he, Gurdon and Harley formed a committee to recommend the surgeon for the Victoria Cross.

They were still in touch with Umra Khan and notes continued to be exchanged, but there was no alteration in the position whatsoever. Some country tobacco was sent in along with a shoulder of mutton, which was first tried on one of the dogs to make sure it wasn't poisoned, and another unsuccessful attempt was made by Mir Hamza to pass through the enemy's lines with a note. The garrison was feeling secure at this point because, with the young moon, the sky at night was so light everything outside the fort could be seen, though the vast snow-covered mountain to the north looked as unsympathetic as ever. The moon had a melancholy effect on the Englishmen, whose chief wish was to get word to their families that they were alive.

The news of the Reshun disaster had depressed them all and the depression was deepened by vague rumours of another disaster to a force marching to the rescue of Edwardes, and the fate of the two captive officers was constantly in their minds. Superstitions abounded. Robertson, who was keen on playing patience, found that whenever the cards came out properly there immediately seemed to be a noisy demonstration by the enemy, and in the end he abandoned patience for good. In the same way, sitting over a charcoal fire in the evening, he was in the habit of getting one of the young Chitralis to bring his sitar and sing with Wafadar, but though the music must have been quite inaudible to the besiegers, this again always seemed to be followed by an alarm and in the end the musicians were also discouraged.

Tempers were growing short, particularly that of Townshend. He was overworked like all of them, and he took it out on the Kashmiri brigade-major who, he said, 'had been simply funking for the last ten days under the excuse of fever'.[1] Whitchurch had reported him well and, sending for him, Townshend asked him bluntly when he proposed to do some duty. 'This isn't the time for a fever,' he snorted.

With the damp and the cold and the monotonous food, they were beginning to get on each other's nerves a little; especially since by this time Robertson had come round to the view held by Harley that they should make a sortie. Townshend didn't agree, and when Robertson felt they might rush two of the sangars in front of the fort and then go up the ridge to the west, he was aghast.

'Up the ridge?' he asked himself. 'Why? What to do but come down again?'

Robertson went on that he thought it was their duty to do something to help those coming to help them, but none of Townshend's undoubtedly extensive military reading suggested that sorties were a good idea. He thought they might possibly sally out when they saw the relieving force, however, and when Robertson insisted – 'We must think what others will think of us' – Townshend finally exploded. They had already done their duty, he felt – at least *he* had – and he didn't care what anybody said.[2]

Despite the bursts of edginess, spirits didn't remain low for long. Fixing tins to the tails of stray dogs which found their way into the fort, they sent them clattering off towards the bazaar to alarm the besiegers. On another occasion, dummies – atrocious caricatures of a British officer and his turbaned orderly – were raised on the rampart to start a furious fusillade which, to the delight of the garrison, left the dummies quite untouched. They were well aware, however, that they had been raised at a spot where they couldn't be hit by the men close to the walls.

Since the fireballs they had made for dark nights had proved only limited in their success, Wafadar showed them how to thrust out little platforms through horizontal slits cut in the parapets, on which heaps of pine chips could be kindled and kept alight with nothing more than a hand or a wrist visible to the enemy. The result was good but when a breeze was blowing they could only be used on the lee side of the fort. If the flames had gone the wrong way, the whole place would have gone up like a torch.

By this time they had decided that the rations would last until 11 June but, with their casualties and sick, there were now only just over three hundred men to man the walls. Because the Sikhs responded better to tough handling and the Kashmiris were always a doubtful quantity, discipline was carefully maintained, and bugle calls were blown as regularly as in a normal camp. At first the calls had been answered by the enemy, and when this ceased they assumed the bugler had joined one of the little bodies of men they saw occasionally moving towards Mastuj along the skyline just out of range.

The Sikhs remained eager and cheerful. Commanding them was an elderly subadar called Gurmokh Singh who lacerated everyone's nerves with his constant haranguing of his men whom he turned out with full ceremonial to present arms whenever Robertson appeared. Though Robertson had only been given the honorary rank of 'colonel' because it was hard for the Chitralis to pronounce 'British Agent', the Sikhs insisted on promoting him to 'general'.

They were always gay and friendly, and kept up their spirits with silly jokes, in great contrast to the Kashmiris, Dogras and the normally-smiling Gurkhas whose faces now remained heavy and uneasy. Most of the latter knew little or no Hindustani, which the British officers used, and as there were no Gurkha officers to lead them, they had to be left to the ill-instructed Kashmiri officers.

In the darkness of Sunday 31 March, at the end of the fourth week of siege, a rattle of stones was heard by the Sikhs on the north-west corner of the fort who immediately replied with shots. Daylight showed that a new fortification eight or nine yards long had been erected, together with another exactly opposite the end of the water-way. Though they were studied with field glasses, they were so cleverly contrived not a single loophole could be seen in them and, since cartridges were too precious to waste, they were not fired at.

That afternoon white flags appeared once more and there was another parley, though the sangar across the river continued to fire. An old woman brought a message from Sher Afzul, offering them all the honours of war if they would leave. Nobody believed the offers of safe passage but they were cheered when the old woman let slip a hint that a relief was being mounted from Gilgit.

The old woman's message was followed by another of the ridiculous incidents of this extraordinary siege when a group of men hurried up to the fort. Robertson at once imagined a variety of reasons for their haste but they brought nothing more than an invitation to

Robertson's clerk, Amir Ali, to play polo with Sher Afzul. The invitation was politely declined.

Nobody was taking any chances. Futteh Ali Shah warned that the little companies of men they had seen travelling down the valley were very likely from Mastuj and were moving to Chitral because a British relief force was heading towards Mastuj from Gilgit, in which case Sher Afzul would inevitably make an attempt to capture the fort before it arrived. It made sense and the defences were carefully inspected yet again.

Another attempt was made by the besiegers to get a message into the fort in the darkness on the morning of 1 April. Shouts were heard and a group of Jandolis near the gun tower claimed to have a letter for Robertson, but when numbers of men began to gather round the messengers, Gurdon grew suspicious. It was possible, of course, with the treachery that was always going on in Sher Afzul's camp, that someone was trying to make sure of his future by getting a message secretly to Robertson in the dark, but it also might well have been a trick to get close to the walls. Gurdon took no chances. As his men opened fire, the messengers scuttled for safety.

One of the things the old woman had let drop the previous day was that Sher Afzul's men were making huge ladders for a determined attack. The Chitralis in the fort told Campbell that they thought bullet-proof nests would be made in the trees which closely surrounded the fort to harass the defence. So Robertson and Wafadar brought out a supply of long spears from the store room. These were placed conveniently near the loopholes on the south and weaker side, in case any attackers got close enough to shoot through them, while the Kashmiris regularly fired into the upper branches of the trees.

These trees had been a source of anxiety all along, and would have been cut down before the siege started if the garrison had possessed either good axes or the skilled woodsmen to use them. But they had neither and in any case expected the siege to end while the trees remained bare of foliage. Now, however, the trees were coming into leaf and providing cover for the enemy, but remembering the price they had to pay for their direct assaults on Edwardes and Fowler at Reshun, the Chitralis never summoned up enough courage to try climbing along the boughs that actually overhung the walls of the fort.

It was none the less clear that the defence had now entered a more desperate phase, and Sifat and his men were accordingly armed with Snider rifles and swords. For while everyone in the garrison knew that the Indian government must have stirred itself on their behalf by now, they were equally aware that the besiegers must realize that they too had no time to lose.

The siege throughout 19
was anachronistic

It was as well known to General Low and Colonel Kelly as it was to Robertson that any advance to the relief of Chitral would increase the danger of a determined attack on the fort. They were as aware as anyone of the theories of Skobeleff, whose activities had caught the imagination of many British soldiers in India. 'Do not forget,' Skobeleff had said, 'that in Asia he is the master who seizes the people pitilessly by the throat and imposes upon their imagination.' Whatever they felt about the first half of the theory, there were no two opinions about the second half.[1] The frontier tribes were always swift to respect power but, as they had shown with Ross and with Robertson's sortie on 3 March, they were equally swift to detect any signs of weakness. It was essential, therefore, that to be successful any advance that was attempted should be bold and made without delay.[2]

The government was still awaiting the end of the month before setting Low in motion. They were having to move cautiously to please both ends of the political scale. They had been bitterly criticized in the legislative council on the one hand for pursuing a policy that had put Robertson in his present position and on the other by critics of the budget on the cost of the relief which, the merchants of gloom claimed, hung 'like a cloud over the future'.

Though General Low's troops were held on a leash, however, no such restraint had been placed on Colonel Kelly whose force, after the disasters to Ross and Edwardes, was the only one on the frontier that could dictate events.

Apart from Kelly's men, the only other troops in a position to move were forty Kashmiri Sappers and Miners, led by Lieutenant L. W. S. Oldham, of the Royal Engineers, who were also marching to

Ghizr where they had been ordered to wait for Kelly. All other troops between Gilgit and Chitral were tied down, either blockaded at Mastuj with Lieutenant Moberly or at Ghizr with Lieutenant Gough, while no reinforcements had yet reached Gilgit from the south or were likely to do so for some time. With his few Sikhs plus the survivors of Ross's ill-fated party and 235 men of the 4th and 6th Kashmir Regiments, as well as Colonel Phula, Captain Bretherton and the wounded Lieutenant Jones to help him, Moberly was safe enough at Mastuj. The fort was small and uncomfortable and designed to withstand nothing heavier than matchlock fire, but unlike Chitral it was at least well-sited. At Ghizr, however, Gough had only sixty trained soldiers and a hundred ragged Hunza-Nagar levies. Hourly expecting attack, his situation was precarious and it was essential to push on to him at the best possible speed.

Though Kelly wasn't a young man, he had a dazzling array of junior officers to encourage him. He needed them, too, because he had plenty of problems. There were barely enough pack animals and Surgeon-Captain Luard's pony – 'about as much use as a headache', according to Lieutenant Beynon – proved a brute. Always ready to see the funny side of anything, Lieutenant Beynon suggested he should 'let it rip' and promised to bury Luard's remains if he came a cropper. He did let it rip, and in Beynon's words, 'you couldn't see the pony's heels for dust as he disappeared across the plain'.

On the second day they reached Suigal in Punial, the home of the local rajah, Akbar Khan, an enormously fat man renowned despite his size as a polo player. He lived in a castle across one of the longest rope bridges in the country, and since some of his family were shut up with Robertson in Chitral he offered his services at once.

The next day the rain stopped at last but by this time they were on one of the *paris*. 'A desolate place,' Beynon said, '. . . when there is any wind blowing, it is like camping in a draught pipe.' Pushing on, they reached the fort at Gupis, which the irrepressible Beynon described as 'perfectly untenable, if attacked by three men and a boy with accurate long-range rifles'. Here Lieutenant Stewart caught them up with his mountain guns.

Beynon considered Stewart 'the most bloodthirsty individual' he had ever come across but, judging by his own sober account, it seems

F

more likely that he was just a good soldier who enjoyed playing the traditional role of a fire-eating Irishman. He had been in the habit of complaining at Gilgit, Beynon said, that the Chitralis wouldn't provide him with a fight every day of the week, and he was now 'turning catherine wheels at the thought of taking his beloved guns into action'.

The next march was to Pingal, where they were met by the hakim, or governor, Mihrbhan Shah, 'a bit of an authority in the murder line', who was supposed to have been employed by Nizam-ul-Mulk as chief executioner. He provided afternoon tea and Shah Mirza, the Wazir of Sai and Gor, a useful Puniali ally whose followers – 'splendid mountaineers, sure-footed as goats' – were enlisted as levies, was roped in as interpreter. So far the weather had not been cold and the soldiers were wearing sheepskin coats. But at the villages en route, shelter had been scarce and when it was wet they had, with the exception of Kelly, to bed down in cattlesheds or huts whose only ventilation was the hole cut in the roof for the smoke to escape. 'At least,' Beynon said, 'that was the idea, but the smoke generally preferred to remain inside.' They shared these places with the cows and goats, and there were always other occupants 'of a more agile nature, armies of them', so that whenever possible they preferred to sleep outside. Stewart, in particular, had avoided the huts, complaining bitterly about the low lintels on which he knocked his head every time he went in or out.

They had set off with a good supply of bacon and had enjoyed starting the morning with bacon and eggs because it would 'carry a man through a long day most successfully'. When the bacon finally ran out 'there was more mourning than over all the first born of Egypt'. Mutton never ran out. Like the poor, Beynon said, it was always with them.

Though the going had been rough, up to now the journey had not been too difficult, but on 28 March they began to enter the snowdrift area which they were not to leave for fifty miles, and their chief concern became to keep the mule battery going over the dangerous hill tracks. The antiquated 7-pounders might only have a limited range of about 1200 yards, but they were expected to have great moral effect and Stewart was determined to get them into action, whatever the cost.

It was to prove high. At one point, two of the mules, one carrying a gun and the other a pair of wheels, fell 150 feet down an incline into deep snow. Stewart and one of his men had to slide down after them and kneel on their heads while their girths were loosened and the heavy saddles freed and carried back up the hill. Tarpaulins were then placed round the frightened animals and they were hauled back to the track. The battery eventually arrived in camp without further mishap, except that the Dogra major in command and several of his men were beginning to show signs of snow-blindness. By this time every Indian soldier in the force had begun to regard the stalwart Stewart as a superman, and one officer of the Pioneers spread the story that he had dived naked into the snow and carried the mules back up the slope on his own.

The snow was beginning to bother the mules by this time, balling under their feet as it melted in the hot sun. Nevertheless, the force reached Ghizr on the last day of the month, having covered the distance in excellent time.

Ghizr was 10,000 feet high and terribly exposed. It was in an ancient lake-bed, the upper end of which narrowed to a steep gorge flanked by wild rocks where Gough had stationed his Irregulars. Even in April the cold was dreadful and there were three feet of soft new snow, while the post consisted of a block of fortified houses only large enough for the garrison, so that Kelly's force had to billet themselves outside.

It was here that 1000 Hunza and Nagar levies were picked up. These men, all strong and often fair-complexioned and red-cheeked, confidently claimed descent from the soldiers of Alexander the Great who had crossed their country in his march to the east.[3] Though only subordinate to Britain for so short a time, they had marched into Gilgit on 7 March and had been issued with Snider carbines and ammunition by Beynon who thought them 'splendid . . . thickset mountaineers, incapable of fatigue'. Their only distinguishing badge was a strip of red cloth worn in their caps. The Hunzas were led by Wazir Humayun and the Nagars by Wazir Taifu and they were employed guarding the passes round Gilgit, though fifty of them now joined Colonel Kelly.

Things still looked promising and everyone was in good heart.

The Shandur Pass was a formidable obstacle at any time and particularly at that period of the year when it was deep in snow and almost
impassable, but there was not time to worry about what might go
wrong. The hill tribes were always sensitive to movements threatening
their lines of retreat, and they all knew that the crossing of the Shandur
would have great moral effect. The difficulties were not even considered, and the fact that the Chitralis were confident that it was
impossible for Europeans to cross in April seemed almost an advantage – so long as they succeeded. Once again Skobeleff had a word
for it: 'To conquer you must know how to surprise.'

As the main column moved off through the snow on 1 April,
however, it was discovered that a number of ponies and a hundred of
the baggage porters had disappeared during the night. These wretched
men lived a harrowing life. No provision was ever made for their
shelter en route or for the bitter cold of the passes, and every year a
high proportion of them died of overwork or were blinded by
blizzards, buried by avalanches, attacked by plague, dysentery, small-
pox or cholera in insanitary camps, or were swept to destruction as
they tried to cross the rivers on rafts. Their backs were worn raw by
their loads and a man condemned to carry to Gilgit was mourned by
his friends as sentenced to death. They weren't even popular and
animals were always preferred if they could be obtained because, to
quote Brigadier-General Gatacre, they were 'unsatisfactory . . . easily
frightened, very independent, have to be fed, and foul the camping
ground'. Without them, though, it was impossible to get Stewart's
guns over the pass if the mules failed, and at once, Beynon dumped the
load of the nearest pony in the snow and rode ahead to warn Kelly at
the head of the column while Stewart jumped on a battery animal and,
terrified of being left behind with his guns, rode furiously back along
the breakneck paths for fifteen miles to round up forty of the unlucky
villagers with gestures and revolver shots. By this time his pony was
at a standstill with exhaustion, but he managed to persuade a passing
traveller to exchange mounts and returned to Ghizr where Lieutenant
Cobbe, of the Pioneers, was waiting with the rearguard. More porters
were found hiding in a village but, as they set off again, they met the
dispirited Kelly returning with the main force.

He had forced his way through the snow for eight miles but his animals had become so exhausted they could only flounder in the drifts up to their girths, and the little force was now dejectedly having to retrace its steps in the darkness and cold to Ghizr.

There was a great deal of bitterness, particularly among the younger officers who began to complain that everybody else would get to Chitral before them. Then snow began to fall again, blotting out the dark sky and the wild horizon, and when someone less exhausted than the rest brightly remarked that it was like Napoleon's retreat from Moscow, he was rounded on angrily.

Kelly was gloomy but inevitably the moment produced the individual. Captain Borradaile, a sturdy man of thirty-five of 'unswerving mind and iron resolve',[4] asked if he could move with his 200 Pioneers on to Teru, a bleak hamlet three miles further up the slopes from Ghizr along a steep path littered with fallen rocks, and try to push over the Shandur to seize Laspur, the highest village on the other side. Eager to press on, Kelly agreed and Borradaile chose Lieutenant Oldham to accompany him with his forty sappers and the Hunza-Nagar levies, while the rest of the force continued back to Ghizr. The confusion caused by the transfer of kits in the dark was 'something dreadful' and they had to post sentries to stop the porters bolting again. By now everyone was covered from head to foot with mud and slush, dripping wet and half-frozen, but Borradaile determinedly set his face to the north, taking with him every available porter, now more precious than ever since it was clearly impossible for the animals to get through. They were already exhausted after a sleepless night, and they were carrying rifles, ammunition and haversacks. In places the snow was five feet deep, but after hours of struggling when the men sank up to their armpits they reached Teru. There, Borradaile, Oldham, Surgeon-Captain S. Browning-Smith, medical officer to Kelly's Pioneers, and Lieutenant Cobbe – who arrived later – got their men under shelter and settled themselves in a dirty hut with a roof like a sieve.

All that night and all the next day the whirling snow never stopped, and at Ghizr, Stewart – 'seated on a rock like Rachel mourning for her children', because his precious guns had come to a halt – frantically discussed with Gough's Kashmiri adjutant how they could get them over the pass.

They, too, were exhausted. They had marched sixteen miles through the snow and had been on their feet for fifteen hours and now they were back exactly where they had started. They had been wet through since midday and the wind and cold had peeled the skin from their faces 'till it hung in flakes'. Stewart was furiously impatient. Kelly had been inclined to accept the difficulties – 'It's no good trying to get the guns on, Stewart; they'll have to wait until the snow melts' – but Stewart refused to agree. 'My guns,' he told his friends, 'are going over that pass even if I have to carry them myself.'

'Try sledges,' the British officers suggested.

'Or digging a new road,' Gough's Kashmiri said.

A new road would take too long so a rough sledge was built, the runners made of young poplars covered with the tin linings of old commissariat chests. Down an incline where the snow was only a foot deep, the sledge would carry eight ammunition boxes, a weight of 1000 lbs. It behaved badly when dragged uphill, but Stewart and Oldham decided that the problem was solved and appeared plastered with white but 'flushed with success . . . swearing . . . they would have the guns over the pass in no time'.

While they argued, Shah Mirza appeared through the storm. There was a mullah in the village, he said, with an infallible charm for stopping the snow. He managed to inveigle a couple of rupees from Beynon as a bribe, and in the afternoon Stewart, Gough and the gunners, as well as forty of the Ghizr Kashmiri garrison, started for Teru, carrying entrenching tools and wooden spades commandeered from the village. Among them was the mullah's, who was loudly indignant, though Beynon blandly pointed out that even if his prayers hadn't had much effect on the snow perhaps his shovel would have. He later saw it sticking up in a drift with the blade snapped off.

For the first two miles the going was easy, but when they met deep snow the feet of the mules went through what track had been made and they sank in up to their shoulders, struggling so violently Stewart thought they would break their legs. Yaks were sent for in the hope that they might tread a firm path, but when they could be kept in single file they trod so exactly in each other's footprints the result was merely a line of deep holes.

The gunners were growing frantic by now. Envious of the medals worn by some of the Sikhs, they were as eager as Stewart to bring the guns into action so that they could win one or two themselves. In desperation, the mules were taken down to the river in an attempt to wade up its margin. But the river bed was uneven and covered with rocks, and the cold was so intense the animals refused to stay in the water. They were sent back to Teru, and the sledges were tried.

They proved useless. Thirty men dragged at each of them but the labour was terrible and the men sank up to their chests; and as the sledges proved too wide for the narrow track, they constantly overturned. As a last resort, Stewart was just about to ask the Pioneers to carry the guns when not only the senior native officer of the Pioneers but also a subadar of the Kashmiri Sappers – quite individually and separately – made the suggestion that the guns simply could not be left behind and that their men, despite their own rifles, ammunition and equipment, would carry them.

Poles were shaped and on 3 April the two 7-pounders, together with ammunition which Kelly had sent on from Ghizr, were hoisted up. The snow had stopped at last, but since the sun was glaring down and baggage porters were scarce, even the barest necessities, including eight boxes of ammunition, were left behind. Even so, the men were soon streaming with sweat in the heat and every time one of them stumbled and fell he brought down every other member of his group. The pace grew slower and slower, and many of the eighty-two gunners were suffering badly by this time from snow-blindness. Even in the easiest parts of the route only a quarter of a mile was covered in an hour. At 8 pm the darkness was as intense as the cold, and icicles were hanging from beards, eyebrows and moustaches. But Langar, which Borradaile had occupied ahead of them, was still several miles away. Everyone was worn out but, as a last resort, a battery sergeant took one of the little cannons on his shoulders and, with two others to steady it, began to stagger off.

Stewart went to the sergeant's help. 'I was no chicken,' he said, 'and proud of my strength,' but by now he could hardly stand for fatigue. He went down 'like a child' under the weight, and all four men fell gasping into the snow.

It was the end.

Guns, carriages, wheels and ammunition were stacked and the poles jammed upright into the drifts in case more snow fell. Then, leaving them behind, the soldiers stumbled through the darkness into the shelter of the camp.

By this time at Chitral the besiegers had worked to within thirty yards of the walls, which meant they could easily rush forward to set the walls alight and could also fire into the loopholes with such accuracy that it was unwise for the defenders to allow themselves to be seen for a second.

Nevertheless, the strange Union Jack which had been hoisted seemed to have brought fresh confidence. The week of the truce had been the low point of the garrison's morale and spirits had now picked up a little, even the setbacks bringing out a new determination in them. On the night of 1 April, Sifat and his men had endeavoured to build a new sunken road to the waterway to protect the water-carriers and this was strengthened with a line of heavy beams standing on end. Unfortunately a steady downpour of rain had started almost at once and by the next morning all the beams had fallen, the sunken way was full of water, and the indefatigable Sifat had to start all over again.

The morning of 2 April also saw the arrival of envoys with another letter from Sher Afzul. This repeated all the familiar demands for the evacuation of the fort while the envoys themselves 'simply cooed with his protestations of friendliness and loyalty'. 'As oily tongued as ever', they also brought news of the massacre of Ross's Sikhs at Kalak, some tobacco for Robertson's clerks, and a goat intended as a bribe.

It was becoming clear, however, that Sher Afzul was batting on a sticky wicket. Captain Townshend had taken note of the numbers of men moving down from Mastuj, bringing with them quantities of sheep and goats, and his observations had led him to believe that help was at last being organized and that in all probability a relief column from the north had already set off for Chitrel.

Robertson was likewise coming round to the view that Sher Afzul was growing more than a little anxious. It so happened that in the fort was one of Afzul's half-brothers – an elderly man whom Robertson looked on as an old friend. Afzul now demanded the services of his relative as an intermediary, sending him a letter claiming that as everything was quiet elsewhere – and the tribes united in his favour – he could immediately attack the fort without fear. To Robertson this was an obvious piece of bluff which only served to encourage his belief that a relief force was on its way. He showed his reaction by informing Afzul that any future armistices must be paid for at a daily rate of six goats and 480 pounds of flour!

Many of the ancient rifles in the fort had now become useless, however, and food was getting low. There were only thirty-six pounds of ghi left, which had to be kept for the wounded. Since ghi to the Indian soldier was as meat to the European, this was very serious, but with the tea and rum rations, they were still hoping to keep the sick list down for at least another three weeks.

On 5 April, while it was still dark, there was a great deal of noise and firing. The enemy bugler, who had suddenly reappeared, blew 'Assembly', 'Fire' and several other calls. When daylight came it was seen that two new sangars had been built, and rumours of a new attack accompanied by mining began to spread. Rab Nawaz Khan, the little cavalryman terribly wounded in his self-sacrificial stand on 3 March, was making a miraculous recovery by this time and, though one of his arms remained permanently crippled, he was already alert and constantly warned of the possibility of a shaft being dug against the gun tower from the summer-house.

A new form of assault that started at this time was abuse. The summer-house corner was only twenty-five yards from the gun tower and, since both sides had perfect cover at this point, they were able to hurl insults at each other. One of the Gilgiti noblemen, who considered he had shown certain defects of courage during the sortie on 3 March, now saw a chance of making up for it with 'hitherto hidden talents' and hurled the foulest of abuse from the top of the east tower. 'All this,' Robertson acknowledged, 'sounds archaic, but the siege throughout was anachronistic.'

At 9 am on 5 April, an explosion was heard from across the river.

A few of the garrison believed it was the first sign of relief, but it was finally decided it was merely a device to persuade the garrison that the besiegers had cannon; a not uncommon ruse along the frontier where artillery had tremendous moral effect. That night, in spite of it being clear and not very dark, an interchange of shots was followed by yells and war cries from the garden walls and the besiegers made a series of not very determined rushes which came to nothing. Pipes were sounded, insults were exchanged, and the racket became incredible as the garrison replied with volleys. Though the initial uproar died down, the shooting continued until daybreak when the reason for it all became clear. Three new works had been built: one large sangar not thirty yards away; a second half-finished sangar in the middle of the garden; and what looked like a covered road leading from the sangar upstream to an outdoor durbar place known as the chabutra, just outside Sifat's enclosure. The defences were strengthened again and loopholes made in the enclosure opposite the big new sangar. Twelve Sikhs were detailed to guard them during the night, while two of the Gilgiti rajahs stationed themselves at sundown in a position where they could watch for a charge across the sand and against the waterway.

The besiegers worked hard all that day at the summer-house position, clearly up to something though it was impossible to tell what. They were also busy on the new covered road, and it was finally decided to send out a patrol that night to find out what was happening and – if necessary – build a protective sangar. In the larger of their two new sangars the besiegers were now not more than twenty yards from the loopholes of the fort. Even as Townshend and Robertson were discussing the problem near the old filled-in gun port, a bullet came through one of the gaps between the stones to smash itself to fragments near Robertson's leg.

Annoyed, he borrowed a rook rifle but as he peered round the edge of a loophole, he exposed too much of his face and a bullet struck the wall outside. Peeping through again after a pause, he realized there was an enemy opposite, also peeping through *his* hole, and they both jerked away in alarm. Shifting to another loophole, Robertson watched carefully and after a while he saw a man's face behind the tiny gap in the enemy sangar. He pulled the trigger immediately and, though he couldn't tell whether he hit his target or not, certainly the loophole remained empty for the rest of the day.

By this time they were down to about 250 rounds per man with grain for seventy-four days if supplied in half-rations, and it was becoming clear that the food situation was such that they could not hope to hold out beyond the middle of June. The first attempts to eat horse on 22 March had been a disastrous and repulsive failure, but they had persevered and, perhaps because of their growing hunger, the revulsion Whitchurch and Gurdon had initially shown was overcome; so much so in fact that Whitchurch had taken charge of the slaughtering. Fortunately there was a large stock of salt in the fort so that the meat could be pickled and none was wasted. Nothing, of course, could persuade the Hindus to touch it and they lived entirely on the gritty flour. As a result, by 6 April, Whitchurch had more than seventy patients to deal with. It had been found in the past that the Indians could always be persuaded by a good officer to put aside their ritual prejudices in an emergency, and if a firm order had been issued it is possible they would have accepted the meat. But Robertson did not want to accept the responsibility; Townshend continued to distrust the Indians, and the wastage of men continued.[5]

Since there was plenty of coarse rum among the stores, it was decided that the British officers might have a little without depriving of their share those Indian soldiers whose religion permitted them alcohol. Morale still remained surprisingly high, but most of the talk at mealtimes concerned food and the dinners at the Savoy they intended to eat when they were relieved. 'This theme never staled.' Whitchurch, who was contemplating marriage, was often heavily chaffed, and another topic which occupied a lot of their table talk was the mystery of how the Indian servants, without a scrap of butter, fat or any other form of grease, managed to fry horse-steaks and other small delicacies.[6]

A far less trivial matter that filled their minds was the problem of disease. Cooped up in the restricted fort with the weather constantly improving, it was something that worried Townshend a great deal. 'What will happen when it gets hot I do not know or care to reflect much,' he wrote in his diary. 'The stenches in this awful fort are simply appalling already. How the men in the stable picket do not get ill I can't imagine. I feel sick every time I go . . . . to inspect. . . .' As a gloomy afterthought, he added once more, 'We have no more tobacco left.'

In the absence of tobacco – a shortage that most affected Whitchurch who was a heavy smoker – they were experimenting with cloves, chopped straw and the bark of plane trees. Though the result was usually awful, the very act of smoking helped to take their minds off the general situation and the increasing threat of a major assault.

Colonel Kelly knew time was short, too, but in Borradaile's force which had managed by this time to push on to Langar, nerves had reached snapping point.

Lieutenant Gough, who had been sent on ahead of the main party, was little more than a boy and had been carrying loads through the whole of the dreadful struggle from Ghizr, so that when he arrived he was in a state of collapse and in pain with snow-blindness. It was a long time before he could be brought round, and it had been Browning-Smith – another splendid doctor who like Whitchurch and Robertson could take on military duties at the drop of a hat – who had to set up markers where the loads had been left. With the dour, dogged Stewart he had brought in the rearguard, which reached Langar, 11,000 feet above sea level and utterly without shelter, at midnight. Even with everyone safely in, the work still hadn't ended. It was freezing hard and the men had arrived too tired even to cook so that the British officers had to inspect their feet for frostbite and – when necessary – work to restore circulation. The more affected younger men were then literally put to bed, though the older men preferred to pass the night stamping up and down, half-frozen, or sitting by the fires which could hardly be kept alight because the only fuel was green scrubwood.

When Stewart had arrived he had found one of his N.C.O.s and three of his men were missing and was told by one of his officers, 'We left a guard, Sahib. The men did not wish to leave their guns lest the enemy should find them forsaken.' With thoughts of the four men becoming victims of the bitter cold, Stewart was horrified but as it happened they survived without much harm.

The next day, guns or no guns, Borradaile decided to take his men over the Shandur. The Kashmiris and the gunners were to stay behind in the hope that they might after all bring on the guns. Leaving them three days' food, Borradaile handed over thirty porters to Stewart with the promise to send back more when he reached Laspur. He then left with Cobbe, Oldham and Browning-Smith. They had no idea whether the Chitralis would hold Laspur in strength or fight on the pass itself. The levies, who knew the route, led the way and, by the time the rest followed, the path had become fairly firm from their feet.

The Shandur was less a pass than a mountain plain, indented by two frozen lakes, and its highest point was 1200 feet above Langar. During April, as a spotless sheet of snow, it presented enormous difficulties and by the time Cobbe, an athletic young man, began the descent to Laspur, only half his men were with him. The others had all fallen out into the snow.

The indefatigable Browning-Smith kept the stragglers on the move, however, and fortunately they were well supplied with dark glasses so that they escaped snow-blindness. Though they all had blistered faces and suffered dreadfully from thirst, everyone eventually struggled over the pass and reached a stream on the other side which brought them back to life. Ten hours after leaving Langar the detachment reached Laspur. There was only a little snow on the ground at this point and everyone was able to find shelter except the pickets. Next morning, huts were fortified in case of an attack. Word came in that the enemy was close by, and when Borradaile, Cobbe and eighty men made a reconnaissance, a group of them, about a hundred strong, were seen running away.

While Borradaile was establishing himself at Laspur, back at Langar Stewart and Gough had finally got the guns and ammunition into camp by late afternoon. The exhausted porters swore that another day of such work would kill them, and there were growing doubts that the guns could ever be got over the pass. Axles were removed from the carriages to lighten the load, and it was decided to leave behind much of the ammunition. Then, by wheedling and promises, the porters were persuaded to try again.

On 5 April a bitter wind was whistling down the pass but guns and carriages moved off at 7.30 am, nine men to each load. Most of the soldiers and some of the officers soon became snow-blind, and to ensure there would be someone fit to lay the guns when the time came, four men who possessed dark glasses were ordered not to take them off under any pretext whatsoever. Before midday the porters sent back by Borradaile began to arrive and better progress was made; especially as the track had frozen hard during the night.

Even so, they were all worn-out by the time they reached the summit of the pass; but, worn-out, snow-blind or not, Stewart and the gunners insisted on taking the guns from the porters before entering Laspur, which was reached late in the afternoon, and carrying them into camp themselves. Stewart brought up the rear with Gough, dirty, unshaven and scarcely able to open his bandaged eyes. They had been practically given up and the Pioneers turned out quite spontaneously to cheer them in. 'You have done a *big* thing, sahib,' one of the officers told Stewart, while Humayun thought it 'a very good business indeed'.

Borradaile had had many cases of frostbite, they found, but there was to be no halting, and for the next part of the journey, all ponies and saddles in Laspur were requisitioned. The assortment of animals varied from a raw-boned, half-starved creature of fourteen hands and with a pitifully sore back, down to six donkeys not more than thirty-two inches high. Of them all, only five were of any use, and with their owners, together with forty villagers impressed as porters, these five animals came to be regarded as pure gold because on them depended the mobility of the mountain guns.

On the morning of 6 April, Borradaile tried to communicate with Moberly at Mastuj, pushing down the valley as far as Gusht with 170 Pioneers and the levies. Two miles beyond Gusht he found the enemy strongly posted on both sides of the river at Chakalwat. There was a brief skirmish during which one of Humayun's levies was captured and Borradaile realized he could do nothing without reinforcements. But when he returned to Laspur after dark it was to find Stewart's guns useless because every one of the gunners, even the layers, were wearing bandages round their eyes because of snow-blindness, while Stewart and Gough, both now quite sightless, were being led along the road by their men.

Once more the advance had come to a full stop.

The route is completely blocked

Though Colonel Kelly's advance was once more held up, Captain Borradaile's dogged march in the rarified air had been a tremendous feat of endurance, and its effect was more valuable than the suffering men realized. The Chitralis had refused to believe that infantry could cross the Shandur, let alone guns. In Laspur letters were found stating that the British were still in Ghizr unable to move because of frostbite and snow-blindness, and that since fresh snow had fallen, no forces would be able to cross for several weeks. The surprise effect of the arrival of the British force on the other side of the Shandur was therefore, as Borradaile had expected, all the more complete.

While Kelly had been driving doggedly on, to the south Major-General Low was having problems. Not only had the policy which had brought about his presence been criticized, but the Indian press was taking the view that no intervention in Chitral should have been attempted until the Chitralis had settled for themselves whom they desired as mehtar. There was a great deal of pessimism. 'The route is completely blocked . . .' *The Times* correspondent reported. 'Information . . . is scarce, but opposition . . . is certain.'

It certainly was. But the tents, the waggons, the guns, the animals and the servants continued to gather. Within seventeen days the 15,000 troops, with 'rather more than that number' of followers and servants, and over 20,000 transport animals, had been concentrated at Hoti-Mardan and Nowshera, and forty days' supplies collected and pushed forward. When the Gordon Highlanders arrived, the place 'swarmed with people, and the fields were covered with hundreds of cattle carts and transport of every kind'. British and native hospital attendants were erecting their tents. There were elephants and camels –

bubbling wetly as they disgorged and gurgled – and hundreds of mules, horses and donkeys. The stink of ammonia, sharp and pervasive, reached into the dusty tents. The usual inter-regimental jokes flew back and forth. Staff officers on horseback, jostling the moving troops in their haste, galloped from area to area while their seniors bent over maps.

By now they had heard of the fighting at Reshun, and were entertaining little hope for the safety of Edwardes and Fowler. They knew, however, that Robertson had estimated he could hold out until the end of April, and Low's staff thought the journey would take them only twenty-four days. They were all eager for a fight; especially the Bedfordshires who had not added a battle or a campaign honour to their colours since the days of Marlborough and were being jeered at, after the manner of soldiers, by the other regiments. With them was Private George Pridmore who had never heard of Chitral until 17 March – an appropriate day, he thought, since it was St Patrick's Day and he was Irish. He wasn't enjoying himself because the nights were chilly and there were legions of ants, scorpions and centipedes. By 1 April Waterfield's brigade was camping near the Shahkot Pass, while a party of cavalry pushed ahead towards the Mora Pass about seven miles away with the object of stirring up the dust to deceive the enemy. Dust was something all frontier fighters knew about. It bedevilled everything they did and there was a jingle they all knew:

> They ask us 'What is dust?'
> It's all right when you know it
> But you've got to see it fust.

The cavalry clattered off among the bare scrubby hills, drab figures with only their turbans and the pennants of their lances adding a splash of colour to the prevalent ochre of the rocky slopes. They had already been seen. According to the *Indian Field Service Pocket Book*, the tribal system of intelligence was always 'very complete', and sharp fanatical eyes were even now staring down from the heights, assessing numbers and counting guns. In their arrogance the tribesmen did not believe there were enough of the infidels to dislodge them.

As the main body moved up towards the Malakand Pass, reaching a point about twenty miles from it in the afternoon, it was Low's intention that they should march to a forming-up position next morning and attack in the afternoon. Brigadier-General Blood argued that the Malakand was a strong position and should be attacked by fresh troops the following morning. Low insisted that they press on, but that night the sky filled with clouds and a violent storm blew down all the tents and made the horses stampede. There was hardly a man who was not 'drenched out and out'.[1] Blood was grateful for the resulting delay, and remarked to Low that he ought to thank the Almighty for intervening. Low didn't think it very funny.

But Blood was right. The Malakand was no place to attack without preparation. The enemy – chiefly Ranazais, Utman Khels and Adinzais – lay along the ridges, with a series of stone sangars pushed down the main spurs. The valley they overlooked was about four miles long, and down it ran a dry watercourse. Their position stretched for a mile and a half and was tremendously strong. Approximately 12,000 tribesmen swarmed among the rocks with their flags and banners, about half of them armed. Some had Martinis and Sniders, but most had muzzle-loaders, jezails, swords and even slings. The rest were there to carry wounded, or fetch water, or were so placed as to send the very hillsides crashing down on the attackers.

Among them were the mullahs, with their wailing prayers, their visions and their talk of the Prophet. The adjuration, 'Prayer is better than sleep', had given way to fiercer urgings, and they claimed to have seen the souls of the faithful rising to paradise, while the spirits of defeated infidels sank into the dank caverns of hell. Those who doubted not were immune to British bullets and the British lines would break as the faithful reached them. Victory would be theirs. Paradise would be theirs. Their names would live in glory for evermore.

The warriors had heard it all before, of course, but the words were still potent enough to rouse them to wild enthusiasm. Death had no more meaning than defeat. The howls and yells of militant Islam broke out along the crest – 'Ya Allah! Glory for all, and Heaven for those who bleed' – and the tribesmen seized swords and ancient muskets as the mullahs laid prayer on prayer and text on text.

Low's plan was to launch two battalions against the extreme right under cover of a concentration of twenty mountain guns. The First

Brigade, supported by the Second, was to make the attack, and the infantry would advance up the spurs towards the enemy's main position on a front as broad as possible. In readiness, the artillery moved along the foot of the hills on the east and the infantry up the centre of the valley. At the same time an advanced guard drove back parties of the enemy, and the sappers cleared a way for the guns through the brushwood and into the fields. The operation went 'like clockwork'.

The detailed artillery programme allowed for a moving curtain of shrapnel spattering the hillsides ahead of the infantry. Although there were 7000 Pathans directly opposite Low, the clever handling of the guns by Major Dacres Cunningham, who dropped crushing salvoes wherever they massed, ensured that they were never allowed to concentrate. A nearby jungle hid the weapons, which had been pushed forward to within 800 yards of the enemy.

As the guns opened up, someone noticed one of the Pathans, who had obviously served at some time with a British-Indian regiment, contemptuously using a coloured standard decorated with scripts from the Koran to signal with military precision to the gunners – 'Miss. Low to the right. High to the left' – until eventually a shell was sent 'where it would do most good . . . and blew the signaller to pieces'.

The Guides Infantry of the Second Brigade had been sent up the steep hills on the west towards the Swat valley to a peak some 1500 feet above, where the enemy was in considerable strength. As they climbed, it was seen that more tribesmen held high ground on their left and the 4th Sikhs were sent forward to strengthen the flank. Since these men could not carry out their attack in time, two companies of the King's Own Scottish Borderers went forward as an advance guard; the guns came into action again and a Maxim gun detachment of the 1st Devons began to fire across a ravine from a point nearer the enemy.

The Guides and the Sikhs had completed more than half the ascent and had made a decided impression on that flank by taking several sangars when, at noon, the Gordons were sent in by Waterfield to make a direct attack in the centre of the position, their objective a small village on the crest of the ridge. Kinloch sent in the King's Royal Rifles lower down. The crest was about 1000 feet above a little stream at the foot of the slope, which was broken by ravines, in many places quite precipitous. It was necessary to advance on a very narrow front, sometimes even in single file, and often the men had to use their hands to pull themselves up. Their difficulties were increased by bushes, trees and rocks on the slope, while all the time they were under fire from the sangars, each of which, as it was captured, came under the fire of the next above.

The Borderers were attacking up two spurs and, moving up a narrow ravine on their right, the Gordons came under fire from both sides. Men were sent up the slopes to silence it, while others worked their way up the watercourse, sheltered by crags and rocks. One young officer trying to pull up a corporal lost his grip as the man's foot slipped, and the N.C.O. rolled towards a forty-foot drop. Fortunately he managed to grasp a bush on the brink and haul himself to safety.

Slowly the men advanced, using their rifles when they could and dashing across the exposed stretches. Then, in the teeth of a 'perfect avalanche of stones' and accompanied by the rapid ping-ping-ping of the Maxims, the two regiments went ahead 'like greyhounds loosed from a leash'. Awaiting them in the sangars on top of the ridge were 2000 picked swordsmen who stood out clearly against the skyline. Small parties kept making rushes down the hillside to the sound of drums and shrieks of '*La illa lah wa Mahomed rasul allah!*' – 'There is but one God and Mohammed is his prophet!' They were a terrifying sight and their shouts echoed among the crags along with the clatter of musketry.

While the Borderers were still only halfway up the hill, a banner-man, carrying Umra Khan's large triangular white standard with its bloody hand insignia, called on the men around him to charge. But the infantry stood firm and the advancing tribesmen, leaping down like deer among the rocks towards them, were met with devastating volleys that shattered their ranks until the banner-man alone was left standing. Pushing on with fanatic determination for a place in paradise, he was several times hit before he was finally shot dead close to the line.

As the soldiers struggled on, one of the enemy drummers climbed to a roof high above them and began to pound his drum. When he was hit and fell off, he persisted in climbing back again. Again he was hit, and again, stopping only to staunch his wounds before recommencing to beat his drum, until he was finally shot through the heart and fell headlong 300 feet down the cliff. Under the last great scarp the Gordons waited, safe from fire and the boulders that were being hurled down at them. Then, climbing a narrow ledge, they reached the top of the slope just as a burst of cheering from the village announced its capture.

Racing to be first for the honour of their regiment, the Borderers had climbed the worst patches literally 'on their hands and knees', closely followed by the Rifles. Lieutenant Watt was the first man to reach the summit where, finding himself facing a horde of howling tribesmen on his own, he thought it sensible to retreat a little until his men joined him. Behind him an eighteen-stone quartermaster-sergeant, sweating with exertion in the heat, was almost in tears with fury. 'You bastards,' he was shouting in his distress. 'If ye was on the flat, I'd eat you!'

The Gordons now plunged into the fight. One officer, struggling with a tribesman found his revolver wouldn't fire and his sword too blunt to pierce the man's sheepskin coat, so that he was in some difficulty until another officer appeared and shot the tribesman down. Those few of the enemy who refused to flee were killed, and the village was soon in flames.

Lieutenant Warre was the first man of the Rifles to reach the top where his regiment, fighting a private battle alongside the Borderers, stumbled on an old Graeco-Buddhist road probably dating from Alexander the Great but forgotten by later generations. The very steepness of the slopes had saved them from too many casualties, whether from bullets or boulders, and soon they were joined by the cavalry. Then the guns raced forward across tracks prepared for them by the sappers, to pepper the tribesmen as they ran, and the pursuit was taken up by the Bedfordshires and the 37th Dogras who had followed the Gordons up the ravine. By 2 pm it was all over and the path became choked with transport, animals slipping and stumbling and falling over the rocks. Field ambulances were set up and hospital tents erected, and here and there the first fires were lit.

Ten thousand tribesmen had been dispersed with 600 killed and another 1400 wounded and the road into the Swat valley was open.

The British casualties were said to be eleven killed and forty-seven wounded, though it was later said in Simla that there were fifty in the Second Brigade alone.

The tribesmen had behaved with great courage, withstanding a searching shell fire from three batteries for five hours, and then meeting bayonet charges by the Gordons and the Borderers hand-to-hand with spears. A remarkable amount of blood was found on the paths at the top of the ridge where bodies had been dragged away. To prevent them being defiled, the British dead were brought in on ponies – torn, stained sacks, their hands rusty with dried blood. Those wounded tribesmen who had been left behind were attended by the British doctors, their wounds of great interest because they were among the first to be caused by the new Lee-Metford rifle the British were using. One captured boy said he came from Barwar, and that he had been given a rifle and five rounds and told to go to the Malakand. His home was nearly a hundred miles away and officers of the brigade passed the hat round and he was sent off with thirty rupees and a blanket. Another boy, with his arm splintered by a bullet and in a terrible state of mortification, was given the choice of amputation or slow death by gangrene. He chose the latter and within a few days was better.

Another man had had a chupatti applied to his wound, with the skin of a freshly-killed chicken bound round it. The wound was in a horrible condition. The Pathans had a shrewd idea how to use splints, however, and men with wounded arms were found with them in well-constructed cradles. One man with three bullet wounds, two in the leg, had walked three miles to be attended. Another with wounds in the shoulder had walked five miles, while a third, with no less than six bullets in him, later walked to Chakdara – a matter of nine miles.[2]

A clinical consideration of the wounds decided the officers that the nickel-plated Lee-Metford bullet, though accurate in flight and giving clean wounds, did not have the stopping power of the heavy lead bullets of the Martini or Snider, unless it hit bone, and the soldiers learned to file the bullets down to the less accurate but more lethal dum-dums.[3] The judgement was sound because the tribesmen called the Lee-Metford 'a child's rifle'. 'We never feared it,' they said. They were far more worried by the Maxims – what they called 'the rattle guns' – and the mountain artillery.

On 4 April Low's division moved on, those who had not been in action before feeling better and braver after the fight. As Churchill later observed, the first time a man was under fire he imagined himself to be the target of every bullet in the area but experience gave him some idea of the odds in his favour.

The soldiers were in good spirits. 'Pull up his shirt, mate,' one of them was heard saying as an elderly Pathan appeared, 'and see if he's the same old Moses we had our bayonets in yesterday.' As they moved forward, however, the hills started them grumbling. 'If these be the bloody hills, give me the plains,' was the cry.

The only available path was a single steep track littered with boulders and very small progress was made until the end of the day when the old Graeco-Buddhist road, stumbled on by the Rifles during the battle, was used. This led down a good gradient to the plains, and every available man was immediately employed in improving this 2000-year-old relic of another civilization. In twenty-four hours the brigades were on their way.

There was another brisk fight at Khar but the place was deserted, though plenty of rice, flour, sugar, calves and goats were found to give a fillip to the rations. They were entering 'the deep green cultivation' of the Swat valley now, a hot fertile place, well watered and green with corn, interspersed with fruit trees and wild flowers, and overlooked by the snowcapped mountains beyond. They were not certain what they were going to meet there. The Pathans despised and distrusted the Swatis, stigmatizing them as cowards; but they were expected to resist, and Blood pushed forward with the cavalry, knowing the tribesmen were terrified of horsemen.

News arrived that Fowler and Edwardes were still alive and now near Barwar, just ahead of the division and 120 miles from where they had been captured. The tribesmen were seen gathering ahead again, and it was reported that the Hamira ferry was held by two brothers of Umra Khan with 3000 men. Brigadier-General Kinloch had all the waggons and pack animals brought up, and the 3rd Mountain Battery took up a strong position to defend them. The Bedfordshires, still itching to add to their honours, were told off for similar duties, and the 37th Dogras and 15th Sikhs were pushed forward to clear the hills. Though the work was difficult, the men were making good headway until the transport animals became jammed. Seeing their opportunity, the tribesmen quickly concentrated and rushed down the defile in a spirited charge.

Sir Ian Hamilton has described such a fight. 'Those armed with the tulwar . . . would catch the bayonet point on the shield and then slash. The most dangerous were those trusting simply to their long . . . knives. . . .' It was the habit of these knife-men to get among the troops and break them up, an occurrence which could turn a battle which had begun well into a bloody disaster. This time, however, only a few reached the lines.

Mountain guns and machine guns roared, and the Bedfordshires were at last in action. They were quick to notice that the tribesmen had sighted their weapons on marks previously set up to give the range, and, watching where the bullets kicked up the dust, gave the area a wide berth. They checked the screaming tribesmen, and then the Guides Cavalry – 'swords drawn, lances at the ready' – were launched from the right in one of the charges so dear to the heart of British officers.

The tribesmen fought cavalry in 'little knots, or . . . lying on their backs whirling their big knives to cut off the legs of . . . horses, a hell of a scrimmage, in fact, until the sowars got to work in couples, one with sword uplifted, the other pulling his carbine out of the bucket and making the enemy spring to their feet and be cut down or be shot as they lay'.[4] In the dust and shouts and clash of steel, the enemy were scattered. The British loss was three killed and twelve badly wounded.

Reconnoitring as far as the river on 5 April, Major Roddy Owen of the Lancashire Fusiliers, a well-known rider and sportsman who was also acting as special correspondent for *The Pioneer* of Lucknow, splashed across to become probably the first European to enter the territory undisguised. Blood, who was up with a covering party, thought the river was fordable in several places but that it would be necessary to build a bridge to get the ammunition and supplies across.

The tribesmen followed their usual tactics and crowded the heights to fire on the working parties, and Umra Khan's brother, Mahomed Shah, was reported to be present with many cavalry and infantry. At this point the First Brigade was left behind on the chilly heights – 'with little to eat and less to wear' – to guard the communications. The Official History says that Low selected his senior brigade for this duty because of the importance of the task, but according to the Bedfordshires' records it was because Kinloch was a difficult man to get on with and had proved troublesome.[5] Blood claimed that Kinloch was 'seriously indisposed' but Lieutenant Warre of the Rifles wrote home bluntly that 'trouble arose between the generals'. 'The reason is,' he said, 'Low is a Scotchman and there are two Scotch battalions with the Second Brigade.' While Brigadier-General Waterfield was still struggling to push through, the enterprising Blood rode across the river, whereupon the tribesmen 'were silly enough to assume, because they could not see any troops behind . . .' that he had not covered his line of retreat. But Blood was too old a hand at the game for that and, rushing out, the tribesmen found themselves under the muzzles of 500 rifles in the hands of concealed British infantry. They left many dead as they retreated.

On 7 April, with the Swat bridged, Waterfield took his brigade forward, supported by the 15th Bengal Infantry and the Ludhiana Sikhs, and advanced to force the river at Chakdara. Mountain and Maxim guns belonging to the Borderers began to fire. The infantry made a dash forward and three and a half squadrons of Guides Cavalry and four of the 11th Bengal Lancers, pushed ahead by Blood and supported by the Sikhs, crossed at a little-known ford. Since the cavalry brigadier weighed eighteen stone and was 'mounted accordingly', Blood had foreseen the possibility of trouble. Sure enough, just when speed was essential, the brigadier became stuck in the boggy rice fields where he remained for some time so that it was Blood, who had taken care to be close by, who launched the horsemen in another spirited charge. Only a few of the enemy cavalry facing them tried to defend themselves with gun and tulwar; most of the rest were lanced in the back as they turned tail and galloped hard for the hills. One who stood his ground shot a trooper. He was transfixed immediately by half a dozen lances and then literally hacked to pieces by the razor-sharp swords.

Among the enemy was Mohamed Shah. He got away but 400 of his men didn't and were pursued for nearly eight miles. One lancer saw a Pathan take refuge in a tree and went for him, standing in his stirrups and holding his lance by the butt so that he could just reach the climbing man. Unfortunately he hadn't noticed a well under the tree and as the tribesman fell from the tree to disappear into the hole, he was followed a moment later by the lancer's horse, hind legs foremost, together with its rider. Both horse and rider were rescued. As the cavalrymen rode back every one of them had one or two swords picked up from fallen tribesmen.

Hullo, Gurdon's had to light up

21

Constantly expecting a major assault, the garrison at Chitral had remained alert for some time. When nothing happened, they had begun to feel that the worst had passed and all they had to do was sit tight and wait. Just before dark on the night of 6 April, however, while General Low was studying his move across the Swat, some forty or fifty men were seen from the fort moving from the bazaar to the river. In Captain Campbell's opinion, they were in for a lively night.

About 10 pm Robertson, Wafadar and Sifat were watching the enemy structure near the chabutra and after a discussion they decided to dig a hole through the enclosure wall with a view to pushing out a defence towards it. Two hours later they had made a hole large enough for a man to crawl through, and beams and boxes of earth were passed out. Soon an effective little sangar had been built. Its walls were so low it could only be used in a crouching position, but it provided cover for the whole of the west wall of the enclosure.

On the parapet overlooking the working party were the Sikhs under Gurmokh Singh, the elderly subadar, who had been told of what was happening. Despite the noise made by the diggers, no notice was taken of them by the enemy in the big sangar opposite. Their silence became so uncanny that Robertson edged forward to a huge chenar tree, which stood in the middle of the chabutra, to see what lay beyond. As he did so, a hubbub broke out among the Sikhs behind him and a warning was hissed. Gurmokh Singh had sent word that the enemy had been seen on the fort side of the tree and that he was going to have to open fire. Clearly, however, it was Robertson who had been seen and he blessed the 'splendid thick-headed old gentleman' for sending his caution.

It was now past 2 am, and Robertson had hardly left for bed when there was a heavy rattle of musketry from the north tower and the Sikhs began to volley against sharpshooters. Shouting started from a point beyond Sifat's enclosure and a wounded Sikh was brought in from the outer works. In the darkness he had not noticed that the old gunport was only roughly blocked up, and he had been shot in the leg in the very spot where Robertson had almost been hit that afternoon.

By the time Robertson reached the party of reserves waiting with Captain Townshend and Surgeon-Captain Whitchurch, the noise on the west side was terrific. Silent and reserved as usual, Whitchurch had a double-barrelled rifle in his hand and the long Chitrali robe he was wearing was tucked into his belt in a businesslike way. He was always a quiet man but now Robertson noticed that his silence and motionlessness in the middle of the excitement seemed to suggest 'immense reserves of strength'.

Lieutenants Gurdon and Harley were on the parapets – Gurdon on the south side, Harley facing the river – but neither Robertson nor Captain Townshend could make up his mind as to whence the attack would come. They had finally decided it was going to come from the garden side when a bright glow appeared at the south-east corner of the fort by the gun tower. Since the wind was blowing strongly from that direction, the fires on the little platforms there had not been lit, and so it was initially assumed that the crisis was such that they had now been thought necessary.

'Hullo,' Townshend said, 'Gurdon's had to light up after all,' but at that moment a man came running across the yard with a message that the besiegers had managed to do the one thing the garrison had always dreaded – set light to the fort. They had placed bundles of faggots against the gun tower which was now well ablaze.

It was a terrible moment but fear quickly turned to anger and energy. Shouting, Robertson collected every available servant, groom, porter and unarmed man except the Chitrali nobles with Shuja-ul-Mulk. Townshend organized lines of men from the reserve, the water-carriers and the Punialis, to pass buckets, pails and pots of water, and – on the advice of the indefatigable and resourceful Wafadar – to carry earth in their coats. Already a great fire was blazing noisily on the outer walls of the gun tower. The one facing the summer-house was the larger of the two, and looked big enough to have been going for hours. As there was no aperture on this side in the lower room, they had to fight it from the apartment above where the machicoulis gallery was situated. At the other side, looking straight down on to the garden, an enormous beam projected several feet from the window and on it a small waist-high barricade had been erected. From here the other fire was being fought by an elderly tracker and servant of Campbell's called Sultan Shah who sat out on the beam and poured water and soil on the flames faster than he could be supplied. He had almost put the fire out when he was shot through the hip and arm and flopped across the beam in agony.

On the summer-house side it was hard to get at the fire from the machicoulis gallery without being hit by the enemy riflemen only twenty-five yards away, and it was now roaring like a furnace. The noise was astonishing; the rush of the flames, the splintering of the boards of the gallery as they were volleyed into at short range, and the triumphant yells of the besiegers combining with the high-pitched wailing of their mullahs chanting prayers.

The loose boards at the sides of the gallery were jumping up and down under the impact of the bullets so that one of the Gurkhas, squatting on the floor to fight the flames, had to keep breaking off his work to replace his own defences. More bullets smashed into the great timbers supporting the roof but everyone worked quickly and without panic. The wounded tracker was shouting for help, men were staggering away half-blinded by flying splinters, and Wafadar was screaming barely-heard instructions and information into Robertson's ear. For a while it seemed as if they were fighting a losing battle amidst the acrid stink of burning and the throat-catching whorls of smoke, and every time they quenched the fire it reappeared with redoubled fury.

When the badly-injured tracker was finally dragged aside, it was decided not to replace him; but as the fire increased in fury Robertson had to send down for more help. Townshend dared not send up any of the reserves in case an attack should develop elsewhere, but Whitchurch brought up six Sikhs and then went back to urge on the water-carriers. Then the gallant little Gurkha working in the gallery was hit twice, the bullets piercing the wooden walls. Because the gallery would hold only one man at a time, he had to be dragged out before anyone else could get in. Trying to decide who could replace him, Robertson's eye fell on Badrinar Singh who had fought so well with Gurdon on 3 March and had afterwards stuck so nobly to Whitchurch. As Robertson's hand touched his shoulder, he visibly changed countenance. He was an intelligent man and knew the danger, but he nevertheless crept on to the gallery and replaced the boards which by this time were 'leaping about as if alive'. Fortunately he was not hit.

Every now and then someone had to push his head over the side of the gallery to examine the blaze. This was always the signal for an outbreak of furious firing, redoubled yells and the whack of bullets against the wall. The defenders were soon so tired they lost all sense of excitement, and though Gurdon's men tried to keep down the enemy's fire by volleys, they were well protected and the loopholes in their sangars could only be hit at an angle.

Gurdon came up to ask if Townshend should send out a sortie, but by this time it was almost daylight and, though the tower wall itself was blazing, the original fire was almost dead. Robertson decided a sortie would be useless. Moving to the room below the gallery to tackle the fire from there, it was found to be just as dangerous. They would have to knock holes in the walls to get at the burning timbers, and as the gun tower contained more timber than any other part of the fort, the chief fear was that it would collapse.

Always cool and helpful, Wafadar, who knew the fort like the back of his hand, was able to point out where the walls could be perforated. But the first hole, about a foot square and breast high, immediately became a target for the besiegers. As most of the bullets were travelling upwards, they caused more alarm than damage.

The yelling outside swelled up again and again, and every time the men inside expected an attack. Ignoring the howls, one of the Sikhs steadily ladled water through the hole on to the fire, smiling all the time – in spite of the bullets – at the praise that was being showered on him for his courage. The lower part of the wall at the south-east corner was now almost red hot. Gurdon's Hunza servant, Rajab, and others broke into the masonry to discover that the fire had penetrated between the inner and outer frames. Stripped to his cotton drawers, Rajab sawed away at the timbers to make a hole wide enough to pour water through.

Because of the cold, Robertson had thrown a fur coat over his pyjamas as he had jumped out of bed but by now the heat was so great he had to fling it aside. As he did so, a bullet which had been fired at long range thumped into a wooden pillar just behind him. He was immediately reminded of a story of Marryat's about a sailor in a sea fight who always thrust his head in the first hole made in the ship's side because he felt shots never struck twice in the same place. He smiled at the recollection, confident that the enemy had been frustrated, but bullets kept coming through the hole where the Sikh was ladling water, to whack into the ceiling and bring down showers of fragments. And then, as Robertson bent to give instructions to Rajab, something struck him heavily on the shoulder so that he stumbled and fell. It was only the expression on Sifat's face which made him realize he had been hit.

Thinking of the horrible injuries he had seen Whitchurch dealing with, Robertson struggled to his feet and stumbled across the roof to his room. Dragging off his pyjama jacket in front of a tiny looking-glass, he began to examine with an expert's touch the bony projections of his shoulder, expecting them all the time to give way beneath his fingers. Fortunately, they had not been harmed, but the wound was large and deep and the bullet had torn away a great deal of flesh.

As he was put to bed, he was brought reports of the progress of the fire. Every time the flames died away, a blast of rising wind would stir them to life again, but about 9.30 am Townshend arrived to say it was almost out. Rajab and the smiling Sikh, together with three or four others, had been badly hit, and just as the tired defenders were beginning to withdraw a last shot mortally wounded Duffadar Mohamed, Campbell's orderly, the handsome soldierly Punjabi of the Central India Horse.

While the garrison were still getting their breath back in the blackened tower and counting the cost of the fire amidst the stink of dust and smoke and the fading scent of fear, Colonel Kelly and his staff had crossed the Shandur and had reached Laspur.

They were all in poor shape. Even before they had left Teru, Lieutenant Beynon was suffering from fever and his face felt like a furnace. It hadn't a bit of skin on it and because of the cracked state of his lips it was painful either to eat or laugh, but he felt better as they prepared to start next morning. As they began to climb they passed the wreckage of Stewart's sledges and pieces of broken spade. The slightest divergence from the track plunged them into waist-deep snow, so that the only member of the party who could move without difficulty was Beynon's mongrel bull-terrier.

That night they reached a camp guarded by the few men left in charge of Stewart's abandoned ammunition. They were all suffering from snow-blindness. As soon as they had scraped a hole in the snow to erect Kelly's tent, Beynon went round with quinine dosing them and all the servants and orderlies against fever, and then took a good dose himself as an insurance against a recurrence.

They were up before dawn the next day to start on the last leg of the pass. There was a strong wind whistling into their faces and Beynon thought nothing could be so cold. 'It simply went clean through you,' he wrote, 'and I quite expected to hear my ribs sing like an Aeolian harp.' They were so high now he began to suffer from what he called 'mountain sickness'. It was undoubtedly lack of oxygen because by this time they were about 12,000 feet high, and the minute they crossed the pass and began to descend it disappeared.

On the other side, they found Laspur garrisoned by 'the maimed, the halt and the blind' – Borradaile's party suffering from frostbite and glare – while Beynon's own face felt 'as if it had been dipped in boiling water'. Curing it with Vinolia baby-powder given to him by Kelly, he offered 'an unsolicited testimonial' to the fact that, although it was supposed to be used only to sprinkle infant's behinds, it also made him look like a human being again.

They were all stiff from their exertions. Even Beynon's dog was snow-blind and had to have its eyes opened every morning and bathed with hot water. They looked a 'thoroughgoing set of ruffians', and Stewart and Gough spent most of their spare time with their heads over basins of hot water dabbing at their aching eyes. Nobody had much skin on his face, and what remained was 'of a patchwork description'. Nobody had shaved for days – 'We couldn't have stood the torture,' Beynon said – and their clothes were in tatters.

7 April was spent treating the frostbite cases and the men with inflamed eyes, who were confined to a darkened room, bringing up the ammunition Stewart had had to drop at Langar, and in holding what Beynon called a 'political tea' for the leaders of the levies and one or two princelings who had come up in the hope of a fight. The levies had proved invaluable. Because many of them had blood relations among the Chitralis, they always brought the first and best information and they always knew where to look for hidden grain.

They set off again on 8 April towards Gusht, leaving Gough behind at Laspur, cursing 'his bloody luck'. As they descended, they soon left the snow behind and, moving through narrow valleys between high stony hills topped with snow, they stopped at the house of the Hakim of Laspur, a hoary-headed old rascal who was firmly believed to have murdered an English traveller called Hayward in 1872. Beynon set the Puniali levies to ransacking the old man's home for food, but though they discovered several hidden mounds of grain, they found nothing else except an old spectacle case. As the old man had never worn spectacles in his life it was probably Hayward's, and Kelly, who had just lost his, promptly annexed it.

From men interrogated by Shah Mirza and Wazir Humayun, they learned the enemy was waiting for them at Chakalwat under one of Sher Afzul's generals – Muhammed Isa, the man who had tricked Edwardes and Fowler and murdered the Sikhs at Kalak – and urgent messages brought up the Puniali levies from Laspur. Chakalwat was a darband like Ghizr and Gairat, and posed a tremendous barrier. Its only drawback was that Mastuj, under the vigorous Lieutenant Moberly, lay in its rear.

The Chitralis held both banks of the river at a point where it swung in an inverted S. Each concavity of the S was filled by a ridged, turtle-backed plain, while across the river in each of the convex curves lay a mighty shale slope. The one on the left was quite impassable while the one on the right could be blocked simply by rolling stones down its incline from above. Everywhere it was difficult – in places impossible – to descend to the river because the shale slopes ended in abrupt cliffs. There were crossings near Gusht but, to stop Kelly, the only bridge had been destroyed and sangars had been built to command the ford. More sangars had been built to cover the road to Mastuj on the opposite bank. This was also blocked by a long loopholed barricade and was threatened with destruction by men waiting above to start the stones and debris rolling as soon as an advance was made, while sharpshooters were posted to harass anyone reaching the plain across the river.

On the evening of 8 April, Kelly sent Beynon forward with a party of levies to make a reconnaissance. Army officers had always declared Chakalwat to be impregnable if held in strength and, after taking one look at it, Beynon saw what they meant. Through his glasses he could see the defenders of the sangars cooking their evening meals, the thin columns of smoke rising in the still evening air, blue against the dark slopes. He stayed long enough to sketch the position in detail.

Next morning the Hunza and Nagar levies, led by Beynon, left at 6 am, and headed up the hills on the left to turn the right flank of the enemy, while the Punialis crossed the river to climb the hills and dislodge the Chitralis posted to roll down rocks. Three hours later the main force moved out of Gusht for a frontal attack. Beynon had put on puttees and rope-soled canvas shoes because he knew the going would be bad. The going turned out to be *very* bad and it grew worse, so that every step they took looked like setting the whole shale slide in motion. The best way, Beynon found, was to rush at whatever slope he had to cross and scramble over it before the whole lot started moving. Seeing a grassy bank, they crossed a saw-edged ridge to it only to find that the clusters of rocks along its edge were occupied sangars, and a few bullets kicked up the dust near them. They continued to push forward, and, as the enemy began to retreat, Beynon sat down to watch the fight which was just beginning below.

A mile below the village, Oldham and his sappers had improvised a temporary bridge, and Stewart's guns had crossed the river on ponies and were being carried up the other side by porters.

'We saw the advance guard get on to the plain and extend,' Beynon wrote to his mother, 'and presently they were joined by the main body and the whole lot formed up for attack.'

G

The advance was led by Lieutenant Cobbe with half a company. His men had to be commanded in dumb show or by whistle, since Cobbe was nearly speechless as a result of the exposure he had suffered on the march across the Shandur. Next came Oldham and his sappers, followed by the main body under Captain Borradaile – one and a half companies of the 32nd, with Stewart's guns.

'We saw the sangars open fire,' Beynon continued, 'answered by volleys from our men. Then came a large puff of smoke and a murmur from the men around me, as a shell . . . burst over a sangar. It was as pretty a sight as one could wish for, and I felt as if I should have been in a stall in Drury Lane.'

The guns had been brought into action by their gunners to the great relief of the village drivers. The distance was discussed by Cobbe, who could scarcely whisper, and Stewart, who could barely see. When Kelly asked what range they were going to use, Stewart replied, 'Four hundred yards.' Kelly thought he was joking. 'Don't be foolish, Stewart,' he said sharply

But Stewart insisted. He had only eight rounds of common shell and knew he daren't waste them. When Kelly pointed out that there were bound to be casualties, he agreed but said it couldn't be helped. One of the precious common shells had to be used to get the distance, so he ordered the range and put up his glasses to observe its fall. To his surprise nothing happened and, turning towards the gun, he saw all the gunners 'engaged in salaaming to it, and to the shell, and to the cartridge. Even the fuse came in for its salutation by way of bidding "God Speed" to their first round fired fighting.' Stewart waited patiently until the performance was over and then gave terse instructions that in future only the first round was to be salaamed. The gun banged and the shell fell short of the sangar nearest the shale slope. There were a few derogatory remarks from the levies but Humayun knew Stewart better. 'Wait and see,' he said. 'This is only the first.'

The next shell struck the foot of the sangar and the third caught it square in the middle, knocking a big hole in it. After a few more rounds, the defenders took to their heels while the men in the other sangars began to sneak away. 'You've won your medals,' Stewart roared to his delighted gunners.

Fire was still coming from some of the other sangars and Kelly asked Stewart to silence one on the right. Only two or three common shell were left by this time so the guns limbered up, advanced straight on the sangar down the slope to a range of 400 yards and blew a hole in it with the first shell.[1]

As the firing slackened, the infantry advanced. Then, at the right moment, Beynon's Hunzas and Nagars appeared above and the tribesmen began to waver. The river was forded by the main body, without opposition, and as the men scrambled up the precipitous slope opposite, the fight was over. As usual the Chitralis had under-valued the British-led troops, assuming them to be the same cowed Kashmiris they had so often defeated on previous occasions.

When Lieutenant Beynon arrived, sliding down the slope – 'chiefly on all fours' – the enemy had bolted. By 10.30 am Colonel Kelly's whole force had reformed and the enemy were being chased down the left bank of the river. Anticipating that the Mastuj troops had already sortied to intercept them, they moved with great speed but as it happened, through some trick of the atmosphere, the guns had not even been heard by Moberly and they escaped. Kelly had four men wounded, only one badly, while the five or six bodies left behind by the enemy were the only clues to the Chitrali casualties, which were estimated at fifty or sixty.

The Chitralis 'had shown great effrontery', however, to fight at all with Mastuj so close to their rear, and Muhammed Isa had withdrawn his men very neatly, distracting Moberly's attention as he slipped past by firing on the fort. By the time Moberly realized what was happening he was gone.

There burst over us a mighty light

22

Meanwhile, to the south there had been another clash, this time with three of Umra Khan's brothers and a cousin.

By now, the whole of Swat knew Low was coming. Indeed the size of his column was enough to make hostile the friendliest of tribesmen. The number of pack animals had grown by now to 35,000. In addition there were elephants to pull the guns, and these enormously intrigued the Swatis who had never seen them before. The size of the force made foraging difficult, to say nothing of camping, because they were now in country where flat areas of land were at a premium. Tents were pitched on rocky saddles – or kotals – along the spines of the hills; draughty places that baked in the daytime sun but were freezing cold at night.

The main body had crossed the Swat at Chakdara – using local watermen and inflated skins – with the loss of only two or three men. The 4th and 5th Sikhs had occupied the town while the Borderers forded the river higher upstream to capture a fort belonging to Umra Khan at Thanna. The whole force was now clear of the Malakand and, still using the old Buddhist road, they pushed on to Ramora. There another large stone fort, strong enough to dominate the whole Swat valley, barred their path. It was captured after a short resistance but attempts to blow it up ended in complete failure. It was therefore by-passed and, as the enemy retired north, General Low's next obstacle became the Panjkora, a formidable and treacherous river which could be fordable one day and a roaring torrent thundering between steep narrow spurs the next.[1] Beyond lay Jandol and Umra Khan's stronghold at Mundiah.

On 12 April, despite continual sniping, the sappers managed to fling a rough footbridge across the river, thus enabling the Guides infantry under Colonel Battye to move over to the western bank. During the night, however, tribesmen took advantage of one of the Panjkora's sudden floods to launch logs into the surging waters, which carried away the newly-erected bridge, leaving the Guides isolated and with an estimated 9000 of the enemy only a few miles further on. Major Fenton Aylmer, RE, who had won theV.C. by blowing in the gate of the fortress at Nilt during the Hunza-Nagar campaign of 1891, advised Low that it would take forty-eight hours to replace the bridge. While this was being done, Battye and the Guides were ordered to make a limited advance and destroy the enemy positions immediately ahead. But after demolishing one or two villages near the river, Battye pressed on into the hills. In the opinion of Major Owen of *The Pioneer* he went too far.

Their movements were constantly watched by the tribesmen, and an unknown Pathan who was later captured and interviewed at Miankilai described how they appeared from the peaks. 'We saw the floating roadway break up,' he said, 'and its pieces swept away on the rapid waters. Our watchmen signalled the news from hill to hill and the clans gathered for the fray, for we believed that the soldiers separated from their fellows were delivered into our hands. . . . Then our mullahs . . . showed that Allah was mindful of his children by placing 1000 rifles and their ammunition within our hands to grasp . . . and we believed victory was certain.'[2]

At midday two large bodies of men were seen pouring out of the hills and sweeping down towards the Guides. Brigadier-General Waterfield sent a signal advising Battye to retire and he accordingly fell back – in Owen's opinion too late. From the opposite side of the river the Guides' withdrawal down the spurs towards their camp was watched by men powerless to help, but the Second Brigade was moved to the water's edge to give what support they could and Brigadier-General Blood saw everything that happened.

Pressed heavily all the way as the tribesmen swept forward, the retreat was so expertly handled that the Guides' losses were small. One of the enemy banner-men was a boy who stood courageously exposed in full view on the crest of a low ridge, urging his comrades forward and leading them from time to time. Suddenly realizing his danger, he dived for shelter at the very moment that a bullet struck him in the head. Blood saw his skull cap fly off, and then he fell from sight in a whirl of arms and legs.

By this time the Guides had reached the foot of the hills where they had to cross a stretch of plain covered with waist-high green barley. Here two great masses of tribesmen chanting '*Allah Lo Akbar! Din! Din!*' thundered into the fray to cut off their retreat. As they surged forward with their banners to within yards of the line, Waterfield's men had to slacken their fire for fear of hitting their own men. There was no panic, however; the Guides continued to halt and fire volleys while their mountain battery opened up on the tribesmen who had almost reached the very muzzles of the guns.

Battye had been calmly giving orders throughout the action but, just as his men reached the shelter of their camp, he was seen to fall. He had been shot in the stomach and, as the tribesmen swept up to hack at his body and snatch his weapons, the guns across the river came to life.

'We could never get close to them,' the unknown Pathan said bitterly. '. . . and when the sahibs across the river began firing upon us, too, we went back to the hills for shelter.'

As they retired, the dying Battye was carried through the cornfields to the camp. The tribesmen were reported to have lost 500 in killed and wounded, but Battye's family had given yet another son to the frontier.

Still cut off from the rest of the army on the wrong side of the river, the Guides made preparations to withstand the night attack they knew must inevitably come. To strengthen them, Waterfield sent two companies of Sikhs with additional officers across the river on rafts, with a Maxim gun under Captain A. L. Peebles of the Devons, an expert machine-gunner and an inventor whose improvements to the weapon had been adopted by the army. At the same time a mountain battery equipped with high explosive and magnesium star shells – something the Pathans had not seen before – was pushed up to the near bank.

The evening set in wet, and as darkness came the rain increased until it fell in torrents, soaking the watchful men as they strained their eyes for a sign of their enemies. The Pathans had not been idle. The mullahs and chiefs had decided their men should creep up on the stranded soldiers and fall on them when the night was at its blackest, so that the vicious knives could do their deadly work unseen. The rifles the soldiers carried were great prizes and the tribesmen went more than willingly.

Two thousand of them, including the man later interviewed at Miankilai, were concealed in standing corn just beyond the Guides' pickets. 'We lay for hours in the wet fields with the rain falling steadily,' the Pathan reported. 'Word came round from chief to chief.' As they rose to their feet, however, they were heard and the mountain battery across the river exploded into action.

'A devil's gun boomed forth,' the Pathan continued, 'and lo! instead of bullets there burst over us a mighty light, so great we thought the night had suddenly become day.'

With the star shells falling slowly to the ground, the attack came to nothing and casualties proved small. But the Guides' camp remained under fire for some time. Peebles was mortally wounded in the stomach, while a native ambulance bearer squatting down in the manner of his tribe was struck by a single shot which went through both arms and both legs.[3]

The following day Aylmer's new bridge was towed into place. It was strong enough to support cavalry, artillery and loaded camels, but during the work one of the rafts was overturned and two soldiers were swept away. One of them was drowned but the other was rescued by Aylmer who had himself lowered in a basket to grab him as he shot past.

The river continued to rise, as did the Swat where a pontoon bridge on which Low depended for supplies was also in danger. By this time, however, Low had opened up friendly relations with Muhammed Sharif, the Khan of Dir, who held the country to the borders of Chitral and had submitted after the initial fighting at Malakand. It was proposed to send a small force on a flanking movement through his territory and over the Lowarai Pass, some twenty miles to the north, into the Chitral Valley. Meanwhile the main column would deal with Umra Khan's forces at Mundiah, about seven miles away. To Blood's annoyance, instead of acting on his own initiative, Low fussily referred the plan to his superiors in Peshawar. They considered it far too risky, and as a compromise, it was arranged that the Khan of Dir himself should carry out the move with 1000 men. Once through the Lowarai Pass, he was to spread rumours that he was only the advance guard of a vast force which had already defeated Umra Khan.

The arrangements were hastily made but as the khan's troops hurried off an unexpected figure appeared in the British camp. It was Edwardes – fit despite his ordeal, blond-bearded, bronzed and turbaned – and with him he had brought a request for an armistice from Umra Khan.

The letter was couched in the usual fulsome phrases of the frontier but the appeal was a plaintive one. 'What have I done,' Umra begged, 'that government is angry with me?'

As General Low had already discovered, Edwardes and Fowler had turned up a hundred miles from where they had been captured at Reshun. They were being well treated, and Umra Khan appeared to be doing all he could to make them comfortable. Indeed, with no idea of what they contained, he had even offered them the bottles of medicine captured during the defeat of Robertson's sortie on 3 March, explaining, 'I know the sahibs find it very hard to get along without wine.' It had become one of his pleasures at Barwar to sit, dressed in spotless white with a blue shawl over his shoulders, admiring his territory, asking the officers how they liked it, and enjoying their comments on its beauty. Edwardes' sepoys were told on 1 April that since they were now regarded as Mohammedans they were at liberty, and their guard was removed. These Hindu soldiers had already been forced to have their hair cut in support of this forced change of religion.

Though their men had been freed, the two officers were still confined to the fort, and they now became aware that the villagers around them had become alarmed and were discussing the British army's movements to the south. If Umra Khan was still friendly enough, some of his followers were not, and one of his officers complained bitterly that the British were only holding Chitral to deny it to the Russians. There was a new nervousness in the air because, with the defeats to the south and east, things had started to go badly for Umra Khan and Sher Afzul. Despite their reputations and undoubted skill, neither of them appreciated the advantages of acting on interior lines, and even if they had, their men were too unreliable to undertake operations that required a high degree of discipline and co-operation. Scattered over the whole theatre of war, they were nowhere strong enough to achieve real success.[4]

Taking advantage of the increasing dismay and confusion about them, Fowler and Edwardes managed to smuggle out a note written on the leaf of the notebook in which Fowler had kept a diary of their captivity – 'Fowler RE and Edwardes 2nd Bo. Grenadiers are shut up in Barwar. Can you get us out? Give bearers Rs100. J.S.F. ps. Shall we try and bolt? People here panic.'

Many of the villagers had already disappeared, in fact, but the two officers were still in great danger. Fanatical Pathan tribesmen prowled about in increasing numbers, sullen and angry, and Fowler and Edwardes were therefore kept out of sight.

When news of more successes by Low arrived, the tribesmen began to take to the hills. On 12 April, the two officers were put on ponies and despatched to Mundiah. Their escort – which always seemed to include men who had served at some time in the Indian army and were therefore willing to share their meagre rations – had to be quick-eyed; not for fear they would escape but in case some sullen warrior took a pot shot at them. For safety they wore Afghan dress but after an hour or two it was decided that the risk of continuing was too great and they returned to a nearby village until sundown. Even then a group of wild fighting men barred their path by a stream, and the escort had to level their rifles to compel the tribesmen to lay down their arms and allow them to pass.

Arriving at Mundiah fort, they were pushed through an armed crowd into a courtyard and then into a room beyond, where they found Umra Khan seated with his holy men and secretaries. Edwardes' terrier bitch, Biddy, now almost recovered, was lost in the crush outside, and they had just accepted that they would never see her again when a Pathan appeared carrying the excited wriggling animal in his arms.

Though he must have been well aware by now that his rule was in the gravest danger, Umra Khan managed to put on a show of confidence, and after attending prayers he gathered his followers round him in a clump of chenars below the fort.

'I have just received a letter from the commander-in-chief of the Afghan army,' he announced. 'His proposal is that I shall invade the Peshawar valley by way of the Malakand with 30,000 men and that he will co-operate through the Khyber Pass with 10,000 more.'

The whole assembly rose with a tremendous shout of 'To Peshawar!', but it seemed to Edwardes and Fowler that Umra Khan was merely bluffing in order to get his men into a warlike state for the final battle with Low, and that the enthusiasm they showed was far from genuine.

By this time negotiations had been started by Major Harold Deane, Low's political officer, for the release of the two men and that evening a Mohammedan noble from Peshawar, sent by Deane, appeared in the fort to take Edwardes away and over the hills to Low's camp. Carefully disguised, he carried with him Umra Khan's request for an armistice and the sword taken from him at Reshun, which Umra Khan had managed to retrieve. Fowler had to remain behind as a hostage.

That sangar was a death-trap

23

As they had taken stock of the damage done by the fire, it had been quite clear to Robertson and Captain Townshend at Chitral that the sentries on the gun tower, men of the always unreliable Kashmir Rifles, had not been keeping a good look-out. From then on the Sikhs and the eager Sifat's men were given the post. Both groups were keen-eyed, and Sifat's men could even often divine what was happening from the noises they heard. The machicoulis gallery was strengthened and a small window in the east tower – not previously manned because of the danger of men on the south parapet being hit by fire from it – was now provided with a marksman.

The blaze had been alarming and Captain Townshend made plans against another by organizing a fire-fighting party. Surgeon-Captain Whitchurch was to be in charge with Sifat as his lieutenant. Heaps of earth and stones, for lobbing on to arsonists, and containers of water were collected on all the towers, while miniature tanks were devised by letting waterproof sheets into holes in the ground. 'I do not think it would be possible for me to take more precautionary measures than I do,' Townshend noted worriedly in his diary.

Rumours had come in during the day that the Chitralis were about to swim the river and attack the covered way. Just after dark, when the officers had made their rounds for the night, firing broke out all around and Townshend appeared in Robertson's room, his face covered with surprise, to say that in spite of all their care, live embers had once more been thrown against the foot of the gun tower. Fortunately no fire had resulted, but the incident had apparently taken place under the gaze of a dozen pairs of eyes. 'It was like witchcraft,' Townshend said.

It was decided that the besiegers had made their move during the changing of the guards, so the times of the reliefs were altered and a trustworthy Sikh was ordered to lie on his face in the gallery from then on to watch through the floor.

The following night was one of the most miserable of Robertson's life. He was in low spirits from the pain of his wound and a new aching depression that had seized him. There had been more desultory firing during the hours of darkness, but hardly enough to rouse interest. Yet after being so sure they had defeated the enemy in everything they could do, the fire and the casualties it had brought had made him realize just how uncertain their defence was. When he woke the next morning he felt he had been through a nightmare.

In the light of what had happened, Townshend and the others had decided to pull down Sifat's enclosure and erect a new defence closer to the walls. This small retirement, together with visits from Sifat, Wafadar, his clerks and others who arrived with long faces to announce that his being hit was a bad omen, finally drove Robertson to his feet, feeling there were already quite enough sick and wounded. By this time the hospital was a terrible place, with eighty-five patients, including Captain Campbell's dying orderly trying in his agony to bite back his groans – anything seemed better than his drab repulsive little room.

Townshend's diary recorded his reappearance: 'British Agent all right in spite of his wounds, and told me to tell Subadar Badrinar. Singh . . . and Sepoy Awi Singh (wounded severely) that they would both be recommended for the Order of Merit for bravery.' Since Badrinar Singh had already been recommended for the third class of the order for his bravery during the sortie, he was now likely to find himself promoted to the second class also, with a further increase in pension.

Because of the shortage of men and despite his wounds, Robertson spent the afternoon supervising the making of loopholes in the gun tower for downward fire. This could only be done in daytime because lights in the darkness would have made the working men targets for the enemy. The timber frame had to be sawed through and it was as the saw pierced the wall that the danger began. As soon as the masonry was cleared the besiegers started shooting.

Lieutenant Harley's Sikh carpenter quite naturally 'did not much care for the job' but Robertson made him tie the saw handle to a stick and, sitting in the hole with his knees and ankles jammed against the sides, he was safe even if uncomfortable. But the enemy marksmen had keen sight and he had no sooner settled in, with the hole in the outer wall no more than five inches wide, when a bullet smacked into the earth between his legs. He could not be hit but every time a bullet came, he stopped work and gave Robertson an 'aggrieved' look.

Another long loophole was made – carefully, in case they undermined the rickety gun tower – to prevent any one approaching close enough to set fire to it again. By this time, the rumour was somehow getting around the fort that the comparative quiet was due to the be-siegers' having moved off to take up positions to oppose the relief force.

9 April *was* a quiet day, but now the besiegers began to fling large stones from behind a wall near the summer-house into the officers' mess on the verandah of a court in the south half of the fort. Many of these landed with remarkable accuracy, causing numerous casualties among the garrison, and had to be carried away by the basketful. It was a constant source of irritation to have to dodge them during the day and no less unnerving to have them falling unseen through the darkness at night. In addition, it was considered 'inglorious' to figure in a casualty list as 'badly wounded by a stone'.

One of the Gilgitis, a Pathan by birth, claimed to be an expert with a sling and suggested that he and his friends should repay the enemy in their own coin. The garrison collected to watch while he carefully selected his stone and began to whirl it round his head with a great deal of arm waving. Unfortunately, instead of flying over the parapet, the stone shot off at an angle between the heads of two of the watchers and the project was hurriedly abandoned.

During the afternoon, Robertson climbed to the gun tower to talk to the Sikh sentry. The Sikh, who was staring with tremendous intensity at a gap in the garden wall, suddenly announced that two men, a Chitrali and a Pathan, had just gone by. Since they had to return, he ought to be able to hit one of them. Some time afterwards, his rifle cracked. The Chitrali had run back, doubled up and at full speed; but the Pathan had stalked past slowly, his nose scornfully in the air, and he was dragged away dying.

That evening a Pathan was heard close to the gap. His brother was dead, he wailed, and since his own life now meant nothing to him, he too wanted to die. Gurmokh Singh reacted promptly. 'All right, father-in-law,' he yelled, using a Sikh term of opprobrium, 'take two steps to the front, and you shall go to your brother.' Chivalry, Robertson decided, was 'not . . . the feeling that generations of war between Sikhs and Pathans had developed'.

Though nothing was known of the hardships and the courage of the men in the besieged fort, or even of Colonel Kelly's dour struggle to the east, suddenly the activities of Major-General Low's relieving force became of great interest to the newspaper-reading public. On 9 April both a reserve brigade, which had been formed at Rawalpindi under Brigadier-General M. W. Gosset, and a moveable column at Abbotabad had been ordered to mobilize to join Low. Offers had also poured in from native states maintaining imperial troops, as well as from other states and chiefs, and the Jaypore and Gwalior transport corps had been told to stand by. Almost as if this activity were the signal for an upsurge of excitement, a whole flood of stories had begun to appear in the press.

So far Britain had remained largely indifferent to what was happening in India. With war in the Far East, an insurrection in Peru, massacres in Armenia and fighting in Cuba, a trivial frontier scuffle like Chitral hadn't seemed much to get worked up about and the newspapers had only accorded it a parsimonious paragraph or two. Now the capture of the Malakand Pass had changed all that, and the country woke up with a bang to the fact that what they had assumed to be a skirmish, engaging a mere company or so of some obscure Indian unit, was in fact a conflagration occupying a whole division and some of Britain's finest regiments.

And in 1895 the Victorians were beginning to love their army. The days of the Crimea when the common soldier had been despised as the scrapings of the gutter were over. The army had brought millions of people under Britain's benevolent hand and the time was very close when the country would sing 'Soldiers Of The Queen' and 'God Bless You, Tommy Atkins' – and mean it. And now British officers had been killed, more were prisoners in the hands of savages, and still more were holding out heroically – doubtless bandaged and backgrounded by the Union Jack – against incredible odds in a beleaguered fort. The newspapers came to life overnight and the threadbare paragraphs became whole columns. A rash of pen portraits of the leaders involved began to appear. Old photographs taken by explorers, soldiers and surveyors were dug out and, to titillate their readers, the illustrated magazines produced spirited 'artist's impressions' of the campaign. The garrison at Chitral and Kelly's force came out of all this rather badly, because most of the news of what was happening came south along the telegraph via Peshawar and no one really knew what was happening to the east.

As the furore in the British press grew, the first real information of what it was all like arrived when Jemadar Lal Khan, one of Fowler's sappers, appeared in Peshawar after escaping from his captors and travelling through hostile country disguised as a fakir. For the first time the world began to realize that the fighting was vicious and deadly, and France's jealousy blazed from the pages of *Le Temps*. 'Chitral,' it stated, 'is not unlikely to become an extreme outpost of the Anglo-Indian Empire.'

The protests of those Liberals who felt that Chitral was of no strategic importance, and that the British were intruding unnecessarily into neutral territory, were derided by those who felt they saw a danger from Afghanistan or Russia. As more hard news began to arrive, the columns given to Chitral became pages and everybody of note who had ever fought or administered on the frontier sprang into print with their views on the righteousness of the British cause. 'It is incomprehensible to me,' Lord Roberts observed, 'how anyone conversant with our position in India can arrive at any other conclusion than that Chitral is of great strategical importance.' General Sir Neville Bowles Chamberlain, another Indian army hero, took an opposite view, while the future Field Marshal Sir Charles Henry Brownlow put forward the theory that, instead of being crushed, Umra Khan should be used to found a buffer state. 'A title,' he wrote, 'a subsidy, a present of ... 1000 obsolete rifles, a couple of honeycombed guns, and some bales of half-worn tunics as uniform would complete the equipment of a new dynasty.' Though the idea was sound, the letter was a clear commentary on British arrogance.[1]

The men directly involved were not so much talking as doing, and Colonel Kelly's indefatigable young officers were by now champing at the bit at Mastuj in preparation for the next step forward.

After Chakalwat, Lieutenant Beynon saw Lieutenant Stewart arriving 'as pleased as Punch' at having had a fight at last. He had seemed pained to hear that the enemy was unlikely to be brought to another fight that day and Beynon decided that only twelve hours' bloody fighting with intervals for refreshments would ever satisfy him.

He was now engaged in checking his beloved guns for the next move while the rest of them swopped yarns with Lieutenant Moberly who, as they had marched up from Chakalwat, had finally sallied out followed by the survivors of Captain Ross's party, their long hair streaming behind them as they rushed forward to greet Kelly's men.

For the change in the climate after the heights Kelly's force thanked God, but they were still not very comfortable. Moberly was delighted to see them, however, for though the siege of Mastuj had never been close, it had always been tricky. The enemy had soon built sangars and occupied houses about 300 yards from the walls. The garrison had silenced the fire from them with volleys and on one occasion had made a sortie to drive out the enemy and then whitewash the outside of the loopholes so that they could be seen better in the dark. When the tribesmen had returned they had never been able to understand why the night-time firing of the Puniali levies had improved. Thanks to Moberly's driving energy no one had been hurt but, with its shaky walls and drab dust-covered rooms, Mastuj had been no rest cure and the eagerness of Kelly's men was damped a little when they learned from Lieutenant Jones the details of Captain Ross's death.

As they were sitting down for their first meal, there was a minor alarm when a picket of Sikhs let fly at a group of men along the river bed. The Englishmen dropped cups and knives and forks, and dived for their weapons and equipment. 'Cuss those niggers,' someone

The Southern Relief Force

Top: General Sir Robert Cunliffe Low and his staff. Robertson, arm in sling, is on Low's right and Blood on his left. Hamilton is seated on ground at left

Bottom: Brigadier-General W. F. Gatacre (seated centre) with the Khan of Dir and their staffs

The country

Top: The bowl of the Malakand

Bottom: Camp of 1st Bedfordshires at Tang-o-Bagh

The enemy

Top: 'Ambush', painting by Vereker Hamilton, brother of Ian Hamilton. The tribesmen are armed with rifles and jezails

Bottom: Capture of the Malakand, 3 April 1895. The Gordon Highlanders reach the summit. Illustration from *St Paul's Magazine*

The crossing of the River Swat

Top: Charge across the river by the Guides Cavalry and the 11th Bengal Lancers, launched by Blood. Drawn by John Charlton, after sketch by Lionel James

Bottom: Low's main army fording the river. The village of Chakdara is in the background. Sketch by A. D. Greenhill Gardyne from *Illustrated London News*

The Panjkora River on 13 April after the breaking of the bridge that isolated Battye and the Guides

Cliff road built at Khairabad by Low's Third Brigade. Such roads sometimes hung over drops of 100 feet or more

Graphic war artist's drawing of the descent by Oldham, Beynon and the sappers into the
nullah during Kelly's fight at Nisa Gul, 13 April

Gurkhas crossing the Lowarai Pass

The garden entrance to Chitral fort from which Harley launched his sortie on 17 April.
The fort's construction can clearly be seen in gun tower on left

The exploded mine below the gun tower

Funeral service for Captain J. McD. Baird. The gravestone was erected and carved by his friend, Major Fenton Aylmer, VC

yelled in exasperation. 'Why can't they let us have our tea in peace?' They hadn't missed much because the food at Mastuj was no great improvement on what they'd already endured, but Beynon found a bottle of whisky which had belonged to Lieutenant Fowler, and, 'as he was either a prisoner or dead', and 'wouldn't require it', they settled down to enjoy it.

On 10 April, the second detachment of Kelly's 32nd Pioneers marched in under Lieutenants Peterson and Bethune with the re-maining gear and ammunition for the battery, and Stewart tried a parade to see what his animals could do. It wasn't much. They could hardly crawl under their loads, several fell and all were unreliable.

After the excitement of crossing the Shandur and the fight at Chakalwat, spirits had slumped a little. The fact that Mastuj was a 'horribly dirty and tumbledown old place' didn't help and a hint of what might have happened but for their arrival was given when in a nearby house they discovered a hollowed-out tree trunk that the enemy had been trying to convert into a cannon. Beynon thought the Pathans unduly pessimistic about the strength of the walls. 'A good strong kick would have been sufficient,' he said. Soon afterwards, in fact, part of one of them did fall on a sleeping sepoy and Beynon decided the man must have sneezed.

While the force was still recovering its breath, the Hunza and Puniali levies were sent forward to reconnoitre towards Nisa Gul, with fifty more Punialis heading up the Yarkun valley. Akbar Khan and Wazir Humayun returned with wide grins. The enemy had been seen just ahead and were clearly more than willing to dispute the passage of the ravine. By this time, knowing of Muhammed Isa's treachery towards Edwardes and Fowler, everyone was eager to get to grips with him again and Lieutenant Beynon was once more sent ahead with the two chiefs to reconnoitre.

Climbing from the river bed to a narrow ledge 200 feet above, he and his party left their horses and scrambled among the fallen rocks for about 800 yards to reach a spot where he could see to make his drawing. Muhammed Isa's position, which was extraordinarily strong, was another darband similar to Chakalwat, and the old Mehtar of Chitral, Aman-ul-Mulk, had often shown it to British visitors.

Below Mastuj there were two paths, one a hill track across dangerous rocky slopes on the right bank, the other running over boulder-strewn patches and through an endless series of winding water channels where the road could only be used when the waters were low. After the crossing, this latter track traversed the hill on the right bank to a rolling plateau which stretched from extremely steep slopes on the right to a perpendicular drop to the river on the left. The plateau's most notable feature was an immense fissure, or nullah, which bisected it from right to left, had precipitous sides and was hundreds of feet deep. The road descended by a narrow pathway to the river at the left extremity of this huge cleft and there was an equally stiff climb up the opposite side. At its other end the cleft lost itself in the hills where the unstable shale slopes seemed quite impassable.

While he was sketching this formidable position, Beynon could see heads bobbing up in the sangars, and eventually some of the men came out to watch him so that he was able to identify the weapons with which they were armed. As he worked a bullet struck the ground nearby and he saw that two 'young sparks' on ponies had worked their way towards him. He went on sketching but when one of the two new arrivals started potting at him with a rifle at about 1000 yards – 'Unpardonable waste of ammunition,' Beynon thought coolly – he was obliged to take cover. Humayun, who had been vowing vengeance for the man captured in the skirmish near Laspur ever since they had crossed the Shandur, borrowed his rifle and he and Akbar worked their way down the hill until they were below and only 800 yards from the unsuspecting rifleman. The marksman's friend had joined him now, but Humayun missed what ought to have been a simple shot and the two young men hurriedly mounted and were soon 'legging it . . . as fast as they could go'. The shot had set the sangars 'humming like a beehive', however, and as Beynon's party again came under fire, in another of his inimitable understatements, 'things were quite lively'.

Humayun had a great reputation for courage and was skilled in war and the use of weapons, and Beynon was just chaffing him on the quality of his shooting when a commotion started below them and men began to appear from the sangars. 'Presently,' Beynon said, 'I saw a crowd of men, mostly mounted, with others on foot carrying flags. Then came a fat man in white, with a standard bearer all to himself.' Obligingly every man in the sangars turned out to greet him, and Beynon used his telescope to count them – around 1500 of them.

The fat man was Muhammed Isa and, shutting his telescope, Beynon suggested moving across the river to view the position from the other side. The idea clearly alarmed Humayun.

'Why do you want to cross the river?' he demanded.

'I want to see the end of the nullah,' Beynon said.

'The cavalry will get you.'

'What cavalry?'

'You've just seen two of them.'

He was clearly referring to the two young men who had been potting at them and Beynon grinned. 'Get out,' he said. 'You're pulling my leg!'

But Humayun was serious. Like all hillmen he had an exaggerated fear of cavalry – extraordinary in that rocky country which hardly ever provided level ground – and the two horsemen had clearly unnerved him.

'Don't go,' he warned.

Beynon, who had an infantryman's contempt for horsemen, was adamant. 'Any young buck on a long-tailed screw is a Chevalier Bayard to them,' he wrote home. 'Why, you've only to move ten yards . . . and no cavalry could reach you, while you could sit and chuck stones at them.'

Humayun gave in. 'Where the sahib goes, I follow,' he said gloomily, and they crossed the river to study the nullah – as Beynon had expected, without trouble.

With Muhammed Isa now known to be just ahead, a start was planned for the next day, 13 April, and Lieutenant Oldham set his men to making ladders and collecting ropes to deal with the nullah. The start was made at 7 am on a brilliant morning, a company of the 32nd Pioneers under Lieutenant Peterson leading off with another under Lieutenant Cobbe in support. The main body, under Captain Borradaile, consisted of the rest of the Pioneers, with the levies on their right, followed by Oldham with his sappers, a hundred men of the 4th Kashmir Regiment under Moberly, and Stewart with his mountain guns. Stewart's animals were beginning to recover a little now, with good care and food, and he had an imposing string of them carrying guns, carriages, wheels, and ammunition.

'The first man into Chitral gets a C.B.,' Borradaile shouted cheerfully as they moved forward.

By 11 am the leading companies had extended on the plateau. It was obvious from the sound of bullets that the enemy had a good proportion of Snider and Martini rifles, and their fire brought down a native officer with a bullet in his leg. The Pioneers pressed on without firing back, and the levies were the first on the British side to open fire – at 300 yards. Their instruction in volley firing had only just begun, however, and they were still not very skilled. Every time a man fired before the final word of command the section commander rushed down the line in a fury, slapping him hard with both hands. Since they were all lying down, the slaps fell across their behinds.

As Peterson's and Cobbe's companies attacked the sangars in front, Stewart brought up his guns and Borradaile tackled the hill sangars and scattered groups of Chitralis on the left of Muhammed Isa's line, while Beynon sent the levies across the dangerous shale on the steep inclines at the upper end of the cleft to attack the sangars on the opposite slope.

At first there was difficulty in bringing up the guns because the fire was 'very heavy and trying', and Stewart realized that, owing to the nature of the ground, they would have to go up close to their objectives. But the bullets were falling so thickly that the villagers driving the ponies refused to budge, the man with the leading animal pointing out that he'd be shot if he moved. Stewart drew his revolver and, putting it to the man's head, told him that he'd certainly be shot if he didn't, and that while he might be missed by the enemy he would not be missed by Stewart. The driver 'saw the force of this grim logic' and the guns were brought to a range of around 400 yards. Then the wretched driver fell shot through the stomach, just as he had anticipated, and a guard of Kashmiris had to be rushed up to stop the others bolting.

The animals and spare ammunition were sent to the rear, and Stewart began pounding the main sangar with shells plugged with sand, which burst after entering the target and were more effective than the normal kind which burst on impact. They got a hit with their second round and continued until that particular sangar ceased firing. The concentrated return fire of the enemy was intense for a while, however, and Stewart deliberately walked thirty yards off to the flank to draw their aim from his men. He was careful not to stand still, but issued his orders while walking up and down. He could hear the bullets singing past and striking the ground at his feet but he was 'too busy to pay much attention'. The earth around him was literally jumping under the fusillade but he was cool enough to hear men of the Pioneers warning their friends to keep clear of the artillery.[2]

Situated on a steep slope, the sangar was hard to demolish, but as it fell to pieces the stones rolled clear. In the middle of the firing, a big dog ran out to dash delightedly at the dust kicked up by the bullets, until it was finally hit by a stray and bolted away yelping, with its tail between its legs. The sangar was a ruin by now and its garrison began to slip away. They didn't get very far.

'That sangar was a death-trap . . .' Beynon said. 'Their only line of escape was across some open shaly slopes within 400 yards of our firing line. . . . The result was like rabbit shooting. You'd see a man jump from the sangar and bolt across the slope, slipping and scrambling as he went; then there would be a volley and you'd see the dust fly all round him – perhaps he'd drop, perhaps he wouldn't; then there'd be another volley and you'd see him chuck forward amid a laugh from the sepoys, and he'd roll over and over till he'd fetch up against a rock and lie still. Sometimes two or three would bolt at once; one or two would drop at each volley, and go rolling, limp and shapeless, down the slope until they were all down, and there would be a wait for the next lot.' Only one man escaped.

As the fire slackened and the guns were limbered up, the trembling villagers and their ponies were sent for to move them to the opposite end of the line. Only the top of the central fortifications could be seen and the range was close enough to count the stones on top. Deciding he must get the guns into position before the defenders realized what was happening, Stewart led them up personally. The battery sergeant-major, two ponies and a driver had already been hit and he warned the gunners they would have to be quick, but, as they ran forward, crouching against the bullets, Stewart saw daylight through the loop-holes of the sangar and realized it had already emptied. Since the sangar at the other end of the line had come to life again, however, two shells were fired at it 'just for the look of the thing', but another N.C.O. was hit, a third shot dead, and a young gunner, little more than a boy, wounded in three places. By now, fifty per cent of the men on the two guns were out of action so Stewart retired them and asked Kelly for permission to look for a route down the precipitous nullah across their path.

Oldham and Beynon had also asked for leave to find a crossing; eventually they found such a spot and the dashing Oldham brought up his sappers while Beynon reported the find to Kelly. For the first forty feet the descent was fairly easy so that a man hanging on to a rope could hack rough steps with a pick. But after that came a vertical drop where a descent could only be made with ladders.

All the time the little group was under galling fire. A sapper was mortally wounded and a havildar was shot through the groin. Oldham scrambled down the rope, however, and placed a ladder with his own hands. A dozen men followed him down and, by cutting foot-holds, reached the bottom. The lower they climbed the safer they were and the thirteen men now began to attack the opposite side. To their delight they found a rough goat-track which they scaled 'on all fours'. It was tremendously risky to climb up to unreconnoitred ground to face an unknown enemy but, reaching the top, Oldham saw that Cobbe had been quick to support him by lining the opposite side of the nullah with his Pioneers, and he waved a handkerchief to identify himself and shouted to them to hurry over.

Seeing the first of the British across, a few Chitralis began to slip away but, as they did so, a chance bullet struck one of a few slabs of gun cotton Oldham had brought forward in case he needed them and laid on the ground by the nullah where he had made his descent. The gun cotton began to blaze a few yards in front of Cobbe's men and he prudently retired his company which had been on the point of following Moberly and Beynon. The Kashmiri infantry were also ordered back and might have continued marching enthusiastically all the way to Mastuj if they hadn't been halted by Browning-Smith, the surgeon, who, once more slipping easily into a military role, wheeled them about and sent them forward again. These backward movements were regarded as a retreat by the Chitralis and they surged forward again, cheering.

Beynon, who had followed Oldham into the nullah and up the other side, chased by his orderly and Moberly, reached the top just as Oldham realized he was on his own with his few men in front of the advancing Chitralis. They were in an incredibly dangerous position: three British officers, Beynon's orderly and eleven sappers armed only with carbines – the orderly the only man with a bayonet. Fortunately there was a low ridge just in front which they could line, but as they moved forward the strap of Beynon's sandal broke and he had to cram it into his haversack and lollop along with one bare foot. When they reached the ridge the Chitralis in the sangar began to retreat once more, racing over the steep hillside. Horsemen posted on the plateau by Muhammed Isa drove them back yet again, but fortunately Borradaile had seen the danger by this time and pushed Cobbe forward. As he and his men crossed, the enemy finally took to their heels, 'a stream of horse and foot . . . about 500 yards away' in front of Oldham, Beynon, Moberly and the few sappers. Delighted to find themselves on the winning side again, the Kashmiris fired volleys after them as fast as they could. As they fled, the levies arrived just at the right time and slid down to occupy the sangar. Colonel Kelly's force still had to cross by the road. As the Chitralis retreated they paused behind every large stone to fire and, because the climb into and out of the nullah was a difficult one, they were able to get away with only a small loss.

The fight had been a brilliant piece of work even allowing for the enemy's lack of guns, because the sangars proved to be immensely strong affairs of huge logs and boulders that required many men to move. In one of them a man in a red robe was clutching a native jezail, and Beynon had just whipped out his revolver when he identified himself as the levy captured in the skirmish at Laspur. His carbine and clothes had been stolen and he had acquired the red robe and the jezail to take their place.

'Humayun,' Beynon shouted, 'your levy is over there.'

'Is he alive?' Humayun demanded fiercely, ready to vent his spite on the prisoners he had taken if he weren't. Assured that he was, he seized hold of Beynon's hands to kiss them violently, and Beynon skipped out of reach just before he could kiss him on the lips.

Most of the British casualties had occurred when the men were grouped together and only one British officer, Moberly, was touched, the palm of his hand being grazed by a bullet which passed between it and his thigh. It was his second close shave. Two years before he had been wounded by a bullet which had grazed the top of his skull and knocked him unconscious.

By this time the garrison at Chitral had been besieged for six long anxious weeks and had fought off several determined attacks. To the south, Major-General Low could easily guess that ammunition, food, energy and probably even hope must be running out but, with Lieutenant Edwardes safe, his problem now was to bring Lieutenant Fowler to safety as well. Away to the east, Colonel Kelly – also well aware of the urgency of the problem and with Muhammed Isa still in front of him, still unbroken and across an appalling road – was trying to decide his next move. His force had bivouacked on 13 April beyond the captured fortifications of Nisa Gul at Sanogher where a deputation of villagers came to meet them, half-naked, their clothes stolen by Humayun's vengeful levies in return for the clothes of the man who had reappeared at Nisa Gul. The headmen offered 'the usual yarn' about being *compelled* to fight the British, and the British made 'their usual reply' by demanding porters.

When the column moved on again in the afternoon of 14 April, rather than risk the defile where Captain Ross's force had been annihilated, Kelly decided to follow the route over the hills, and the track of Stewart's battery was soon dotted with the stiff ugly carcasses of dead ponies. So many died, in fact, that eventually drag ropes had to be fastened to the guns and the men had to pull themselves to prevent the remaining overloaded brutes staggering from the path.

Nearing Drasan in an area of cornfields and apricot and peach trees in bloom, Beynon went ahead with the levies to see if the fort there was occupied. It was deserted, like the villages around, and using a tree as a battering ram the levies broke down the door and 'went through the place like professional burglars'. Beynon had hardly reached the courtyard by the time they found the grain store.

To repair the broken bridge for the following troops, they tore down a verandah, and when Kelly arrived with the main column it was in working order. 'It was pretty rickety,' Beynon admitted '. . . but only one man fell in.' The battery forded the river and the baggage animals were swum across, their loads being carried by hand.

They set off again the next day, their main problem now the terrifyingly narrow roads along the cliffs. One battery pony rolled down a slope with a gun on its back without much harm, and soon afterwards two donkeys disappeared down a hundred-foot drop. During this day's march and the next they saw decaying bodies floating down the river or stranded on shoals, which they assumed to be the remains of the Sikhs killed with Ross or perhaps some of Edwardes' party. Jaded and exhausted, they reached Baranis on 17 April. The road had been entirely demolished and the bridge over the river burned to a cinder. The stream was forded, however, the soldiers crossing in parties of four or five, their packs carried on their heads and the water up to their waists.

'Most of the coolies,' Beynon said, 'crossed in parties of a dozen or more, holding hands, but now and then a man tried by himself, generally with the result that half-way across he was swept off his feet and went floating downstream, vainly endeavouring to regain his footing.' Then there was a rush of two or three of the levies who had been stationed downstream on horseback especially for that purpose; the man was swung on to his feet, and his load fished out. 'One man I thought was bound to be drowned,' Beynon went on. 'He had somehow tied his load to his head and . . . his head was kept . . . below the water while his legs remained waving frantically in the air.' Inevitably Stewart refused to be parted from his guns, while the other British officers, sometimes carrying as many as eight rifles, struggled through the current, dragging long lines of exhausted sepoys hanging on to the tails of their ponies.

In the afternoon, Kelly arrived with the main body and at 5 pm the rearguard came in. There was still no news of the garrison at Chitral.

General Low was equally in the dark about Chitral but at least he knew what Umra Khan was up to, because on 16 April Fowler had followed Edwardes into his camp.

Because of the hostility of the unruly hillmen, Fowler had been kept hidden during daylight in what had formerly been the harem at Mundiah and was only allowed exercise on the roof after dark. There had been bad news for him on the night of 15 April when a letter arrived to say that the Indian government had sent back a firm 'no' to Umra Khan's request for a truce and negotiations for Fowler's release had been broken off; but the next day, Umra Khan, despite the knowledge that he had been ruined by the adventure in Chitral, decided that Fowler must leave. Dressed as a Pathan and protected by a few horsemen and tattermedalion foot soldiers, Fowler was sent off, and, 'as lighthearted and as gay as if they were marching to the sack of Indian cities', the party moved towards the British outposts. After a while the British were seen and the horsemen turned back so that only the armed scarecrows on foot remained as escort. Fowler tied a white rag to his cudgel and began to wave it over his head. Finally all his companions except two halted 600 yards from Low's men, Fowler fervently hoping that the Pathan idea of a joke would not persuade them to shoot him down at the last moment.

A group of Sikhs ordered him to stop, telling him they were looking for a British officer. Then, as he dismounted, they realized he was not a Pathan at all and crowded round him excitedly, grinning and shouting.[1]

With both Edwardes and Fowler released, it was now possible for Low to press on without fear of jeopardizing their lives, and with Aylmer's suspension bridge at last across the Panjkora, his column got on the move again on 17 April.

By this time, with the campaign reaching its climax, the government of India was growing concerned that if Umra Khan was deposed, Jandol, like Chitral, would become a bone of contention among neighbouring states and involve them in a whole series of wars, so they were now offering him asylum in India until they could decide what to do about his future. He was still said to be at Mundiah and to discover exactly where he was, Brigadier-General Blood rode into the

Jandol Valley and advanced upon the fort with an escort of Guides cavalry and Lancers. There wasn't a soul around as the walls of the fort came into view, and the first person they saw was a man ploughing his fields.

'Could you tell me where the Sardar Umra Khan is?' Blood asked.

The man pointed. 'The Sardar is at Mundiah Fort. His army is at Miankilai.'

He agreed to carry a letter, and Blood summoned Captain Nixon, of Intelligence, who to his dictation wrote a letter telling Umra Khan that he would be wise to give himself up. The main column would be arriving in two hours, he said, and then Umra Khan would have to decide whether to fight, surrender, or escape over the Afghan border. If he took the first or third courses his life would probably be short. If he took the second, however, Blood would see he was well treated.

The ploughman ran off, and Blood planted a lance bearing a Union Jack in the ground while his escort dispersed to find what shade they could. Meanwhile, Umra Khan's men came streaming out of the village and took up a position about half a mile away at the other side of a small river. Though they made a lot of noise, they made no move to attack.

The ploughman returned an hour later with a letter from Umra Khan, which said he would be glad to surrender but that he had 3000 ghazis around him who wouldn't let him. 'You, too, I notice, are accompanied by those cut-throats of yours,' he continued – a reference which delighted the Guides – '. . . Now I propose that you send away your cut-throats and I will send away mine, and then you and I can have our conference alone in the field.'

It seemed a friendly enough offer, but then Blood noticed that the tribesmen by the river were beginning to threaten the flanks of his cavalry, a move which made any meeting out of the question. At this moment Brigadier-General Gatacre arrived in his usual tearing hurry with the Third Brigade, the 11th Bengal Lancers, and the Derajat Mountain battery. Blood asked him to make a quick frontal attack on Umra Khan's men while he personally led the cavalry in a wide sweep to cut off their retreat to the north and east. Gatacre, who was senior to Blood, refused in his fussy manner to co-operate. Blood was no respector of seniority or rank and was an old hand at frontier fighting.

He also had little love for Gatacre, and his hot Irish blood rose during the argument that followed. While it was still going on Low himself rode up with the remainder of the column. To Blood's fury, he supported Gatacre.

As the mountain battery opened fire, Umra Khan's men began to move away, and Gatacre followed them until evening. His brigade halted for the night well ahead of the rest of the column, and the Second Brigade were ordered up in the expectation that the Pathans would make a stand the next day. Blood's judgement had been the better one, however, because they were already streaming away up the Nawagai valley. Next morning, when Low and his staff rode forward, they found the fort abandoned, and spies came in with the report that Umra Khan had crossed the Afghan border with eleven mule-loads of gold, silver and jewels – worth over £50,000. Blood always felt that if he had been the senior officer Umra Khan would never have got away.

The sole occupant of Mundiah fort proved to be one deformed half-wit. Books, grain, stolen rifles, and £10,000 worth of coin sealed in government boxes were discovered, and there were also several dismounted cannon. On one, a big eighteen-hundredweight weapon, was inscribed the name of the maker, Ustaz Gholam Khan, who had also worked into the metal a scrap of verse which, when translated, read:

> The iron voluntarily being produced,
> This heavy gun, a most tremendous sound,
> What can I say? Is this a gun or is it a dragon?
> In Hindustan or Kabul no such gun is to be found.

Other guns were similarly inscribed, and several interesting documents were found. Among them was a letter written by a mullah seated at the head of the Malakand Pass watching Low's force camp below, which went, 'We see the infidels, the sons of pigs . . . in the plain below us. There are very few of them and we shall easily send them all to Hell.' According to George Younghusband, the mullah had probably spent the next few days 'breaking the record towards Upper Swat'.

There was also correspondence from a Scottish firm in Bombay offering Umra Khan anything he required in the way of arms and ammunition, and even enclosing photographs of quick-firing guns. 'Our price for Maxim guns,' one of the letters ran, 'is 3700 rupees each and our revolvers at thirty-four rupees a piece.' The documents were sent at once to Peshawar, and the firm in question hurriedly decided to transfer its offices to Cairo.

Time was still desperately important as they reformed, and that day the sense of urgency became even greater because, even as Colonel Kelly was fording the Chitral river far to the north, Low received fresh news of the garrison at Chitral itself from the Khan of Dir. From this it seemed that, beaten to their knees, short of rations and having to fight for every drop of water, they were now about to be finally overwhelmed by the use of mines which had already been burrowed to within fifteen feet of the towers of the fort.

Low had already sent Gatacre ahead in the direction of Dir with two battalions, several guns and twenty days' rations, in pursuit of Umra Khan. As the champion record-breaker of the expedition, it was believed Gatacre could force his way through if anyone could. He had already thrust beyond the Janbatai ridge, but was still five days' march from Chitral, and though Churchill was to describe it two years later as 'a triumph of engineering', the road to Dir was still appalling for an army. The hanging galleries at Baitari ahead of Kelly were repeated here along equally daunting cliffs, while at other points the road zigzagged round spurs in the most alarming fashion.

The situation did not permit of any hesitation, however, and, flashing the information to Simla, Low ordered Gatacre to press on as rapidly as possible. Gatacre neeed no urging. Hourly expecting to hear the distant explosion that would announce all was over at Chitral, he nagged his men forward. Dir, a tumbledown fort surrounded by a dirty straggling village, was taken, but the road beyond was once again 'awful' and 'a drizzling rain started'. At one point, men and mules had to slide down a long shale chute where one officer found himself being pursued by a mule moving considerably faster than he was. He just managed to throw himself aside as the kicking animal shot past. Various methods of descent were used. Litters for the wounded were converted into hammocks slung between two men, and a nineteen-stone Bengali commissariat clerk was wrapped in a tarpaulin and simply pushed off into the void. Picking themselves up at the bottom, order was restored and they set off once more.[2]

Inside the fort at Chitral everyone had grown very tired by this time and Surgeon-Captain Whitchurch's health had been badly affected. Overwork and exhaustion in the stinking, pain-filled hospital had brought him down and he was racked by a fever, though he could always overcome the high temperatures from which he was suffering to help in an emergency.

Robertson was also depressed by the pain of his wound and his nerves were very much on edge. Captain Townshend and the others suggested that some of the men of the mixed company he commanded were not entirely trustworthy and asked him to bolster them up with a few Kashmiri Gurkhas. But these 'irregular regular' soldiers were horrifyingly clumsy and difficult to order about because they couldn't speak Hindustani and Robertson couldn't speak Gurkhali, and they so exasperated him that he hurriedly dispensed with their services.

By this time, with the fortifications that had to be manned and the repairs that were always a matter of grave concern in the tumbledown old fort, there were simply not enough men to do everything. And with everyone awkward with weariness or weak with illness, walls put up one day fell down the next, and an aperture being made for a loophole would suddenly crumble until it was large enough for two men to push through abreast.

There was another lively night on 10 April with firing and shouting from all sides of the fort, and an attack from the west seemed imminent. To the weary garrison the night alarms were growing unbearable by now and, though the shooting from the fort had greatly improved, the enemy was also learning tricks, and this time instead of the usual ragged firing, a shouted order was followed by a flash and the thunderclap of a disciplined volley. Since they had heard that scaling ladders wide enough to support three men abreast had been constructed, this was thought to be the start of a big attack and Wafadar made sure once more that the long spears were at hand. During this little battle the untrustworthy Chitralis had seemed unusually perturbed and little

Shuja-ul-Mulk was so terrified that for once he abandoned his dignity and burst into tears.

The next day was glorious with the sun nailed to the sky but, instead of lifting the jaded spirits of the garrison, it only served to increase their misery. Lovely and pale, Tirich Mir showed its unruffled outline against an unclouded sky, in sharp contrast with the strident greys, browns, yellows and purples of the surrounding hills, but its serene beauty only filled Robertson's mind with thoughts of human insignificance.

Townshend also noticed, as he and Lieutenant Gurdon drank their tea together on the parapet and watched the dawn break, that the mountain looked 'very imposing and solemn'. He was feeling a little gloomy because his dog had been shot as it strayed out of the fort below the stables. He was also still troubled by the unreliable Kashmiris. One of the sentries had been found asleep, and Townshend had informed the Kashmiri officers that the man must be tried by court martial and sentenced to death. 'We are not safe with this damned regiment,' he said bitterly. 'They seem utterly callous as to what happens!'

By evening, the calm had ended and, though the stone-throwing stopped, the besiegers were drumming away again for polo or dancing. A solitary voice flinging abuse was interspersed by trumpet calls, and the watch-fires on the walls were lit.

On 12 April groups of men on foot and on horseback were seen moving up the valley carrying banners and apparently setting off towards Mastuj. The move seemed too ostentatious to mean anything because if Sher Afzul had wished to use his men to oppose a relieving force it would have been more normal for him to move them after dark and leave the garrison to believe he was as strong as ever. And when in the late afternoon, one of the Sikhs was found shot dead on the west parapet over the main gate – hit clean through the eye from one of the enemy's nearer works – another sharp fight was expected during the night.

Tirich Mir, its snowy surface glowing with salmon and copper tints in the late sun, was carefully watched as it faded in the dusk because its changing colour was usually the signal for pandemonium to break loose. This night was no exception and a clamour started from the summer-house corner – howls and yells accompanied by drum-beating and the strains of 'some unusually lacerating musical instrument of the horn species', while showers of stones were poured into the fort. The sentries fired a few shots but there was no attack.

By this time, however, mere harassment was sufficient. Enclosed in the four narrow walls, little evils had become mountainous and one of their many irritations was a small monkey which stole official diaries, papers and small cherished articles. In addition the carcasses of the dead ponies lay just outside the walls, repulsive and stinking, and the garrison dogs were in the habit of getting over the walls to feed on them.

Probably noticing how easy they found it, one of the Chitrali youths also suddenly leapt one of the barrier walls and was soon among the trees. It was believed he had been sent out by the other Chitralis to cover themselves with friendly messages in case of defeat, but Sher Afzul 'must have been in a vicious temper' that day because he was immediately put to death. After that no one else tried to desert.

On 13 April the number of casualties in the hospital had dropped to seventy-six, but all were serious, and Robertson was beginning to think that if they were not relieved until May the rations would have to be further reduced. Men were still seen marching up the valley and the evening drumming, singing, abuse and stone-throwing began again. On the morning of 14 April it was noticed that the big sangar on the west had been connected to another by a trench roofed with leaves. These were quite as effective as stronger defences because the garrison could not afford to shoot at anything they could not see. By that evening the garrison had been besieged for forty-two days.

Rab Nawaz Khan was still warning about the possibility of mining against the gun tower from the summer-house and everyone was told to keep his ears open. But nothing was heard and, though one of the sentries thought he heard a pick on 16 April, it was not repeated and, since mining was 'most unusual in a hill tribe', the fears began to recede. That night, however, the enemy began to drum particularly noisily and it suddenly occurred to Townshend that perhaps the racket was less to hide the fact that enemy troops were being detached than to drown the noise of picks. It was known that they had taken prisoner a few of Fowler's sappers who could well have been forced to apply

H

their knowledge, and men had certainly been seen working hard in the summer-house as long ago as the beginning of the month. The thought of how far they might have pushed underground by now was worrying and Townshend warned the sentries in the gun tower and at the main gate again, and sure enough after midnight the sentry in the lower storey of the gun tower reported the noise of a pick from the direction of the summer-house, just as Rab Nawaz Khan had suggested.

Going to the tower, Townshend listened intently but could hear nothing. During the morning of the next day, however – the day Low received his alarming message from the Khan of Dir – he was sent for again and this time he distinctly heard the sound of a tool being used close by underground. He sent for Robertson and from the long loophole they had constructed after the attempt to fire the tower, they could quite clearly make out the muffled thud of a pick in the earth – even the higher-pitched ring as it struck stone.

The enemy was not more than ten or twelve feet from where they stood! [3]

The thing had been pure luck

25

The thought of the enemy burrowing beneath them took their breath away. It would require little in the way of an explosion to crumble the rubble-filled fortifications and only one small breach was needed for the besiegers to pour through.

Townshend and Robertson looked at each other with worried faces, and began to discuss the possibility of a counter-mine. Sifat had followed Robertson to the loophole, and, though he could not understand English, he was intelligent enough to know exactly what they were saying and immediately suggested a sortie. Townshend later claimed the suggestion came from him, but Robertson heard Sifat vehemently whispering over his shoulder – 'Bahar Jana, Bahar Jana' – which was his way of saying they should make an attack. 'I acquiesced at once,' Robertson said, 'and so did Townshend.'

As Townshend went to listen once more to the dull thuds, 'so menacing and yet so full of fascination', Robertson turned again to the resourceful Sifat.

'How many men, Sifat?' he asked. 'Sixty?'

'No, a hundred,' the Puniali answered and Robertson agreed.

Studying the area from which the sound came, it was decided that the mine shaft more than likely originated from the summer-house as they had expected, and a 'forlorn hope' was therefore immediately made up consisting of forty Sikhs under their own officer and sixty Kashmiri riflemen under a subadar, with Lieutenant Harley in overall command. Lieutenant Gurdon begged to be allowed to go, too, but it was felt they dared not risk more than one officer. Under some initial misapprehension that he wasn't to lead his own men, Harley appeared in front of Robertson 'with a terribly aggrieved face, to substantiate his claims to be the first man knocked on the head'. After forty-five days of siege it was reassuring that some spirits were still high enough for two young men to argue their fitness to lead such a desperate venture.

It was felt that the attack should be made as soon as possible, and 4 pm that same day was settled on. Townshend began to write out the orders, while Harley selected the explosives to blow up the mine. He was still the garrison's only expert and had spent a lot of his leisure time filling canvas bags with the gunpowder which had been found in the fort. Into the middle of these bags, which weighed between fifty and one hundred pounds, he had thrust the end of a long narrow canvas tube filled with gunpowder as a substitute for a fuse. The whole thing was then enclosed in a larger bag made of waterproof sheeting to guard against the damp, and from this larger bag the long canvas hose could easily be drawn and used to fire the charge when it had been tamped. Harley had had no particular object in view when he had made the charges, and had thought only that they might be useful for demolitions. Selecting two of the bags, one of fifty and one of sixty pounds, he also arranged to carry a dozen pickaxes in case the mine had to be broken down by hand.

As the men began to gather by the door of the garden entrance to the fort, the heavy stones forming a barricade behind it were stealthily removed. The enemy was so close by this time they had to be handled carefully in case the men outside heard a noise and suspected something. Then Townshend gathered the native officers round him and explained the object of the sortie. They must, he urged, pass on every scrap of information he gave them to the N.C.O.s who in turn must explain everything to the men, so that every single individual leaving the fort would know what had to be done, in case he was the only man left alive to do it. All the officers were to carry matches, and only bayonets were to be used in the attack on the summer-house so that the rest of the enemy forces would not be alerted too soon. The job had to be done quickly, he ended, *and they could expect no support*.

Normally a gay, cheerful young man, Harley wore a quiet look of concentrated energy and self-possessed eagerness. He was dressed like his men, even to wearing a turban, and Robertson reminded him not to get too far ahead of his front line and to keep five trustworthy soldiers alongside him so that he would not be singled out by sharp-shooters. Harley nodded, knowing as well as Robertson that if he should fall the sortie would probably fail through lack of leadership and the mine succeed. Robertson also asked him to bring in prisoners if possible, so they could find out what was happening outside.

The parapets and towers were quietly manned and, hearts thumping, Harley's party pressed closer to the gate in a tight silent group. They all knew the 'awful significance of that incessant pick-pick-picking at the foot of the gun tower . . . approaching nearer and nearer; each stroke with suggestions of overwhelming catastrophe'. Everything depended on the summer-house not being too strongly held, and Robertson felt physically sick with apprehension.

At 4 pm, the gate was swung open and Harley ran out with his men. They could push through only two or three at a time and he had to wait until about a dozen of them had joined him near a built-up area of the garden. Then he made a rush, followed by the rest of his men as they emerged.

Priding themselves on knowing nothing of Pathan methods of fighting, the Chitralis had handed over the defence of the summer-house and the garden wall to Umra Khan's Pathan soldiers. But an 'arrogant childish vanity' was always a part of the Pathan character.[1] They considered themselves superior to Indian troops who, they felt, only beat them because of their superior arms. They had even been known to appeal to the sporting instincts of British generals to send away their artillery and fight their battles with them man to man, and now the persistently defensive tactics of the garrison at Chitral had made them grow contemptuous. This was an attitude Robertson had hopefully anticipated. When he had been shut up in Sherpur in 1879 the defenders had constantly been abused by the Pathans as '*Kila-bund badmashes*' – cowardly rascals who dared not emerge from their defences – and he was hoping that they were simply not expecting a sortie. It was a good guess. In their carelessness, fatalism and arrogance, the Pathans were not even on the alert.

There were about forty of them in the summer-house, together with a few Chitralis, but they were completely taken by surprise and only a few straggling shots met Harley's rush. They recovered quickly and fired a volley into the faces of the charging men, killing two and severely wounding an over-eager Gurkha who had squeezed himself into the front rank reserved for the Sikhs.

There were not even any barricades in front of the summer-house, only a wall of bundles of compressed green twigs, and the attackers were inside the building in a matter of seconds. Bayonet work cleared it, the enemy – apart from those inside the mine – fleeing along the garden wall to the far corner of the garden where, throwing up a temporary sangar, they began to direct a well-sustained fire at the summer-house. Harley's quick success had been dearly paid for, however, and uniformed figures sprawled among the trees in 'the massive limpness of death'. On the back of a dead Gurkha, a copper bugle gleamed in the sunshine.

A violent outburst of firing had started all round the fort as soon as the besiegers realized what was happening, and they raced up from all sides to reinforce the sangars. Believing the sortie to be a despairing effort by a starving garrison to cut their way free, they pressed forward delightedly to wipe them out. As the firing increased, inside the fort the men on the walls became frantic with excitement as they worked their weapons, eyes glaring and everybody shouting and no one listening. Rab Nawaz Khan flourished a revolver with wild gestures and a maniac laugh. Near him a Kashmiri soldier, his head whirling, was actually aiming at the summer-house, now occupied by Harley, when Robertson grabbed him and twisted him round to face the river. Even the Sikhs in the hospital came crawling out. Several had lost part of their feet from frostbite but they dragged themselves up the ladders to the parapets, shouting with joy at the prospect of a fight at last in broad daylight. It took a long time to bring some order to what was going on, and meanwhile Gurmokh Singh, Robertson's 'splendid thick-headed old gentleman', was dancing with rage at the sight of them and shouting that 'it was a soldier's first duty to obey, that they had been ordered to hospital, and that there they must stay'.[2]

It was in the middle of the uproar, with everyone 'literally standing on tiptoe and sweating with excitement' that Robertson saw the point of a remark of Harley's about Gurdon. At critical times, he had said, the young political officer kept so cool he was positively irritating. And now indeed Gurdon calmly reported to him with a quiet, gentle smile which Robertson found 'astonishing to behold' in that scene of frenzied action. 'Is there anything you want me to do, sir?' he asked mildly, and for the first time Robertson fully appreciated just how it was he had managed to bring the relics of Baird's decimated group to safety through the very middle of Sher Afzul's screaming men on 3 March.

By this time the enemy were directing a tremendous fire against the waterway, stables, defences and the south face of the fort. Bullets were kicking up spurts of dust and chips of stone from the walls, and streaming through the open door of the garden entrance. 'The guard formed a respectful lane,' Robertson reported dryly, and only one man was hit there. Wounded men were beginning to reach the hospital, however, one of them a water-carrier, his jaw broken by a bullet. In spite of his injury and the shock he must have been suffering, he picked up his great skin bag as soon as his injury was dressed and was just about to go to work again when Robertson halted him.

Meanwhile, in the summer-house, Harley was being galled by the tremendous fire. His men were replying independently, but not very successfully, and he calmly stopped them and made them fire in volleys instead. These immediately took effect, and he began to look for the mine shaft which was eventually found outside the wall of fascines that had been broken down in the first headlong charge. Frantically clearing away the fascines, Harley called for volunteers from the Kashmiri Gurkhas who he felt would be more use with their kukhris in the confined space of the tunnel than a Sikh with a rifle and bayonet. There were no offers, and only one Dogra dragged out his great knife and jumped into the pit.

The Sikhs pressed forward eagerly, however, and six were selected, to descend two at a time while the remainder stood at the top to drag out the Chitralis as they appeared. The minute a man showed, armed or unarmed, he was bayoneted and hoisted out of the way. By this time, the frenzy of the fighting had roused all Harley's men – Sikhs, Gurkhas and Dogras – to a furious rage of excitement. With frantic yells of 'Kill! Kill!' they cut down the wretched men as they emerged one by one and it was all Harley could do even to save two as prisoners.

Stumbling over the scattered wreckage and the sprawled bodies of the dead and wounded, Harley now brought up his powder bags. Clearing the shaft of men, he dropped into it with one Sikh, quite unaware of how many enemies were still below. A swordsman appeared, but the Sikh grabbed the great curved weapon with one hand and drove home his bayonet with the other. In the noise and the reek and the fury, only death could have restrained the Sikhs; and the mine-workers, guessing what was happening, knew they had to die at the top of the shaft or be blown to pieces inside. Finally believing it clear, Harley began to place his explosives but, as he did so, two last desperate Chitralis struggled out and in their confused hurry their feet tore the long powder hose to pieces.

Harley was in despair. Even if there had been time to break down the shaft by hand the men carrying the picks had flung them aside to use their rifles, and they had disappeared in the long grass. In the fort Townshend was worried sick about the passing of time and, seeing numbers of the enemy gathering near the stables, he withdrew a few Sikhs from the parapet and put them in the east tower and along the garden front. Then, in desperation, he sent three different messages to Harley telling him to hurry.

In fact, Harley was doing everything in his power, and by the greatest of good fortune he now found a twenty-foot length of his tubing-fuse still intact. He was just about to jump back into the shaft to connect it when a violent explosion occurred in front of him, and the blast surging up the tunnel knocked him flat and burned the turbans and hair of the Sikhs. The powder bags he had placed had somehow exploded prematurely, or else been set off by some surviving miner inside the shaft or a stray shot from one of the sepoys.

Watching from the gallery of the gun tower, Robertson saw an enormous puff of smoke rise 'like a huge white balloon'. Then Harley's men came racing back in two parties, Harley himself last of all, bringing with him one of the prisoners. Several of them were hit and fell, but no one was seriously hurt despite the tempestuous fire. As they dashed into the fort the door was slammed shut and quickly rebarricaded.

It had taken just over an hour. [3]

The garden gate area was a confusion of panting men boasting and shouting the names of their friends. The Sikhs, 'still raging with excitement, crowded forward to recite the numbers they had killed, and to exhibit their stained bayonets and blood-splashed faces'. The wounded were carried to the hospital, one of them – an exceptionally brave man who had been among the first to be hit – shrieking in agony and humiliated by having to scream out the remainder of his life like a woman, something he regarded as far worse than death itself.

Wretched with a sense of failure, Harley was downcast and angry because the premature explosion had brought down only about three yards of the roof of the mine. The rest remained intact but, through the 'bitter . . . cold dismay' that shook him too, Robertson realized that there was still no time to be lost. A second sortie was out of the question because the enemy were already crowding back into the summer-house. And so, guided by Wafadar and Sifat, he started the digging of counter-mines, Sifat being promised a large sum of money if his men could penetrate beyond the walls in time to intercept the enemy tunnel.

They were still working with frenzied energy when the imperturbable Gurdon came down from the tower and, in his driest manner, observed casually that the enemy seemed to have dug a trench which reached almost to the wall. Harley's gunpowder had done its work after all. The frail roof of the tunnel, unsupported by beams, had slowly sunk down, collapsing from end to end, leaving only occasional narrow earth bridges where tree roots acted as supports. The Pathans had shown great skill and the tunnel, which was fifty yards long, had been constructed in zigzag fashion to drive the blast against the walls. It was only eighteen inches below the surface, direction being given to the men working underground by sticks driven through at intervals from above under cover of darkness.

The garrison stared silently at its crumbling edges. 'The explosion,' Townshend noted in his diary '. . . had burst out the whole mine . . . the result . . . could not have been better if we had had Engineer officers.'

His heart was full of unspoken relief, and he felt he had finally been proved right in refusing to allow any useless sorties. They had been saved, but he was under no delusions. 'The thing had been pure luck,' he said.

I

Quiet as the ghosts they resembled

26

The destruction of the tunnel[1] left the garrison in high spirits again, with Robertson convinced that his luck had finally turned.

'Back swung the pendulum triumphantly,' he said. 'With the conviction of a zealot, I declared to everyone that our troubles were over.' Nevertheless, to relax would still be dangerous, and he agreed with Townshend that the digging of the counter-mines should not be stopped. The 'butcher's bill' had been a big one. Townshend's estimate of the enemy's casualties was between forty and fifty killed, about thirty-five of them in and around the mine shaft, while Harley's men had lost twenty-one killed and wounded.

Despite the losses, they had been lucky. According to Harley's two prisoners, a major assault had been planned for the following day to coincide with an attempt to burn the water tower. Movable shelters had been constructed, beneath which fires were to have been kindled against the wall and the attack had been postponed only because the Pathans had expected to create a breach in the walls by demolishing the gun tower. There was one other item of news which heartened the garrison. With a reluctance that added to the conviction that it was correct, the prisoners admitted that Mastuj had been reached by a force from Gilgit and that the Chitralis had fallen back ten miles to defend the Nisa Gul cutting.

The awareness that they had regained the initiative made the officers' mess a cheerful place that evening and even the smokers did better than usual. With the air of a conspirator, Wafadar produced about twenty Egyptian cigarettes belonging to Shuja-ul-Mulk which he doled out one at a time. Whitchurch finished his at speed and then watched with 'wolfish eyes' as the others burnt their fingertips and moustaches.

During the early part of the night, the besiegers were heard moving about under cover, cautiously dragging away their dead. Harley's dead sepoys had had to be abandoned. Just before midnight the sound of cheering was heard but the watching garrison could not make out why and apart from a few shots the night was quiet.

They felt that a lot of their troubles were over, and when, shortly after breakfast on 18 April, the brave Bengali commissariat agent who had spent the whole siege overcoming his admitted terror, burst in – his eyes staring, his lips dry – announcing, 'Please, sir, I hear the voice of digging,' the British officers were paralysed by the news. Shouting for silence, quite definitely in the Bengali's store they could hear a menacing thud-thud-thud but, while they were still worriedly wondering where it came from, it was noticed that the sound coincided with a sepoy chopping firewood in another room and the excitement died down. Later in the day another alarm was raised but this time the sound proved to be Sifat's men at work.

Everyone was cheerful now and the Sikhs sat in groups, cleaning their rifles. 'The arm of the government is slow,' one of them said, 'but it reaches very far.' The day remained quiet, with only a little firing at parties of the besiegers carrying off their dead. Since another attack was expected that night, the defenders spent some time devising new fortifications to cover the foot of the walls from above. Then, about two hours after midnight, a worried Townshend reported that a man had actually crept up to the Sikhs' post on the west side, shouted something, and then escaped uninjured. Surely even the Sikhs couldn't be getting slack!

They all turned out, and again a voice was heard shouting. Like magic, the word 'flashed through the fort' that the besiegers had gone and that it was Futteh Ali Shah's brother, Rustum, demanding admission. Townshend was inclined to suspect a trick but the man was eventually admitted through a manhole in the gate and he immediately confirmed that Sher Afzul and the two khans who were driving him on in his venture had indeed fled and that the force from Gilgit was only two days' march away. Muhammed Isa had been heavily beaten at Nisa Gul and had fallen back towards Chitral.

Everyone shook hands delightedly with Shuja-ul-Mulk. The other Chitralis, quick to sense a change of fortune, crowded round shouting 'Mubarik' – victory! – while the Bengali commissariat clerk said heavily to Robertson, 'Sir, I am born again, and if I live for twenty years more I shall never forget this time.'

Townshend immediately put the sepoys on full rations, and fresh supplies of sheep, goats, ghi and eggs were brought into the fort. Wafadar produced the last seven of Shuja-ul-Mulk's Egyptian cigarettes, and a quantity of the dreadful rum was made into grog. They all expected to have hangovers the following day, but that hardly seemed to matter as they sat drinking round a small fire, talking of home, wondering, surmising and guessing throughout the rest of the night.

The Chitralis remained exuberant in their new loyalty until they learned that Sher Afzul had put to death all their relatives and carried off their wives and sisters. Their houses were mere ash-heaps, and all their property was gone. Wafadar had suffered most, and Robertson felt 'a sickening horror about these vile retaliations' against a man who had contributed so much to the defence.

While the garrison at Chitral endeavoured to console Wafadar, Brigadier-General Gatacre struggled on towards the Lowarai Pass and Colonel Kelly's force pushed stolidly nearer from the east. Kelly had devoted 18 April to foraging, and on this day the mutilated remains of the Sikhs murdered at Kalak were found. Muhammed Isa was still falling steadily back one day ahead of them and was now reported to be standing at Gulan Gul. This was a stupendous defile, with a wild stream bursting over rocks into the Mastuj river where the spider's thread of a bridge had now been burned down. The Chitralis were entrenched on the far side, so Kelly ordered Lieutenant Bethune across to take the position in flank. On the morning of 19 April, Lieutenant Oldham moved up in an attempt to use the remains of the burned bridge, but he found its supports gone and the masonry still red-hot. Two of Bethune's men and some of the Hunzas swam the river with ropes but the moment the bridge was repaired word came that Muhammed Isa had received an urgent summons to Chitral and the passage of the Gulan Gul was no longer disputed.

The force crossed, and during the afternoon Lieutenants Cobbe and Beynon pushed forward to make a reconnaissance. They soon met a man carrying letters from Robertson, from whom they learned the siege had been lifted. They also met Chitralis heading for the hills. 'We hate these Pathans,' they said, hurriedly trimming their coats to the new wind. 'They have plundered our houses and carried off our women.' Reaching a house that had been occupied by Muhammed Isa, they found it stuffed with sacks of carroway seeds, 'the stuff,' Beynon wrote to his mother, 'they put in what are called "wholesome cakes for children".' The levies used it for cooking purposes until the whole camp stank of it.

It was on this morning that Captain Townshend finally withdrew his objections to a sortie from Chitral, and at 9 am Lieutenant Gurdon marched out to obtain final confirmation that all they had heard was true. Chitral was denuded of the enemy who had fled to the hills for fear of reprisals, and Bajouri traders came forward with propitiatory gifts of sugar and groceries. They could add nothing to the news of the night before, except that a second force – even greater than the one from Gilgit – was marching up from Peshawar and Hoti-Mardan, accompanied by the ruler of Dir. Sher Afzul and the khans, it seemed, had been uneasy ever since 12 April but had kept up their followers' spirits by reiterating that the Amir of Afghanistan's forces were hurrying to their aid.

Despite the feeling of relief that Gurdon's news brought, work in the fort didn't stop. A letter was sent off to the Gilgit force, while Captain Campbell, who had uncomplainingly spent the whole siege in his dark and wretched little room, was promised that he should be carried out to the fresh air as soon as anyone had time. That night word came from Kelly that he would arrive the following day, 20 April.

They couldn't stay in bed the next morning. For breakfast they had eggs, fresh milk and a skinny chicken they 'could hardly eat for admiration of such delicacies'. The women emerged from the rooms where they had sheltered throughout the siege, one or two of them weeping with relief. By this time the place stank and they stared sombre-eyed at its shabbiness, wondering how they had managed to hang on to it. At 2 pm Kelly's advance guard was seen crossing the bridge, their blaring bugles bringing a lump to the throats of the weary garrison. To Beynon, as they rode up, the garrison looked 'pale and worn thin'.

There were no extravagant greetings. Robertson was so weary, all he could really take in were Kelly's solid dark-complexioned Masbis and two of the officers: Oldham, who was wearing a turban, and Kelly himself, who waved a walking stick from his seat on a sturdy pony. Only twelve of Lieutenant Stewart's animals remained alive, but his men were desperately proud of the way they had overlooked their cherished caste to bring the guns up. 'We did the march, sahib,' one of them told him, 'with fewer cooking pots than the Masbi Sikhs.'

As they tramped up, the little group in front of the ruined outwork of the fort were strangely quiet. 'Nothing short of a Pathan battle cry and the sharp clatter of rifle fire could have . . . roused us,' Robertson thought, 'for the long-sustained stimulus of danger and responsibility was gone and only tiredness . . . of brain and eyes and body remained.'

As Beynon recorded, there was one thing they did enjoy. They revelled in the fresh air 'after the poisonous atmosphere of the fort'. Apart from that '. . . They were walking skeletons, bloodless, and as quiet as the ghosts they resembled, most of them reduced to jerseys and garments of any description.' They were indeed attired in an odd mixture of British and Indian uniform and civilian clothes, and looked a shabby exhausted group even to the battered men of Kelly's advance guard who had not suffered much less themselves.

On 21 April a durbar hall, which had been occupied by Rab Nawaz Khan's wife and two other women during the siege, was turned into a banqueting hall for dinner and Campbell was carried in. It was surely the occasion for a celebration, and one of the long-treasured bottles of brandy was produced as well as a carefully hoarded Christmas pudding. Even now, however, the members of the garrison still couldn't believe it was all over and, with the habits of the siege still strong in them, kept getting up to go round the sentries.

On 22 April, Campbell was at last carried outside, thankful to put behind him the dark grimy room he had tenanted for almost seven weeks. The following day they gave the fort back to the young mehtar and his advisers, and moved into Robertson's old house with the crazy flag they had made flapping on the roof. There they learned that both Edwardes and Fowler were safe with Low's force.

In spite of everything, they reluctantly conceded, Umra Khan had behaved like a gentleman.

It was over. The people in Britain had held their breath in an agony of suspense. It was only ten years since the country had gone through the traumatic experience of reading of Gordon trapped in the Sudan and, as the result of government dilatoriness, being murdered by just such fanatical Mohammedan tribesmen as had now been besieging Chitral. People had even begun to whisper, 'It is Khartoum all over again'.[1] But then the news came that General Gatacre and Colonel Kelly were 'racing for Chitral', and on 22 April the headlines informed the world that, with the garrison 'close to their last gasp', Sher Afzul had fled and the relief had arrived 'just in time'.

Kelly's advance was called 'a brilliant military exploit' and 'one of the most remarkable marches in history', and indeed he had revealed two qualities all too often lacking in Victorian soldiers – speed and decision. Probably because they had never stayed anywhere long enough to foul their own ground, his little force had also suffered far less from illness than Low's army, who were already enduring the dysentery and enteric that would soon crowd ill-prepared and ill-equipped hospitals.

Gatacre came panting up a few days later, his men furious that they had been beaten at the post – especially since they considered that Kelly had had it easy, despite his 220 miles march. The lean hard-bitten Buffs had been pushed over the Lowarai Pass on 25 April in a swift thrust forward that had proved an ordeal for men and animals alike. At one point Gatacre had watched twenty of his mules in succession 'slide on their haunches quite solemnly, some hundreds of feet, turn over in the snow and remain there till extricated' – all fortunately without loss beyond broken boxes and torn bags.[2] He

had just been about to start on the last leg for Chitral when word came
that Kelly had got there first.

Low arrived soon afterwards and photographs were taken for
posterity by Sergeant Mayo and the Bengal Sappers photographic
section; even one of Sher Afzul who was brought in on 27 April with
three of his brothers and a total of 1500 followers including women
and children. The Khan of Dir had driven them into the snow and
starved them into surrender. They were all in poor shape, Sher Afzul
himself – wearing an astrakhan hat and a military cloak – fatigued and
with a drawn face and chapped and peeled lips.

He blamed everything on Umra Khan. 'I had no wish to fight,' he
said. 'I had no alternative. . . . I do not want ever to set eyes upon
Umra Khan again . . . He destroyed us with promises and when he was
called to defend his own home, he fled like a fox.' He was sent south
to become a state prisoner of India.

After a little confusion as to his whereabouts, Umra Khan was reported to be at the walled town of Jalalabad and then a prisoner of the
Afghans at Dangama. Inevitably, *he* blamed everything on Sher Afzul.[3]

Later he was said to be confined at Asmar, but eventually he
appeared under escort in Kabul where his reception by the amir was
said to be 'unfriendly'. Since the amir's son was at that moment about
to pay a state visit to Queen Victoria and likely to be embarrassed
by the Chitral affair, this was probably correct. At Kabul, Umra was
again put in prison, though this was probably no more than a gesture
by the astute Abdur-Rahman to appease the government of India,
and finally he was allowed to go on a pilgrimage to Mecca. The
treacherous Muhammed Isa had gone into hiding, and every other
important chief who had taken part in the rising was in British or
Afghan hands.

At Chitral, however, no one was thinking of anything but the
honours to be done to the garrison and the men who had relieved
them. As Captain Townshend put it rather smugly, the affair 'quite
restores our prestige. Nothing as good as this has been done for
many years, and for some time it should keep the frontier quiet.' He
had been quick to see the good it might have done for him, too, and
had already sent off letters to his titled relatives informing them of his
success.

On Low's first parade, the weary garrison had been too feeble to appear and the post of honour on the right had been given to Kelly's ragged little band, with Lieutenant Stewart's guns, forming the right of the line, played on and off the parade ground by the pipers of the Derajat Battery. A little later, another parade was held at which the garrison of the fort stood in the middle of a hollow square while Low congratulated them on their long defence and Kelly and his men on their courage in surmounting such enormous odds. A funeral service was held over Baird's grave, and his friend, Major Aylmer, erected a stone and carved the inscription on it with his own hands.

When the news of the relief reached India and then England, even more generous tributes were paid. Sir George White, Commander-in-Chief, India, declared – somewhat fulsomely, considering the disaster they had brought on themselves on 3 March – that Townshend and his men had 'greatly added to the prestige of British arms', and that their gallantry would elicit 'the admiration of all'. The Viceroy, Lord Elgin, endorsed his words and spoke of 'the cheerful endurance of all the hardships of the siege . . . in this glorious episode in the history of the Indian Empire and its army'. Queen Victoria joined in the general congratulations and all ranks were rewarded with six months' pay and three months' extra leave.

Kelly was recommended for a K.C.B. and a brevet as major-general. What he got was a C.B. and an appointment as aide-de-camp to the Queen. He never did get the full credit for the relief. Little appeared in the papers about his tremendous march, and most of the kudos went to the better-known Low with his more fashionable regiments and his direct telegraphic link to Peshawar.

Campbell was given the D.S.O., as were Gurdon, Harley, Moberly, Edwardes, Fowler, Borradaile, Stewart, Beynon, Jones and Bretherton. And in fulfilment of Baird's dying wish, Surgeon-Captain Whitchurch received the Victoria Cross. Rather surprisingly, Townshend was given a C.B. and promoted to brevet majority. Seeking as always to further his career by moving from one command to another, he arrived in England to find himself a celebrity and a very popular bachelor in the homes of society hostesses with marriageable daughters. His praises were sung by those who mattered like the Duke of Cambridge, the Queen's cousin and lately commander-in-chief of the army. He was granted an audience of the Prince of Wales, and decorated by the Queen at Osborne where he was flattered to be reminded of his descent from the Townshend who had taken over the command at Quebec. He rather put his foot in it, however, when the Queen, who was inclined to favour Scottish regiments, asked if he didn't think that Highlanders were the finest soldiers in the world and he replied bluntly that he thought the English weren't bad either. There was a dead silence and the Queen hurriedly changed the subject. 'You might have heard a mangle drop,' the ebullient Townshend reported.

It all went to his head a little, in fact, and he immediately started plotting his next promotion. The Prince of Wales offered to back an application for a transfer to the Guards but Redvers Buller, by now a figure to be reckoned with in the army hierarchy, advised him to stick to India. He wisely did, but was eventually invited to join Kitchener on the Nile expedition that ended at Omdurman. He served in South Africa during the Boer War; and then, in 1915, by now a major-general, found himself with the 6th Indian Division in Mesopotamia. Forced by the Turks into Kut, in a bend of the Tigris, he decided to dig in. 'I will hold it as I held Chitral,' he said.

He did – for 143 days, one of the longest sieges in history. This time, however, it was to no avail. He wasn't opposing unorganized tribesmen but one of the toughest fighting races in the world, who stopped dead all attempts at relief and eventually forced him to surrender. It ended his career. Though his men continued to admire their 'Chitral Charlie', he was severely criticized by the government and the army for living in luxury as a prisoner of war while they died of starvation. His reputation never recovered, and he was snubbed by everyone he later appealed to for employment. He died of cancer in 1924, but they said it was caused by a broken heart.

With his Montgomery-like belief in publicity, he was probably years ahead of his time; but he was never popular with the stiff-upper-lips of the army of the day, and there often seems to be a note of sarcasm in those books by his contemporaries which refer to him as 'the hero of Chitral'. General MacMunn was an old frontier fighter who might be assumed to have heard the truth about Chitral, and he seemed to think that Townshend had taken rather too much of the credit for himself. 'The defence of the fort,' he wrote firmly in the Thirties, 'had largely been the doing of Captain Campbell, assisted by Townshend. Campbell had been wounded at the commencement, but was a more important factor in the defence from his bed than popular accounts give credit to. Signor MacStinger, the "Man in the Sangar", otherwise Townshend, was naturally a prominent feature.' But MacMunn later served with the force trying to relieve Kut, and had possibly become disillusioned with Townshend's bitter reproaches and the torrent of trivialities addressed to his theatrical friends with which he used up the radio operators' time. Or perhaps the trouble was that Townshend, as Curzon had noted after their encounter at Gupis, just wasn't cast in the traditional mould. Yet there seems to be a wealth of meaning in that nickname MacMunn gave him and that reference to 'popular accounts', by which he appears to mean Townshend's own; and oddly enough, in *his* account of the siege even Robertson makes remarkably little mention of his military commander.

Gurdon ended up as a lieutenant-colonel and was political agent in Dir, Swat, Chitral, and finally at Gilgit, before moving on to places of increasing importance until he retired in 1918. Harold Deane, who had negotiated the release of Edwardes and Fowler, eventually received a knighthood, as did Richard Udny who was so bitterly criticized by Townshend for not doing anything to help.

Whitchurch went on to serve with the Malakand Field Force in 1897, seeing things from the other side for a change when Chakdara was besieged and he was in the relieving force. He also took part in the relief of the besieged embassies at Peking following the Boxer Rebellion of 1901, as well as in several other actions. He died in 1907 at the early age of forty-one.

Harley served in the Sudan, South Africa and the Great War. He ended up as a much-decorated colonel, with an appointment on the staff of the British Mission to Italy when that country entered the war. He too died young. Edwardes retired as a brigadier and Fowler as a lieutenant-general, both serving in the Great War. Cobbe also became a general with his own Victoria Cross, won in South Africa. The Younghusbands, to everyone's continuing confusion, both received knighthoods, George John becoming a major-general and Francis Edward famous as an explorer. Stewart finished as a brigadier, like

Harley covered with medals. He died as late as 1948, as did Borradaile who had already retired when World War I brought him back into uniform.

Brigadier-General Gatacre proved a damp squib, and that miraculous energy he had shown let him down four years after Chitral at the beginning of the Boer War. Ordered to attack Stormberg, he assumed that green troops recently arrived from England possessed his own powers of endurance and sent them off on a night attack after a nine-mile march in the blazing sun. He left 600 of them behind as prisoners – chiefly because they were so exhausted they had fallen fast asleep.

Of the others, a surprising number turned up in Mesopotamia and involved with Kut. As a general, Aylmer led the relief attempts until, defeated and finally disillusioned, he was replaced. George John Younghusband led the Seventh Division of the relief force and Cobbe the First Indian Army Corps, with Edwardes under him in command of the Eighth Brigade. Moberly, by then a brigadier, became the official historian of the campaign. Beynon also became a general, as did several others who had been with Low – among them Ian Hamilton and Bindon Blood, both famous characters in the British army.[4]

Campbell recovered completely from his wound, but for years afterwards Robertson suffered remorse for his rough treatment of him on the day of the sortie. Eventually, however, he was assured by a famous London surgeon that his enthusiasm with the bottle of carbolic acid solution had probably saved Campbell's leg. And certainly, less than two years later, Campbell was riding with one of the Indian cavalry's champion polo teams. Probably the last survivor of the Chitral campaign was the light-hearted Beynon who later served in campaigns in Tirah, Somaliland, Tibet, Abor, Afghanistan and in World War I. In addition to the D.S.O. he received after Chitral he too was knighted and mentioned six times in despatches. As late as 1943 he was still engaged with his country's enemies as a member of the Observer Corps at the age of seventy-seven. He was eighty-nine when he died in 1955.

Chitral was soon forgotten by the public. All things considered, the Victorians probably rather overdid the congratulations and the honours, and the siege soon slipped out of sight in the preparations for an expedition to put down trouble on the Gold Coast which started even as Chitral finished. There was even another insurrection by the Pathans. Umra Khan was still in Kabul, with the amir under obligation to the British to prevent him raising hell again. This did not stop Abdur-Rahman supplying him with plentiful funds, so that Umra[5] was able to stir up trouble in the Mahmund Valley in 1897.

Perhaps Chitral need never have happened at all – and might not have – if Robertson had not so impulsively installed Shuja-ul-Mulk as mehtar. However, it *did* happen and for a long time after it had passed out of the public eye it still occupied the thoughts of the British and Indian governments, with many famous frontier fighters joining in the debates on its future. As an expert on the matter, Townshend was asked by the Duke of Cambridge for his views, and he offered the opinion that one battalion of British-Indian infantry and one mountain battery was enough to hold the place. Lord Roberts was also worried that the government might back away from its commitment there, and he took Townshend aside at a dance to urge him, 'Mind you vote the right way about retaining Chitral!' One eye as always on his future, Townshend made sure he did.

For the government of India, there were two possible solutions to the problem. Either they must 'abandon any effective control' over Chitral, or they must put a garrison there big enough to hold it. The Viceregal Council decided that to maintain British influence in Chitral was 'a matter of first importance' and in a despatch on 8 May 1895, to the home government they set forth their reasons, at the same time declaring it impossible to garrison Chitral without improving the road from Peshawar.

It was this decision that stirred the emotions of people like the Duke of Cambridge and Lord Roberts. Sir George White and Sir Henry Brackenbury were among other eminent soldiers who also took the view that Chitral was of the greatest strategical importance, but there were as many who did not. Sir Redvers Buller was 'dead against it'; and on 6 June, 1895, with the siege barely over, Sir Neville Bowles Chamberlain wrote to *The Times* that a diversion by the Russians was 'extremely improbable, if not impracticable', because of the absence of food in the barren valleys. In the June number of the magazine *Nineteenth Century*, Sir Lepel Griffin observed that 'a small Russian detachment might occupy Chitral, but the British Empire would not collapse because a few hundred Cossacks foolishly immured themselves in a death-trap'.

In the event, the army *did* remain in Chitral. On 13 June Lord Rosebery's cabinet decided decisively against retention, and left Chitral, in Churchill's words, 'to stew in its own juice'. But 'once more an important imperial problem became the sport of English party politics', and, just as the Union Jack was about to be hauled down, the Liberal Government fell and Lord Salisbury, who replaced Rosebery as Prime Minister, reversed the decision. Thus the retention was sanctioned, and the road from Peshawar opened up. It was the most extensive advance northwards of all, and carried the British frontiers into the heart of some of the greatest mountains of the world.

They were on a firm basis, too, because Robertson's choice of mehtar proved a good one and Shuja-ul-Mulk reigned for forty years, modern in outlook and renowned for his wit and his skill as a chess player. Unlike his elder brother, Nizam, he was a good Mohammedan and a strict teetotaller and, late in life, he was air-minded enough to allow himself to be persuaded by the R.A.F. to complete a trip home from the south in the rear cockpit of a Hawker Hart. He left sixteen sons, all men of considerable ability, and was succeeded by the eldest of them, Nasir-ul-Mulk, a university graduate and scholar who as a young man had been trained in the Royal Scinde Rifles and as an assistant commissioner in the Indian Civil Service. The family's hereditary instincts had not altogether died out, however, and, though some of Nasir's brothers served with distinction in the Indian and Pakistani armies, one of them, Burhan-ud-Din, was in turn a brigand, Indian army officer, air force pilot, and – after being captured by the Japanese during World War II at Singapore – an Indian National Army bully under the Japanese and the torturer of loyal Indian soldiers. The garrison at Chitral was maintained until the state acceded to Pakistan following the partition of the subcontinent in 1947, by which time to the threat from Russia had been added another one from China.

Chitral hadn't been the longest siege in history and its casualties were small compared with those of many campaigns, but it had been the kind of adventure story that everyone loved and, as *The Illustrated London News* commented, it had provided Mr Rudyard Kipling with plenty of material for stirring songs. But, though the newspapers and Townshend made much of it, Robertson took a different view. He had been promptly and properly rewarded with a knighthood (K.C.S.I.) for his special role in the defence of Chitral, but to everyone's surprise, and with his career apparently in full flood, he suddenly abandoned India four years later to return to England where he became Liberal Member of Parliament for Central Bradford. He died on the first day of 1916 in the middle of a war which made the affair in Chitral seem as insignificant as he had often felt himself alongside the bulk of Tirich Mir.

He had never been under any delusions about the siege. They had owed a great deal to the loyalty and courage of Indians like Gurmokh Singh, Badrinar Singh, Rab Nawaz Khan, the splendid Sifat and the ever loyal Wafadar, as well as to many others whose names never appeared in any account and, though the congratulations had helped to check the 'terrible reaction' they all felt after their long and insanitary imprisonment, he modestly never considered – despite its weariness and the 103 casualties out of 370, forty-one of them dead – that the siege had been anything else but small and insignificant. One of the things that had pleased him most about it was the bizarre flag they had made. When they had raised it the first time and every morning afterwards, 'a smile of confidence, one might almost say the smile of adoration for a fetish', had accompanied the action. And though the two most critical moments of the siege – the firing of the gun tower and the fight for the mine – followed, it had seemed to change their fortune. It became one of his dearest possessions.

Sources

BARKER, A. J., *Townshend of Kut*, Cassell, 1967

BARTON, SIR WILLIAM, *India's North-West Frontier*, Murray, 1939

BETHELL, L. A. (Ed.), *Tales from the Outposts*, Blackwood, 1933

BEYNON, W. G. L., *With Kelly to Chitral*, Arnold, 1896

BLOOD, GEN. SIR BINDON, *Four Score Years and Ten*, Bell, 1933

CAROE, SIR OLAF, *The Pathans*, Macmillan, 1965

CHURCHILL, W. S., *The Story of the Malakand Field Force*, Longman 1898

DAVIES, C. C., *The Indian Frontier 1858–1918* (from *The Cambridge History of the British Empire*, Vol. V), Cambridge University Press, 1932

DAVIS, PATRICK, *A Child at Arms*, Hutchinson, 1970

DURAND, COL. ALGERNON, *The Making of a Frontier*, Murray, 1899

FOWLER, JOHN S., *Diary*, Dublin, 1897

GARDYNE, LT.-COL. C. G., *The History of The Gordon Highlanders*, Medici Society, 1903

HAMILTON, GEN. SIR IAN, *Listening for the Drums*, Faber, 1944

JACKSON, A. F., *Heroes of the Chitral Siege*, London, 1897

JAMES, LIONEL, *With the Chitral Relief Force*, Calcutta, 1895

LEITNER, G. W., *Dardistan in 1895*, Woking, 1895

MACFETRIDGE, C. H. T., & WARREN, J. P. (Eds.), *Tales of the Mountain Gunners*, Blackwood, 1973

MACMUNN, GEN. SIR GEORGE, *The Romance of the Indian Frontiers*, Cape, 1931

MASON, PHILIP, *A Matter of Honour*, Cape, 1974

MASTERS, JOHN, *Bugles and a Tiger*, Michael Joseph, 1956

MAURICE, GEN. SIR F., *Life of General Lord Rawlinson of Trent*, Cassell, 1928

MILLAR, RONALD, *Kut*, Secker and Warburg, 1969

NEVILL, CAPT. H. L., *Campaigns on the North-West Frontier*, Murray, 1912

NEWMAN, H., *Umra Khan and the Chitral Campaign of 1895*, Lahore, 1897

PARLIAMENTARY PAPERS: *Correspondence Relating to Chitral,* London 1895; *Correspondence Relating to the Occupation of Chitral,* London 1896

ROBERTSON, SIR GEORGE, *Chitral,* Methuen, 1899

ROBERTSON, CAPT. W. R., *The Official Account of the Chitral Expedition, 1895,* Office of the Superintendent of Government Printing, India, 1898

SHERSON, ERROLL, *Townshend of Chitral and Kut* (Based on Townshend's diaries), Heinemann, 1928

SMALL, E. M., *Told from the Ranks,* Melrose, 1897

SWINSON, ARTHUR, *North-West Frontier,* Hutchinson, 1967

THOMSON, H. C., *The Chitral Campaign,* Heinemann, 1895

WALDER, DAVID, *The Short Victorious War,* Hutchinson, 1973

WARRE, COL. H. C., *Letters*

YOUNGHUSBAND, G. J. and F. E., *The Relief of Chitral,* Macmillan, 1896

ZIEGLER, PHILIP, *Omdurman,* Collins, 1973.

The Chitral Expedition, 1895, Allahabad, 1895

Civil and Military Gazette, Lahore
Hampshire Gazette
Illustrated London News
Lloyds' Weekly
Nineteenth Century
Punch
Bradford Observer
Daily Graphic
The Gazette
The Graphic
The Leeds Mercury
The Pioneer, Lucknow
The Times
The Times of India
Westminster Gazette
Whitaker's Almanack

Notes on sources

Unless otherwise stated, the story of what happened inside the fort at Chitra is based on Robertson's own account and on the Townshend diaries as quoted by Sherson. Kelly's story is based on Beynon; and what happened in the south on Younghusband or on the dispatches of newspaper correspondents.

CHAPTER 1: *The land of mirth and murder (pages 1 to 9)*

1 Before the Mutiny of 1857, in fact, it reached disastrous proportions and left regiments denuded of leaders, while those who remained were regarded as failures.
2 Davis
3 Walder

CHAPTER 2: *That pattern meant war (pages 10 to 15)*

1 An official blinder, in fact, became an important official at his court
2 Abdur-Rahman's biography as quoted by Davies
3 Davies
4 Mehtar: The title derives from the Persian and means rajah. There were others equally endearing and meaning variously 'ruler', 'rajah', 'governor', 'prime minister' – Thum of Hunza, Mir of Nagar, Askogol of Shogot, Sayid of Gupis, Wali of Swat, Hakim of Laspur.
5 Sir Lepel Griffin, an authority on Afghanistan
6 One of them was once seen to summon a courtier so that he could blow his nose on the end of the courtier's turban.

CHAPTER 3: *They weren't there for a change of air (pages 16 to 19)*

1 Davies
2 Major-General H. Essame, in conversation with the author

3 Skobeleff: The Russian general who had reduced Plevna in 1877 after a siege lasting 143 days. He was a violent Anglophobe but a successful general greatly admired by the British army who were fond of quoting him.

CHAPTER 4: *Some subterranean conspiracy had exploded (pages 20 to 24)*

1 Major-General H. Essame, in conversation with the author: 'They were the absolute bottom as soldiers,' he said. 'Almost as bad as the Egyptians.'
2 MacMunn

CHAPTER 5: *This was a bolt from the blue! (pages 25 to 34)*

1 Townshend, quoted by Sherson
2 Blood, Thomson, Younghusband, and others
3 Some years earlier an envoy of the mehtar had met a conquering general in this area and, throwing himself at the general's feet, had clasped the conqueror's knees to implore mercy – before, with a sudden jerk, hurling him off the road into the defile a hundred feet below. The invading force of 7000 was then cut off and killed or taken prisoner.

CHAPTER 6: *The first shot . . . always to be dreaded (pages 35 to 42)*

1 Durand
2 Inevitably he became known to the irreverent soldiers as Sugar-and-Milk. Townshend thought him about fourteen, Younghusband nine or ten. Thomson's estimate – twelve – seems nearest to the truth.
3 Younghusband, Blood, and others

CHAPTER 7: *When you meet an Asiatic, go for him (pages 43 to 49)*

1 According to Thomson, an expert on Pathans who went with Low as a press correspondent and reached Chitral a week after the siege ended, Sher Afzul was virtually a prisoner from the moment he joined forces with the active and ruthless Umra.
2 'On the Gilgit Frontier,' Robertson said, 'a subaltern's equipment can hardly be considered complete without a banjo and a fox terrier.' Townshend, in particular, was a great man with a banjo and had even carried one with him throughout the desert campaign to relieve Gordon at Khartoum. It was almost lost when the camel carrying it fell dead from the heat.

CHAPTER 8: *Like wild dogs round a failing deer (pages 50 to 59)*

1 Robertson

CHAPTER 9: *Impossible ever to improve them (pages 60 to 64)*

1 *Combined Training, 1905*
2 Barker
3 General Sir Redvers Buller, one of the leading figures in the British army at the time, was also a relation by marriage.

CHAPTER 10: *His bright smile haunts me still (pages 65 to 72)*

1 During World War II the author was in South Africa when Singapore fell and the Japanese were expected to pour across the Indian Ocean. There were few arms available for defence, but among them were a few ancient Martinis left over from the native risings of the previous century. Normally when the trigger was pulled the bullet trudged up the barrel to fall at the marksman's feet – a case, surely, of 'the harder you pull the trigger the further the bullet goes' – but on one occasion when one was discharged accidentally the lead bullet made a hole one foot square in a wood, stone and plasterboard wall. The recoil was vicious and it is easy to imagine the difficulties of hitting anything. Of the Snider, Ian Hamilton wrote: 'If you did not estimate the distance to within a few yards, the more carefully you aimed and the more steadily you pressed the trigger the safer your quarry would be.'
2 Essame: Though British officers were expected to eat it, they pronounced it 'very indigestible'.
3 An apocryphal story of the stupidity of Sikhs comes from the last war when one of them thought it was his duty to catch hundredweight bags of flour hurtling down from an aeroplane during an air drop.
4 John Masters remembered seeing a Gurkha havildar kicked on the head by a mule. He complained only of a headache, but the mule went dead lame.
5 Pronounced 'P't'ahns' or, by the ordinary British soldier, 'Paythans'
6 The British didn't hesitate to retaliate with equal cruelty. Masters tells how, after a British officer had been caught, castrated and flayed, a wounded tribesman was pegged out and the men of an Indian battalion were told to kick him in the testicles every time they passed. When he died, his body was left where the British officer's skin had been found.

'It is doubtful if the Pathans . . . gave the matter a second thought,' Masters records.

7 Or 'The Wounded Heart'. It began:

> There's a boy across the river
> With a bottom like a peach
> But, alas, I cannot swim.

The North Staffordshire and Liverpool Regiments both liked the tune and it was used for years by the latter as a regimental march.

8 Masters quotes one as saying after a day of vicious fighting that 'our men had done well'. It turned out he was talking not of the British but of the enemy tribesmen be normally administered.

9 MacMunn

10 'Ghazi – champion, particularly against infidels. A title of honour, chiefly applied to Mohammedan fanatics who devoted themselves to the destruction of infidels.' – *Encyclopaedia Britannica*.

11 Mullah – a priest. During a battle a sort of cheer-leader. Younghusband describes them delightfully as 'a sporting parson type'.

CHAPTER 11: *Still the friend of the British (pages 73 to 79)*

1 Churchill pointed out that there were many Hindus along the frontier who had fled north to escape the vengeance of the British after the Mutiny. They always continued to stir up trouble and many of them reached positions of authority among the tribal chiefs.

CHAPTER 12: *Gallant to the verge of eccentricity (pages 80 to 91)*

1 Essame
2 Edwardes' report in official account, Fowler diary
3 Jones's report in official account

CHAPTER 13: *An ominous absence of all news (pages 92 to 97)*

1 Townshend, quoted by Sherson

CHAPTER 14: *No wild firing (pages 98 to 103)*

1 As the siege progressed, fourteen per cent of the rifles in the fort became useless.

CHAPTER 15: *The red Reshun soil (pages 104 to 111)*

1 Patrick **Davis** was aware of this feeling even as late as the Burma campaign of 1943.
2 *Civil and Military Gazette*

CHAPTER 16: *An outbreak of firing came as a relief (pages 112 to 123)*

1 Robertson thought the incident symbolized the extraordinary difficulties of fighting in Chitral where the countryside could claim victims even among the local inhabitants.
2 This silence was often more worrying to the attackers than rifle fire, as the defenders of the Alcázar at Toledo during the Spanish Civil War later discovered. It was felt by those outside that behind every dark loophole an eye was watching and that it was dangerous to move.
3 Captain Townshend had once received a letter from the Governor of Yasin in return for the gift of a mere cake of Pears' scented soap which ran, 'Wonderful and marvellous!... the smell of musk and of ambergris, mixed with attar of roses, reaches the pores of my soul and has ... scented the brain of our friendship and . . . been the cause of the increase and strengthening of our mutual love.'
4 Harley to Robertson
5 Townshend, quoted by Sherson
6 He numbered Gaiety Girls among his friends
7 The army didn't appear to agree with him and a court of enquiry exonerated both officers. But Townshend was always more inclined to be harsh in his judgments, while Robertson's account of the siege is always kinder, more humorous and full of scarcely concealed affection for the cunningly childish tribesmen.

CHAPTER 17: *There is an excellent road (pages 124 to 133)*

1 Younghusband
2 Nevill
3 Robertson
4 Ziegler
5 *The Times*
6 Reuter report
7 Caroe
8 The Younghusband brothers continued to be confused with each other

all their lives. Both were explorers and writers and since both were present as captains and correspondents for *The Times*, to baffled readers a single Younghusband appeared able by some form of necromancy to appear simultaneously to the east and south of Chitral. Even as late as 1961 Francis was credited with being both with Low and Kelly!

CHAPTER 18: *Illegal, to fight without the Union Jack (pages 134 to 143)*

1 This distrust of Indians continued all his life, and when he was besieged in Kut in 1915–16 he believed his Indian soldiers there were malingering.
2 Townshend's views on sorties remained unchanged at Kut. He was always against them and never willing to mount one to help the troops struggling to relieve him.

CHAPTER 19: *The siege throughout was anachronistic (pages 144 to 158)*

1 Nevill
2 There are several quotations to illustrate the theory of getting there quickly and hitting the enemy hard. 'Git thar fustest with the mostest,' was Nathan Bedford Forrest's dictum in the American Civil War. 'Hit the other fellow as quick as you can, and as hard as you can, where it hurts him most, when he ain't looking,' is attributed to a British sergeant-major and was often quoted by Field Marshal Lord Slim.
3 When the Thum of Hunza had proved so difficult in 1891 and was told to desist, he replied, 'Potentates like myself and Alexander of Macedon answer no summons and acknowledge no rule.'
4 Robertson
5 At Kut, Townshend again failed, despite the advice of his staff, to issue such an order and with the same results. Moberly's men and Stewart's well-led gunners put aside their religious objections.
6 According to John Masters, whenever an Indian cook was given modern equipment, comfort and an ordered routine, his performance varied from good to poisonous. But set him down in a howling wilderness of rock and thorn, in the open, hunched over a tiny fire between two stones with rain or snow falling, and he came up with a miracle 'as surprising as, and far more satisfying than, the rope trick'.

CHAPTER 20: *The route is completely blocked (pages 159 to 169)*

1 They nevertheless considered themselves lucky to be there. Action was

the way to promotion, and everyone wanted to join the relief force. One Irish colonel of cavalry was so determined to see active service that he shouldered a rifle and marched with the infantry to the Malakand where he took part in the battle as a private soldier. The regiment he chose had its full share of the fighting.

2 Blood, Younghusband and others

3 How important it was to stop a tribesman was shown by one man whose ancient weapon had exploded and blown the lock into his shoulder. He walked about with it lodged there for months before it was cut out.

4 Hamilton

5 Kinloch was the only one of the senior officers not mentioned in Low's despatch.

CHAPTER 21: *Hullo, Gurdon's had to light up (pages 170 to 179)*

1 Stewart's account, quoted by Bethell, and MacFetridge & Warren

CHAPTER 22: *There burst over us a mighty light (pages 180 to 186)*

1 On one occasion it rose fourteen feet within a matter of hours.

2 *The Times*

3 *The Times*, the official report and *The Pioneer*

4 Nevill

CHAPTER 23: *That sangar was a death-trap (pages 187 to 200)*

1 *The Times*

2 Kelly, Stewart

CHAPTER 24: *Those cut-throats of yours (pages 201 to 210)*

1 Fowler

2 Gatacre, official report

3 Robertson and others

CHAPTER 25: *The thing had been pure luck (pages 211 to 217)*

1 MacMunn

2 Younghusband

Townshend, quoted by Sherson, noted that he heard the explosion just after 5 pm.

CHAPTER 26: *Quiet as the ghosts they resembled (pages 218 to 223)*

1 Somehow, Simla heard about the mine at almost the same time as the garrison at Chitral.

CHAPTER 27: *The admiration of all (pages 224 to 232)*

1 *Graphic*
2 Gatacre, official report
3 James and *Civil and Military Gazette*
4 Hamilton's reputation continued to grow until it was ruined by Gallipoli, though until his death in 1947 he always remained a well-loved and colourful figure who poured out a string of erudite and witty books. One other who had taken part became Sir William ('Wullie') Robertson, who had enlisted as a private soldier and served through the campaign as a captain on Low's staff. He became Chief of the Imperial General Staff in 1915 and a Field Marshal in 1920. He nearly didn't make it, though, because while at Dir he was almost assassinated by a treacherous guide who was holding his belt and used both his revolver and his sword to attack him. Robertson received a five-inch wound in the head and a cut in the arm which severed several tendons of his fingers.
5 Research does not reveal what finally happened to Umra Khan who seems to have been as slippery in death as he was in life.

Index

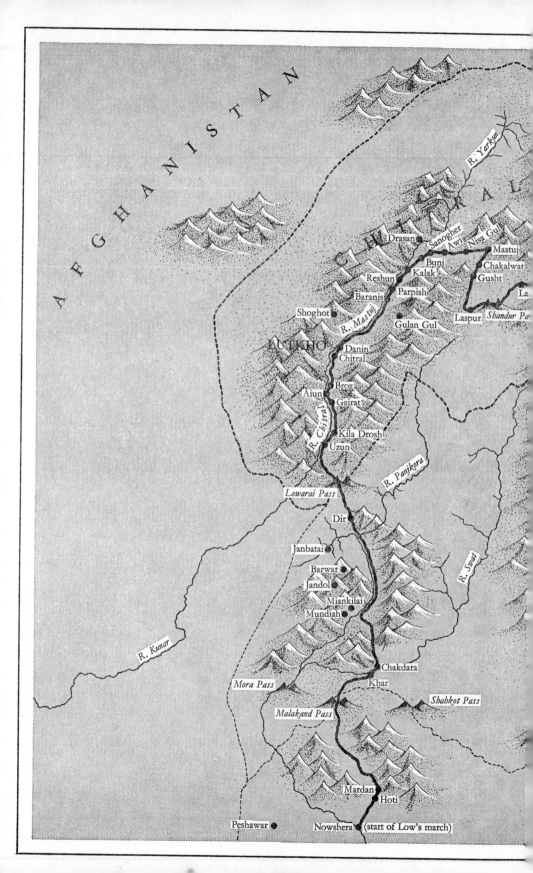